Anarchism and Education

A philosophical perspective

Judith Suissa

Anarchism and Education: A Philosophical Perspective
Judith Suissa
This edition © PM Press 2010
All rights reserved. No part of this book may be transmitted by any means without permission in writing from the publisher.

First published 2006 by Routledge, an imprint of the Taylor & Francis Group
© 2006 Judith Suissa

ISBN: 978-1-60486-114-3
Library of Congress Control Number: 2009912425

Cover by John Yates

10 9 8 7 6 5 4 3 2 1

PM Press
PO Box 23912
Oakland, CA 94623
www.pmpress.org

Printed in the USA.

In loving memory of my mother, Ruth

Contents

Preface

It is nearly five years since the first publication of this book. Reflecting on the work that went into it, and on the discussions that it has prompted with friends and colleagues over the years, there are two points that I would like to make in this preface to the new edition. These concern both the past and the future: the things I said in the book and why I still feel they are important; and the things that were left unsaid that need to be written and, more importantly, acted on.

Firstly, the past: For much of the time I spent researching the book, I was buried in, and entranced by, the world of nineteenth-century social anarchists. Sitting in silent archives, rummaging around second-hand bookshops, retracing the steps of Kropotkin in the East End of London and of Francesco Ferrer in the streets of Barcelona, it was easy to get lost in this world, where so much seemed possible. So it comes as no surprise to have been accused, by some readers of the book, of being "romantic" or "utopian". Yet, annoying though these accusations are, I am not entirely uncomfortable with the label. As I tried to show in the book, engaging with anarchist theory and, particularly with anarchist educational ideas and practice, can help to rescue the word "utopian" from its pejorative connotations and reclaim it as an urgent and committed form of social hope. This project seems particularly timely in our current political climate. Ideas matter, and at a time when we are surrounded by pronouncements about "the death of ideology" and politicians talking about "what works", they matter more, not less, than ever. If, as Susan Neiman has argued (Neiman 2009: 26), one goal of philosophy is to enlarge our ideas of what is possible, then a philosophical exploration of anarchism is surely a valuable exercise. Indeed, as Neiman shows, one of the effects of contemporary political discourse has been to blur the very distinctions between our core metaphysical concepts: ideals and ideology; realism and pragmatism; what is actual and what is possible. Part of the battle to resist neo-liberal ideology and its effects on our lives is a battle to reclaim our ethical vocabulary. I hope that in showing how, for example, the notions of freedom and equality were conceptually intertwined in the thought and political activism of nineteenth-century social anarchists, I can play a small part in this battle.

When it comes to education, articulating and engaging with anarchist positions takes on a particular significance. I am still compelled to draw people's attention to anarchist educational ideas and practice both because the role of education in anarchist theories of social change and human nature is still seriously overlooked in theoretical work on anarchism, and because the unique intellectual roots and political underpinnings of anarchist educational practice are largely left out of philosophical and historical work on education. Yet my urge to tell the story of anarchist education stems from more than a desire to correct theoretical misrepresentations or to fill gaps in the academic literature. We live in a time when educational policy makers in the USA and the UK often talk as if state education had no history. Terms like "parental choice", "child-centred" and "educational opportunity" are scattered across policy documents as if their meaning is straightforward and unproblematic, and the political assumptions underpinning them are rarely made explicit. But as Michael Apple has argued (Apple 2000, 2006), the forces of "conservative modernization", while reconstructing the means and ends of education and other social institutions, are also creating a shift in our ideas about democracy, freedom, equality and justice, turning "thick" collective forms of these (always contested) concepts into "thin" consumer driven and overly individualistic forms. This tendency needs to be resisted if we are to create and sustain the kinds of learning environments and the kinds of just societies where children and adults can truly flourish. Confident statements are made, in the media, in policy documents and in academic literature, about the aims and benefits of state schooling and liberal education as if there was no need to even ask ourselves what these things mean, what values underpin them, and why they have taken on the institutional forms and structures that they have, or to remind ourselves that things were not always thus. Revisiting the educational ideas of anarchist theorists and practitioners forces us to step back and ask these questions; to remind ourselves that there were times where not just the link between the state and education, but the state itself, was contested. But thinking about how our political structures and the educational processes and relationships that inform and are informed by them could look radically different is not just a historical exercise: it is an important reminder that there are other ways of doing things; that even now, within and alongside the structures of the state, it is possible, as Buber says, to "create the space now possible" for different human relationships; different ways of organizing our social and political lives.

And this brings me to the final point: the book I didn't write and the things I didn't say. For, when all is said and done, the writing of this book and the research that went into it was an intellectual endeavour. I make no apologies for being an academic, for I do believe that thinking about the world, particularly thinking critically about it, is an essential part of changing it. However, the real story of anarchist education is still going on, outside the pages of this book. It is unfolding in the nondescript classrooms of under-resourced inner-city schools; in the leafy grounds of independent schools; in grimy youth-clubs; on the streets; in theatre-halls and in seminar rooms. Since the first publication of the book, I have been contacted by countless activists and teachers who, in one way or another, are practising, experimenting with and developing various forms of anarchist education: through street theatre; through anti-racist, feminist and critical pedagogy; through the founding and running of experiments in collective living; through innovative approaches to art education, sex education, political action against oppression, community projects, and numerous other initiatives that challenge dominant mind-sets and political structures and form part of the ongoing chorus of what Colin Ward called "voices of creative dissent". If there is a hope expressed in this book, it is these activists and educators who give it substance and who are, at this very moment, writing its sequel.

I dedicated the original edition of this book to the memory of my mother, Ruth. I would like to dedicate this new edition to the memory of Colin Ward. They both, in their different ways, have inspired me and will continue to do so.

Judith Suissa
London, 2010

References

Apple, M. (2000) *Official Knowledge: Democratic Knowledge in a Conservative Age*, New York: Routledge.

—— (2006) *Educating the "Right" Way: Markets, Standards, God and Inequality*, New York: Routledge

Buber, M. (1958) *Paths in Utopia*, Boston: Beacon Press.

Neiman, S. (2009) *Moral Clarity; A Guide for Grown-Up Idealists*, New Jersey: Princeton University Press.

Ward, Colin (1991) *Influences: Voices of Creative Dissent*, Guildford: Green Books.

Acknowledgements

I have been living with this project for several years and cannot possibly thank all the people who have supported me along the way. Certain individuals, however, deserve special mention.

The staff and students in the School of Educational Foundations and Policy Studies at the London Institute of Education have provided a consistently supportive and stimulating environment in which to work. I am grateful to all my colleagues in the Philosophy Section but particularly to Patricia White for her invaluable supervision, unfailingly thoughtful feedback and support during my PhD research, on which this book is based, and for her ongoing friendship and enthusiasm for the project.

The research for this book was made possible in part by generous awards from the ORS Awards Scheme, the University of London Central Research Fund and the Philosophy of Education Society of Great Britain.

Aside from offering financial assistance, the Philosophy of Education Society of Great Britain has provided a wonderful forum for the exchange of ideas, collegiality and stimulating discussion, and I am grateful to be part of such a community.

I would like to extend my heartfelt thanks to the following individuals both within the PESGB and from the broader community of philosophers, educators, utopian dreamers and anarchists, who have, over the years, offered encouragement, friendship, inspiration and valuable insights into and criticisms of various versions of the ideas and arguments developed here: Harry Brighouse, Ruth Cigman, Jau-Wei Dan, Mike Degenhardt, Ayal Donenfeld, Michael Fielding, Jane Green, David Halpin, Graham Haydon, Hemdat Lerman, Terry McLaughlin, Brenda McQuillan, Yishay Mor, Janet Orchard, Shirley Rowan, Michael Smith, Richard Smith, Paul Standish, Tirza Waisel, Colin Ward, John White and Christopher Winch.

An earlier and much-abridged version of the central themes of this book appeared in 'Anarchism, Utopias and Philosophy of Education', *Journal of Philosophy of Education*, 35 (4), 2001. A version of the arguments in Chapter 7 appeared in 'Vocational Education: A Social Anarchist Perspective', *Policy Futures in Education*, 2 (1), 2004.

My father, Stan Cohen, has not only provided me with the unconditional support which only a parent can, but has, at several points, offered the sharp and thoughtful criticism of an experienced – but not cynical – academic writer. He has my gratitude for both these roles. Although my mother, Ruth, sadly did not live to see this work completed, she has been with me every step of the way.

My husband, Elhanan, has, perhaps more than anyone, followed at close quarters the ups and downs that have been a part of the process of writing this book. Throughout, he has been unfailingly supportive and understanding, and has helped to keep things in perspective.

Finally, I am immensely grateful to my children, Lia and Yonatan – mainly for simply being there and also for being somewhere else at crucial moments so that I could get on with the writing.

Introduction

'To declare for a doctrine so remote as anarchism at this stage of history', wrote Herbert Read in 1938, 'will be regarded by some critics as a sign of intellectual bankruptcy; by others as a sort of treason, a desertion of the democratic front at the most acute moment of its crisis; by still others as merely poetic nonsense...' (Read 1974: 56).

After several years of working on this project, I think I have some idea of how Read felt. Anarchism is rarely taken seriously by academics, and its advocates in the political arena are generally regarded as a well-meaning but, at worst, violent and at best a naïve bunch. Why, then do I think anarchist ideas merit a study of this scope? And why, particularly, do I think they have something to say to philosophers of education?

Part of my motivation is the need to address what appears to be a gap in the literature. Although the anarchist position on education is, as I hope to establish, distinct and philosophically interesting, and although it has been expressed powerfully at various times throughout recent history, it is consistently absent from texts on the philosophy and history of educational ideas – even amongst those authors who discuss 'radical' or 'progressive' education. Indeed, one issue which I address in this book is the failure of many theorists to distinguish between libertarian education (or 'free schools') and anarchist education. I hope to establish that the principles underlying the anarchist position make the associated educational practices and perspective significantly distinct from other approaches in radical education.

Similarly, both academic texts and public perceptions often involve simplifications, distortions or misunderstandings of anarchism. The typical response of contemporary scholars to the anarchist idea – that it is 'utopian', 'impractical' or 'over-optimistic regarding human nature' (see, for example, Scruton 1982; Wolff 1996) – needs to be scrutinized if one is to give anarchism serious consideration. To what extent are these charges justified? And what are the philosophical and political assumptions behind them? Indeed such charges themselves have, for me, raised fascinating questions about the nature and role of the philosophy of education. In what sense are we bound by the political and social context within which we operate? To what extent should we be bound by it, and what is our responsibility in this regard as philosophers? If philosophy is to reach beyond the conceptual reality of our present existence, how far can it go before it becomes 'utopian', and what does this mean? And if we do want to promote an alternative vision of human life, to what extent are we accountable for the practicality of this vision? So while the focus of this work is an exploration of the philosophical issues involved in anarchist ideas of education, these broader questions form the backdrop to the discussion.

The bulk of this work consists of an attempt to piece together a systematic account of what could be described as an anarchist perspective on education. This project involves examining the central philosophical assumptions and principles of anarchist theory, with particular reference to those ideas which have an obvious bearing on issues about the role and nature of education. Specifically, I devote considerable space to a discussion of the anarchist view on human nature, which is both at the crux of many misconceptions of anarchism and also plays a crucial role in the anarchist position on education. I also discuss several attempts to translate anarchist ideas into educational practice and policy. This discussion, I hope, serves to highlight the distinct aspects of the anarchist perspective, as compared to other educational positions, and furthers critical discussion of the way in which anarchism can be seen to embody a philosophically interesting perspective on education.

The thrust of my account of anarchist educational ideas and practice is to show how such ideas are intertwined with the political and moral commitments of anarchism as an ideological stance. One cannot, I argue, appreciate the complexity of the anarchist position on education without understanding the political and philosophical context from which it stems. Yet equally importantly, one cannot appreciate or assess anarchism's viability as a political position without an adequate understanding of the role played by education within anarchist thought.

In the course of this discussion, I refer extensively to other traditions which inform major trends in the philosophy of education, namely, the liberal and the Marxist traditions. While I do not claim to offer a comprehensive account of either of these traditions, nor of their educational implications, this approach does, I hope, serve the purpose of situating anarchist ideas within a comparative framework. I believe it establishes that, while anarchism overlaps in important ways with both liberal and Marxist ideas, it can offer us interesting new ways to conceptualize educational issues. The insights drawn from such an analysis can thus shed new light both on the work of philosophers of education, and on the educational questions, dilemmas and issues confronted by teachers, parents and policy makers.

It is important to stress, at the outset, that this work is not intended as a defence of anarchism as a political position. I believe that philosophers of education and educational practitioners can benefit from a serious examination of anarchist ideas, and that many of these ideas have value whether or not one ultimately endorses anarchism as a political ideology, and even if one remains sceptical regarding the possibility of resolving the theoretical tensions within anarchist theory.

More specifically, I believe that the very challenge posed by what I refer to as the anarchist perspective, irrespective of our ultimate ideological commitments, can prompt us to ask broad questions about the nature and role of philosophy, of education, and of the philosophy of education.

Most contemporary philosophers of education acknowledge that philosophy of education has, at the very least, political implications. As John White puts it (White 1982: 1), 'the question: What should our society be like? overlaps so much with the question [of what the aims of education should be] that the two cannot sensibly be kept apart'. Likewise, Patricia White laments the fact that philosophers tend to avoid 'tracing the policy implications of their work' (White 1983: 2), and her essay *Beyond Domination* is a good example of an attempt to spell out in political terms what a particular educational aim (in this case, education for democracy) would look like. A compelling account of the historical and philosophical context of the relationship between educational theory and political ideas has been notably developed by Carr and Hartnett, who lament the 'depoliticization of educational debate' (Carr and Hartnett 1996: 5) and argue for a clearer articulation of the political and cultural role of educational theory, grounded in democratic values. But even work such as this tends to take the present basic social framework and institutional setup as given. Even philosophers of education such as John and Patricia White, Carr and Hartnett, Henry Giroux, Nel Noddings and others who take a critical stance towards the political values reflected in the education system, tend to phrase their critique in terms of making existing society 'more democratic', 'more participatory', 'more caring' and so on. The basic structural relations between the kind of society we live in and the kind of education we have are, more often than not, taken for granted. Indeed, it is this which makes such theories so appealing as, often, they offer a way forward for those committed to principles of democracy, for example, without demanding an entire revolution in the way our society is organized.

In political terms, the acknowledgement by philosophers of the essentially political character of education seems to mean that, as succinctly put by Bowen and Hobson

> It is now clear to most in the liberal-analytic tradition that no philosopher of education can be fully neutral, but must make certain normative assumptions, and in the case of the liberal analysts, these will reflect the values of democracy.
>
> (Bowen and Hobson 1987: 445)

In philosophical terms, what this acknowledgement means is that discussion of 'aims' and 'values' in education often assumes that the kind of social and political values we cherish most highly can be promoted by particular conceptualizations of the curriculum. Richard Pring captures this idea in stating that debates on the aim of education 'take the word aim to mean not something extrinsic to the process of education itself, but the values which are picked out by evaluating any activity as educational' (Pring 1994: 21). Thus much work by philosophers within the liberal tradition focuses on questions as to how values such as autonomy – argued to be crucial for creating a democratic citizenry – can best be fostered by the education system. Many theorists in this tradition make no acknowledgement of the fact that 'education' is not synonymous with 'schooling'. Even those who do explicitly acknowledge this fact, like John White who opens his book *The Aims of Education Restated* (White 1982) with the comment that 'not teachers but parents form the largest category of educators in this country', tend to treat this issue simply as a factor to be dealt with in the debate conducted within the framework of the existing democratic (albeit often, it is implied, not democratic enough) state. The normative questions regarding the desirability of this very framework are not themselves the focus of philosophical debate.

In short, the sense in which many philosophers of education regard their work as political is that captured by Kleinig, when he states:

> Philosophy of education is a social practice, and in evaluating it account needs to be taken not only of what might be thought to follow 'strictly' from the arguments used by its practitioners, but also the causal effects of those arguments within the social contexts of which they are a part.
>
> (Kleinig 1982: 9)

Critical discussion about the desirability of this social context in itself, it is implied, is beyond the scope of philosophy of education.

The anarchist perspective seems at the outset to present a challenge to such mainstream views in that it does not take any existing social or political framework for granted. Instead, it has as its focal point a vision of what an ideal framework could be like – a vision which has often been described as utopian. The question of why the anarchists were given the label 'utopian', what it signifies, and whether or not they justly deserved it, is one which is hotly debated in the literature, and which I shall take up later. But what anarchism seems to be suggesting is that before we even engage in the enterprise of philosophy of education, we must question the very political framework within which we are operating, ask ourselves what kind of society would embody, for us, the optimal vision of 'the good life', and then ask ourselves what kind (if any) of education system would exist in this society.

Of course, any vision of the ideal society is formulated in terms of particular values, and many of the values involved in the anarchist vision may overlap with those promoted by philosophers writing in the liberal-democratic tradition (e.g. autonomy, equality, individual freedom). But it is not just a question of how these values are understood and translated into political practice; nor is it a question of which of them are regarded as of primary importance; the distinction is not, then, between emphasizing different sets of values in philosophical debates on education, but, rather, of changing the very parameters of the debate. Thus the question of 'what should our society be like' is, for the anarchist, not merely 'overlapping', but logically *prior* to any questions about what kind of education we want.

An anarchist perspective suggests that it is not enough to say, with Mary Warnock, that philosophy of education should be centrally concerned with 'questions about what should be taught, to whom, and with what in mind' (Warnock 1977: 9); one has to also ask the crucial question 'by whom?' And how one answers this question, in turn, has important political implications which themselves inform the framework of the debate. For example, if one assumes that the nation state is to be the major educating body in society, one has to get clear about just what this means for our political, social and educational institutions, and, ideally, to be able to offer some philosophical defence of this arrangement. The view of society which informs the anarchists' ideas on education is not one of 'our society' or 'a democratic society', but a normative vision of what society *could* be like. The optimality of this vision is justified with reference to complex ideas on human nature and values, which I explore later.

The question for the philosopher of education, then, becomes threefold: One, what kind of society do we want? Two, what would education look like in this ideal society? And three, what kind of educational activities can best help to further the realization of this society? Of course, the arguments of anarchist thinkers do not always acknowledge the distinction between such questions, nor do they always progress along the logical route implied here, and untangling them and reconstructing this perspective is one task of this book.

Why, then, to go back to the opening quote from Herbert Read, is anarchism regarded as so eccentric – laughable, even – by mainstream philosophers? Is it the very idea of offering an alternative social ideal that seems hard to swallow, or is it that this particular ideal is regarded as so 'utopian' that it is not worth seriously considering? And wherein does its 'utopianism' lie? Is it just a question of impracticality? Are we, as philosophers, bound to consider only those political programmes which are clearly practically feasible? Yet if we are concerned primarily with feasibility, then we have to address the claim, made by anarchist thinkers and activists, that their programme *is* feasible in that it does not demand a sudden, total revolution, but can be initiated and carried out 'here and now'. For the anarchist utopia, as we shall see, is built on the assumption of propensities, values and tendencies which, it is argued, are already present in human social activity. Is it, then, that philosophers believe that this utopian vision of the stateless society goes against too much of what we know about human nature? Yet there is little agreement amongst philosophers as to the meaning, let alone the content, of human nature. Many anarchists, however, have an elaborate theory of human nature which arguably supports their claims for the possibility of a society based on mutual aid and self-government. Is it, then, simply that we (perhaps unlike many radical thinkers of the mid-nineteenth century) are so firmly entrenched in the idea of the state that we cannot conceptualize any kind of social reality without it? Does the modern capitalist state, in other words, look as if it is here to stay? Have we, similarly, fallen victim to the post-modern skepticism towards 'grand narratives', suspicious of any political ideal which offers a vision of progress towards an unequivocally better world? These are all valid and interesting points against taking anarchism seriously, but they, in their turn, deserve to be scrutinized as they reflect, I believe, important assumptions about the nature and scope of the philosophical enterprise.

Perhaps the very perspective implied by taking a (possibly utopian) vision of the ideal society as the starting point for philosophical debates on education is one which deserves to be taken seriously. It is certainly one which challenges our common perceptions about the role of the philosophy of education. We are already well acquainted with talk of 'the good life' and 'human flourishing' as legitimate notions within the field of philosophy of education. But how broadly are we to extend our critical thought and our imagination in using these notions? If we admit (with John Dewey, Paul Hirst, Richard Peters and others) that such notions cannot be understood without a social context, then is it not incumbent on us – or at the very least a worthwhile exercise – to consider what we would ideally like that social context to be? We are accustomed to the occasional philosophical argument for states without schools. Yet how often do we pause to consider the possibility of schools without states?

An analysis of anarchist thought seems unlikely, due to the very nature of the subject, to yield a coherent, comprehensive and unique philosophical account of education. Indeed, part of anarchism's complexity is a result of its being intellectually, politically and philosophically intertwined with many other traditions. Thus any questions about anarchism's uniqueness must remain, to a certain extent, open. Nevertheless, in the course of exploring the educational ideas associated with the anarchist tradition, and their philosophical and historical connections with other traditions, many – often surprising – insights emerge. Some of these challenge common perceptions about anarchism; some of them suggest important links between anarchist ideas and liberal aspirations; some of them prompt a rethinking of the distinctions between various educational traditions; and some of them prompt questions about how we see our role both as educators and as philosophers of education. All of them deserve exploration.

1 Anarchism – definitions and questions

Before moving on to a discussion of the educational ideas associated with anarchism, we need a broad understanding of what the anarchist position involves – and, perhaps equally importantly, what it does not involve.

As a political ideology, anarchism is notoriously difficult to define, leading many commentators to complain of its being 'amorphous and full of paradoxes and contradictions' (Miller 1984: 2).

One reason for the confusion surrounding the use of the word 'anarchism' is the derogatory meanings associated with the connected terms 'anarchy' and 'anarchic'. The Oxford English Dictionary defines *anarchy* as (1) absence of government or control, resulting in lawlessness (2) disorder, confusion; and an *anarchist* as 'a person who believes that government is undesirable and should be abolished'. In fact, the title 'anarchist' was first employed as a description of adherence to a particular ideology by Pierre-Joseph Proudhon in 1840 and, as shall transpire, the substantial part of this ideology consisted in far more than a simple rejection of government. Indeed, as many anarchists have stressed, it is not government as such that they find objectionable, but the hierarchical forms of government associated with the nation state.

A second reason for the difficulty in reaching a conclusive definition is the fact that anarchism – by its very nature – is anti-canonical, and therefore one cannot refer to any single body of written work (unlike in the case of Marxism) in the search for definitive answers to questions on the nature and principles of the anarchist position. Furthermore, those anarchists who have written extensively on the subject have seldom formulated their views in the form of systematic works – largely out of a conscious commitment to the popular propaganda of their ideas.

Yet in spite of these difficulties, and in spite of the great variance amongst different anarchist thinkers at different times in history, it is possible to approach a working definition of anarchism by asking what it is that distinguishes it from other ideological positions. From this point of view, Reichert is undoubtedly right in pointing out that anarchism is 'the only modern social doctrine that unequivocally rejects the concept of the state' (Reichert 1969: 139).

As the discussion in the following chapters will reveal, as a theory anarchism also addresses basic philosophical issues concerning such notions as human nature, authority, freedom and community. All of these issues have an important bearing on philosophical questions about education, and can be usefully understood in contrast with the views articulated from other ideological perspectives. It is, though, perhaps in light of its rejection of statehood that the theoretical cluster of anarchist ideas is best understood.

Historically speaking, it has been argued (e.g. by Miller, Chomsky and Guerin) that the origins of anarchism as a comprehensive political theory can be traced to the outbreak of the French Revolution. Miller claims that the Revolution, by radically challenging the old regime, opened the way for other such challenges to states and social institutions. Specifically, institutions were now regarded as vulnerable to the demand that they be justified in terms of an appeal to first principles, whether of natural right, social utility, or other universal abstract principles (see Miller 1984: 2–4). Yet anarchism as a political movement did not develop until the second half of the nineteenth century, especially in conjunction with the growing workers' movement. Indeed Joll argues that although philosophical arguments for anarchism can be found in texts of earlier historical periods, as a political movement, anarchism is 'a product of the nineteenth century' (Joll 1979: ix). As Joll points out, 'the values the anarchists attempted to demolish were those of the increasingly powerful centralized, industrial state which, in the nineteenth and twentieth century, has seemed the model to which all societies are approaching' (ibid.).

However, the philosophical ideas embodied in anarchist theory did have historical precedents. Some writers have made the distinction between anarchism as a political movement and 'philosophical anarchism' which consists of a critique of the idea of authority itself. Miller, for example, notes that, as opposed to the political objection to the state, philosophical anarchism could entail a very passive kind of attitude, politically speaking, in which the proponent of this view evades 'inconvenient or immoral state dictates whenever possible', but takes no positive action to get rid of the state or to propose an alternative form of social organization. On this view, one can be an anarchist without subscribing to philosophical anarchism – that is, without rejecting the idea of legitimate authority, and vice versa. However, other theorists, such as Walter, argue that, irrespective of the existence of a philosophical position against authority, all those who identify themselves as anarchists share the positive idea that a stateless society is, however remotely, possible and would be preferable to current society.

Most theorists, in short, seem to agree that, as a political movement, albeit not a continuous one, anarchism developed from the time of the French Revolution onwards, and that it can thus be seen as historically connected with the other major modern political doctrines which were crystallized at around this time, namely, liberalism and socialism. It is indeed around the question of the relationship between these two intellectual traditions that many of the criticisms of anarchism and the tensions within the movement can be understood. In a certain sense, the tensions between liberal and socialist principles are reflected in the contradictions often to be found within the anarchist tradition. While many commentators (see for example Joll 1979; Miller 1984; Morland 1997) describe these apparently irreconcilable tensions as obstacles towards construing anarchism as a coherent ideology, anarchist thinkers writing within the tradition often refuse to see them as contradictions, drawing on particular concepts of freedom to support their arguments. Thus Walter, for example, notes that anarchism

> may be seen as a development from either liberalism or socialism, or from both liberalism and socialism. Like liberals, anarchists want freedom; like socialists, anarchists want equality. But we are not satisfied by liberalism alone or by socialism alone. Freedom without equality means that the poor and the weak are less free than the rich and strong, and equality without freedom means that we are all slaves together. Freedom and equality are not contradictory, but complementary [...] Freedom is not genuine if some people are too poor or too weak to enjoy it, and equality is not genuine if some people are ruled by others. The crucial contribution to political theory made by anarchists is this realization that freedom and equality are in the end the same thing.
>
> (Walter 1969: 163)

Walter, like many anarchist theorists, often fails to make the careful philosophical distinctions necessary to fully appreciate these complex conceptual issues. Presumably, he does not wish to argue that freedom and equality are actually conceptually identical. Rather, the point he seems to be making is that they are mutually dependent, in the sense that the model of a good society which the anarchists are defending cannot have one without the other. I shall examine these conceptual issues in greater depth in the following discussion.

In spite of Walter's observation, it is undoubtedly true that, throughout history, different people calling themselves anarchists have often chosen to place more weight on one rather than the other side of the 'old polarization of freedom versus equality'. Specifically, it is common to find a distinction between anarchists of more 'individualist' leanings, and 'social anarchists', who see individual freedom as conceptually connected with social equality and emphasize the importance of community and mutual aid. Thus writers like Max Stirner (1806–1856), who represents an early and extreme form of individualism (which Walter suggests is arguably not a type of anarchism at all) view society as a collection of existentially unique and autonomous individuals. Both Stirner and William Godwin (1756–1836), commonly acknowledged as the first anarchist thinkers, portrayed the ideal of the rational individual as morally and intellectually sovereign, and the need to constantly question authority and received opinion – to engage in a process which Stirner called 'desanctification'. However while Stirner seemed to argue for a kind of rational egoism, Godwin claimed that a truly rational person would necessarily be benevolent. Although sharply critical of the modern centralist state, and presenting an elaborate doctrine of social and political freedom, Godwin, writing in the aftermath of the French Revolution, placed great emphasis on the development of individual rationality and independent thinking, believing that the road forward lay not through social revolution but through gradual reform by means of the rational dissemination of ideas at the level of individual consciousness.

As Walter comments (Walter 1969: 174), such individualism, which over the years has held an intellectual attraction for figures such as Shelley, Emerson and Thoreau, often tends towards nihilism and even solipsism. Walter ultimately questions whether individualism of this type is indeed a form of anarchism, arguing rather that libertarianism – construed as a more moderate form of individualism which holds that individual liberty is an important political goal – is simply one aspect of anarchist thought, or 'the first stage on the way to complete anarchism' (ibid.). The key difference between this kind of individualist libertarianism and social anarchism is that while such libertarians oppose the state, they also, as Walter notes (ibid.), oppose society, regarding any type of social organization 'beyond a temporary "union of egoists"' as a form of oppression.

Many commentators have acknowledged that leading anarchist theorists did not see individual freedom as a political end in itself (see, for example, Ryth Kinna, in Crowder 1991). Furthermore, central anarchist theorists, such as Kropotkin and Bakunin, were often highly disparaging about earlier individualist thinkers such as William Godwin and Max Stirner, for whom individual freedom was a supreme value. 'The final conclusion of that sort of Individualist Anarchism', wrote Kropotkin in his 1910 article on 'Anarchism' for the *Encyclopaedia Britannica*,

> maintains that the aim of all superior civilization is, not to permit all members of the community to develop in a normal way, but to permit certain better- endowed individuals 'fully to develop', even at the cost of the happiness and the very existence of the mass of mankind . . . .

Bakunin, another leading anarchist theorist, was even more outspoken in his critique of 'the individualistic, egoistic, shabby and fictitious liberty extolled by the school of J.J. [Rousseau] and other schools of bourgeois liberalism' (Dolgoff 1973). Accordingly, several theorists have proposed that it is in fact equality, or even fraternity (see Fidler 1989), which constitutes the ultimate social value according to the anarchist position. Others, like Chomsky, have taken the position that anarchism is simply 'the libertarian wing of socialism' (Chomsky, in Guerin 1970: xii) or that 'anarchism is really a synonym for socialism' (Guerin 1970: 12). Indeed, Adolph Fischer, one of the 'Haymarket martyrs' sentenced to death for their part in the libertarian socialist uprising over the struggle for the eight-hour work day in Chicago, in 1886, claimed that 'every anarchist is a socialist but not every socialist is an anarchist'. (quoted in Guerin 1970: 12).

The arguments of anarchist theorists such as Chomsky and Guerin, to the effect that the best way to understand anarchism is to view it as 'libertarian socialism', are also supported by the work of political scientists such as David Miller, Barbara Goodwin and George Crowder. Goodwin, for example, states that 'socialism is in fact the theoretical genus of which Marxism is a species and anarchism another' (Goodwin 1987: 91), whereas Crowder goes so far as to say that 'from a historical point of view classical anarchism belongs more properly within the socialist tradition' (Crowder 1991: 11).

It is certainly true that the most influential anarchist theorists in recent history, in terms of developing and disseminating anarchist ideas, belonged on the socialist end of the anarchist spectrum. Many of the central ideas of this tradition were anticipated by Pierre-Joseph Proudhon (1809–1865), commonly regarded as the father of social anarchism. Yet the bulk of social-anarchist thought was crystalized in the second half of the nineteenth century, most notably by Michael Bakunin (1814–1876) and Peter Kropotkin (1842–1912). Other significant anarchist activists and theorists in this tradition include Errico Malatesta (1853–1932), Alexander Berkman (1870–1936), Emma Goldman (1869–1940), and, more recently, Murray Bookchin (1921–2006), Daniel Guerin (1904–1988) and Noam Chomsky (1928–).

Apart from the differences in emphasis in terms of the individualist–socialist continuum, one can draw other distinctions within the broadly socialist approach amongst different variants of social anarchism which have been expressed in different political and historical contexts. Briefly, these five main variants are: mutualism, federalism, collectivism, communism and syndicalism. Although this taxonomy is conceptually useful, it is important to remember that the views of many leading anarchist theorists often involved a combination of strands from several of these different traditions.

Mutualism represents the basic anarchist insight that society should be organized not on the basis of a hierarchical, centralist, top-down structure such as the state, but on the basis of reciprocal voluntary agreements between individuals. Perhaps the best-known, and certainly the earliest, proponent of this type of anarchism was Pierre-Joseph Proudhon, who, writing in the mid-nineteenth century, envisaged a society composed of cooperative groups of individuals exchanging goods on the basis of labour value, and enjoying the credit of a 'people's bank'. Proudhon was criticized by later anarchists for appealing primarily to the petit bourgeoisie, and for failing to deal with the basic issues of social structure as regards the class system, industry and capital. Indeed, he often wrote with horror of the increasing threat of massive industrialization, expressing a romantic wish to preserve small-scale trade, artisans' workshops and cottage industry. Nevertheless, his views on private property and his argument that social harmony could only exist in a stateless society, were highly influential and were later developed by leading anarchist thinkers, notably Bakunin.

Federalism is basically a logical development from mutualism, referring as it does to social and economic organization between communities, as opposed to within communities. The idea is that the society of voluntarily organized communities should be coordinated by a network of councils. The key difference between this anarchist idea and the principle of democratic representation is that the councils would be established spontaneously to meet specific economic or organizational needs of the communities; they would have no central authority, no permanent bureaucratic structure, and their delegates would have no executive authority and would be subject to instant recall. This principle was also elaborated by Proudhon and his followers, who were fond of pointing to international systems for coordinating railways, postal services, telegraphs and disaster operations as essentially federalist in structure. What is notable about the elaborate attempts by Proudhon, Bakunin, Kropotkin and other anarchists to show how federalist arrangements could take care of a wide variety of economic functions, is that they illustrate the point that anarchism is not synonymous with disorganization. As the twentieth-century anarchist Voline clarifies:

> it is not a matter of 'organization' or 'nonorganization', but of two different principles of organization....Of course, say the anarchists, society must be organized. However, the new organization must be established freely, socially, and, above all, from below. The principle of organization must not issue from a center created in advance to capture the whole and impose itself upon it, but, on the contrary, it must come from all sides to create nodes of coordination, natural centers to serve all these points...
>
> (quoted in Guerin 1970: 43)

It thus seems appropriate to view federalism not so much as a type of anarchism but, as Walter suggests, 'as an inevitable part of anarchism' (Walter 1969: 175).

Collectivism takes the aforementioned points one step further and argues that the free and just society can only be established by a workers' revolution which will reorganize production on a communal basis. Many central figures of the twentieth-century anarchist movement – notably Bakunin and his followers in the First International – were in fact collectivists. They opposed both the more reformist position of the mutualists and federalists, on the one hand, and what they saw as the authoritarian revolutionary position of the Marxists on the other.

Anarchism and Marxism

Many of the central ideas and principles of social anarchism overlap with those of Marxism, perhaps nowhere more explicitly than in collectivism, the form of anarchism most closely associated with Marxist socialism in that it focuses on the class struggle and on the need for social revolution. However, there are crucial differences between the anarchists and the Marxists, and indeed much of Bakunin's political theory took the form of an attack on Marx. Specifically, the anarchists opposed common, central ownership of the economy and, of course, state control of production, and believed that a transition to a free and classless society was possible without any intermediate period of dictatorship (see Walter 1969: 176).

Fundamentally, the anarchists consider the Marxist view of the state as a mere tool in the hands of the ruling economic class as too narrow, as it obscures the basic truth that states 'have certain properties just because they are states' (Miller 1984: 82). By using the structure of a state to realize their goals, revolutionaries will, according to anarchism, inevitably reproduce all its negative features (the corrupting power of the minority over the majority, hierarchical, centralized authority and legislation, and so on.) Thus the anarchists in the First International were highly sceptical (with, it has to be said, uncanny foresight) about the Marxist idea of the 'withering away of the state'.

The anarchists also argued that the Marxist claim to create a scientific theory of social change leads to a form of elitism in which the scientific 'truth' is known only to an elect few, which would justify attempts to impose this truth on the 'masses' without any critical process. Bakunin, in a speech to the First International, attacked Marx as follows:

> As soon as an official truth is pronounced – having been scientifically discovered by this great brainy head labouring all alone – a truth proclaimed and imposed on the whole world from the summit of the Marxist Sinai – why discuss anything?
>
> (quoted in Miller 1984: 80)

In contrast, a fundamental aspect of the anarchist position is the belief that the exact form which the future society will take can never be determined in advance; the creation of the harmonious, free society is a constant, dynamic process of self-improvement, spontaneous organization and free experimentation. In keeping with this view, anarchist revolutionary theorists insisted that the revolution itself was not subject to scientific understanding, and its course could not be determined in advance, favouring instead an organic image of social change. As Bakunin wrote:

> Revolution is a natural fact, and not the act of a few persons; it does not take place according to a preconceived plan but is produced by uncontrollable circumstances which no individual can command. We do not, therefore, intend to draw up a blueprint for the future revolutionary campaign; we leave this childish task to those who believe in the possibility and the efficacy of achieving the emancipation of humanity through personal dictatorship.
>
> (Dolgoff 1972: 357)

It is in the context of this position that anarchists have consistently refuted the charges of utopianism – charges made both by right-wing critics and by orthodox Marxists. This point shall be discussed in greater detail in the following chapters.

Anarcho-Communism is the view that the products of labour should be collectively owned and distributed according to the principle of 'from each according to his ability, to each according to his needs'. Those anarchists – notably Kropotkin, Malatesta, Berkman and Rocker – who proclaimed themselves to be communist-anarchists shared the collectivists' critique of Marxist socialism, but rejected the title 'collectivist', saw themselves as presenting a broader and more radical vision, involving the complete abolition of the wage and price system. Most revolutionary anarchist movements have in fact been communist in terms of their principles of economic organization – the most notable example being the anarchist communes established during the Spanish Civil War.

Anarcho-Syndicalism is that strand of anarchist thought which emphasizes the issue of labour and argues that the trade unions, as the ultimate expression of the working class, should form the basic unity of social reorganization. There is naturally considerable overlap between the syndicalist view and the collectivist or communist form of anarchism, but historically, anarcho-syndicalism as a movement is closely tied with the development of the French syndicalist (i.e. trade unionist) movement at the end of the nineteenth century. As the anarcho-syndicalist position emphasizes workers' control of the economy and means of production, its proponents have tended to be less libertarian in their sympathies.

In summary, it is abundantly clear that people of fairly diverse political views have, at one time or another, called themselves anarchists. Indeed, as Walter remarks, it is hardly surprising that 'people whose fundamental principle is the rejection of authority should tend to perpetual dissent' (Walter 1969: 172). Nevertheless, a few general points emerge, based on the aforementioned passage:

1   All anarchists share a principled rejection of the state and its institutions; and in doing so they:
2   Do not reject the notion of social organization or order *per se*;
3   Do not necessarily regard freedom – specifically, individual freedom – as the primary value and the major goal of social change, and;
4   Do not propose any 'blueprint' for the future society.

As discussed earlier, it is the work of the social anarchists which constitutes the bulk of the theoretical development of the anarchist position. Likewise it is, I believe, these theorists who offer the most interesting insights into the relationship between education and social change. Thus, in what follows, I shall refer primarily to the tradition of social anarchism and the philosophical and educational ideas associated with it.

However, in adopting this perspective, I by no means wish to gloss over the tensions and apparent contradictions within anarchist theory. These tensions are perhaps an inevitable historical consequence of the fact that, as Joll puts it:

> On the one hand, they are the heirs of all the Utopian, millenarian religious movements which have believed that the end of the world is at hand and have confidently expected that 'the trumpets shall sound and we shall be changed, in a moment, in the twinkling of an eye. [...] On the other hand, they are also the children of the Age of Reason [...] They are the people who carry their belief in reason and progress and peaceful persuasion through to its logical limits. Anarchism is both a religious faith and a rational philosophy...
>
> (Joll 1979: x)

In fact, as I shall argue, it is these tensions which make the anarchist tradition so fascinating and rich in philosophical insights. Furthermore, the process of trying to resolve and understand these tensions is part of the process of making sense of anarchist ideas on education.

Anarchism, philosophy of education and liberal suspicions

At first glance, trying to construct an anarchist philosophy of education may seem to the reader an unpromising line of enquiry, or at least one which, while perhaps being of some scholarly interest, has little to offer in the way of practical or philosophical value.

There are several reasons why this may be so. Some of these concern anarchism's viability as a political ideology, and some refer more explicitly to what are assumed to be the educational implications of such an ideology.

As far as the first group of concerns go, most of these involve, whether implicitly or explicitly, assumptions about the alleged utopianism of the anarchist position. This common line of critique, which encompasses both the charges of utopianism from classical Marxists and the scepticism of contemporary liberal theorists, can be broken down into several distinct questions. Most critics have tended to focus (often implicitly) on one or the other of these points.

1   Are the different values promoted by anarchist theory mutually compatible? Many contemporary liberal theorists, for example, working with the notion of personal autonomy, have argued that freedom, in this sense, is incompatible with the ideal of the anarchist community. Similarly, it is almost a built-in assumption of the neo-liberal position that individual freedom and social equality are mutually exclusive. It is from this perspective that some critics have argued that anarchism, as a political theory, lacks internal cohesion (see Taylor 1982).

2   Is the anarchist vision of the ideal human society feasible given the structure of human nature? This question can be broken down into two further questions: (a) The question of inner consistency – that is, is the anarchist social ideal consistent with human nature as the anarchists understand it? and (b) The question of external validity – is the anarchist social ideal feasible given what we know about human nature? This second line of criticism inevitably takes the form of a challenge to the anarchist view of human nature – a view which, as shall be discussed later, is regarded as unrealistically optimistic, as opposed to the rather more pessimistic view, according to which the inherently egotistical, competitive elements of human nature could not sustain a society organized along anarchist lines.

3   Can anarchism be implemented on a large scale in the modern industrialized world? This line of criticism focuses on the problems of translating anarchist ideas about self-governing, freely established communities based on mutual aid and non-hierarchical forms of social organization, into the world of industrial capitalism, global economy and multi-national corporations. In other words, while the previous two points concern primarily the feasibility of establishing and maintaining an anarchist community, this point is more concerned with the problem of relations between communities.

As this brief summary suggests, the anarchist conception of human nature is the key to understanding much of anarchist thought and thus to addressing the criticisms of anarchism as a political theory. Furthermore, this notion is an important element in the anarchist position on education.

It is harder to articulate the criticisms of anarchism from an educational perspective due to the simple fact that very little has been written, from a systematic philosophical point of view, about the educational ideas arising from anarchist theory. On the face of it, there are many ways in which anarchist theory could have implications for our ideas about education. These concern both the policy level (i.e. questions about educational provision and control), the content level (i.e. questions about the curriculum and the underlying values and aims of the educational process) and what could be understood as the meta level (i.e. questions about the moral justification of education *per se*). In spite of the dearth of philosophical literature on this subject, the remarks made informally by philosophers of education on encountering work such as my own suggest that their suspicions, apart from reflecting the above broad scepticism with regard to anarchism's feasibility as a political programme, reflect problems such as the following:

1   First, the anarchist challenge to the idea of authority may seem in itself to undermine our basic assumptions regarding the very legitimacy and value of education as an intentional human endeavour. If anarchists reject authority and hierarchies, one wonders whether it is possible to develop a coherent theory of education within the context of a commitment to anarchist ideals.

Thus the concept of authority and its interpretation within the anarchist tradition needs to be examined further, with this question in mind.

2   Second, the central anarchist argument against the state in itself goes against the ideal of universal educational provision, which has become an implicit assumption in nearly all contemporary philosophical debates on education. This challenge to the liberal ideal of universal, compulsory, state-controlled education is both implicit in the anarchist critique of the centralist state as a mode of social organization, and explicitly argued in anarchist work, from the time of William Godwin's classic argument against state control of education in *An Enquiry Concerning the Principles of Political Justice*, in 1793. Of course, the anarchist argument for abolishment of the centralist state is based on an understanding of and commitment to specific human values and, connectedly, to a specific view of human nature. If one accepts these values, the rejection of the liberal democratic state as the optimal framework for social organization then prompts the question of what framework is to replace it and whether these same values would indeed be better promoted and preserved under alternative arrangements.

3   Although anarchists – as shall be discussed later – advocate a broadly libertarian approach to education, their normative commitments imply a vision – some would argue a utopian vision – of social change. If anarchist education is to be consistent with anarchist principles, then this suggests the following dilemma: either the education in question is to be completely non-coercive and avoid the transmission of any substantive set of values, in which case it is hard to see how such an education could be regarded as furthering the desired social change; or it is to involve the explicit transmission of a substantive curriculum regarding the desired social order – in which case it would appear to undermine the libertarian ideal. In effect, if the anarchist position is actually a libertarian one, is not all educational intervention morally problematic from an anarchist point of view? This issue poses both internal and external problems: the internal problem has to do with the consistency between a substantive educational agenda and a broadly libertarian outlook, whereas the external problem has to do with the difficulty of accommodating a normative – perhaps utopian – vision with the liberal commitment to autonomy.

In order to address these often interconnected issues, it is important to untangle the conceptual web of educationally relevant concepts in anarchist thought, and to understand more fully the basis for the anarchist rejection of the state. One can then pose the question of whether any qualitatively different educational perspective, or indeed any philosophically defensible advantage, is gained by simply replacing the state with, for example, the community.

Furthermore, it is important to clarify the way in which anarchist ideas on education are connected to anarchist values and ideals and thus to articulate an anarchist conceptualization of the role of education in achieving social change. One important aspect of this project is the distinction, to be discussed later, between anarchist educational practice and other broadly libertarian approaches.

The aim of the following chapters, then, will be to explore the philosophical underpinnings of central concepts in anarchist thought and to articulate the picture of education which emerges from this thought. Specifically, I will address the question of whether anarchists regard education as primarily a means to achieving the political end of establishing an anarchist society.

In the course of this analysis, I will try to establish whether the anarchist position on education is significantly different from other positions, and whether it can shed any new light on common philosophical debates on the nature and role of education.

As mentioned earlier, one cannot begin to answer any of these questions without a detailed understanding of the anarchist conception of human nature – a notion which is central both to the charges of utopianism raised against anarchism, and to the role assigned to education in the process of social change. Indeed, it could be argued that any philosophical position on the nature and role of education in society involves, at least implicitly, assumptions about human nature. A key step, then, will be to unpack the anarchist notion of human nature, and to provide an account of the values associated with it. This task is relatively straightforward as several leading social-anarchist theorists, notably Kropotkin, and several anarchist commentators, have addressed the issue of human nature explicitly and at some length in their writings.

Unpacking the other educational questions is a somewhat more complicated task. The anarchist theorists who wrote about education did so in a rather unsystematic and often sketchy way, so this book is largely a project of reconstructing their position.

It is possible to formulate a further, broad question which links both the aforementioned sets of questions: Does the question of whether or not anarchism is viable as a political ideology have any direct bearing on its educational value? In other words, if it can be convincingly argued that the anarchist vision of a free, equal and harmonious society is hopelessly unrealistic, does this fact detract from its ability to function as an animating force in educational thought and practice? I hope to suggest some answers to this meta-question in the course of discussing the philosophical perspective on education embodied in anarchist theory.

Liberalism and liberal education

In order to create a coherent framework for this discussion, the position broadly referred to as the liberal theory of education shall form my main point of reference for much of the following comparative analysis. Apart from methodological considerations, there are several connected reasons why this approach makes sense. First, as Anthony O'Hear (1981) puts it, many of the central ideas of liberal education have become so common as to be almost axiomatic within the field of educational theory and practice. Indeed, liberalism as a political theory has, as many theorists note, achieved such ascendancy, at least in the West, that in a certain sense, 'from New Right conservatives to democratic socialists, it seems we are all liberals now' (Bellamy 1992: 1). This is hardly surprising when one considers that 'liberal ideals and politics fashioned the states and social and economic systems of the nineteenth century, creating the institutional framework and the values within which most of us in the West continue to live and think' (ibid.). In as much as this is true, it is certainly the case that the central values of liberal theory underlie much contemporary philosophical discourse on the role, aims and nature of education, and most participants in this discourse take it for granted that the education under consideration is education in — and controlled by — a liberal state. In addition, anarchist theory itself, as a nineteenth-century tradition, is often most interestingly and constructively understood when compared and contrasted with the other nineteenth-century tradition of liberalism, with which it is closely connected. Indeed, some commentators (notably Chomsky) argue that anarchism is best understood as a logical development out of classical liberalism. I shall examine this argument in the course of the following discussion for, if anarchist ideas can be construed as a variant of liberalism, then it may be possible to construct an anarchist view of education that can be accommodated within, and perhaps shed new light on, the paradigm of liberal education.

In order to identify some useful points of reference for further discussion, I shall now turn to a brief outline of some of the central ideas of liberalism and the liberal view of education.

Before attempting to outline what is meant by the term 'liberal education', it may be useful to present a brief discussion of some of what are generally accepted as the basic assumptions of liberalism as a political theory and to indicate how these assumptions have come to be associated with certain educational ideas.

Liberal theory

Some theorists claim that liberalism is not, in fact, a single, coherent doctrine, but a 'diverse, changing, and often fractious array of doctrines that form a "family"...' (Flathman 1998: 3). Indeed, one can draw distinctions, within this 'family', between fairly different perspectives — for example, the central distinction between philosophical, or neutralist liberalism (most notably represented in recent years by the work of Rawls, Dworkin, Hayek and Nozick), versus what Bellamy dubs 'communitarian liberalism' (as exemplified in the work of Walzer and Raz). Yet it is possible to identify a few basic ideas — or, as Andrew C. Gould puts it 'aspirations' common to all variants of liberalism:

1   The commitment to constitutional parliamentary government as the preferred form of political rule. This idea developed out of the rejection

of monarchism, reflecting the view that the arbitrary authority of monarchs and their officials should be replaced by predictable, rational decision-making processes established in written laws.

2   The commitment to individual freedoms laid down and protected by constitutions.

3   The pursuit of enlightened self-interest and the idea that such self-interest, if pursued in the framework of free markets, can lead to public benefit. Connectedly, the expansion of markets is usually one aim of liberal theory, although nearly all contemporary liberal theorists acknowledge the need for some regulation of the market.

(Gould 1999)

Meira Levinson, in her overview of contemporary liberal theory, offers an account similar to Gould's, but adds as a further liberal commitment: 'An acceptance – and more rarely, an embracing – of the fact of deep and irremediable pluralism in modern society' (Levinson 1999: 9). John Kekes, writing from a more conservative position, has expressed these liberal ideas in negative terms, arguing that 'essential to liberalism is the moral criticism of dictatorship, arbitrary power, intolerance, repression, persecution, lawlessness and the suppression of individuals by entrenched orthodoxies' (Kekes 1997: 3).

Kekes, citing the classic Lockean position that the only reasonable justification of government is an appeal to the argument that individual rights are better protected than they would be under a different arrangement, supports the view that the individual and individual freedoms and rights are the basic units of liberal theory. While certain theorists, notably Kymlicka, have defended an interpretation of liberalism which, while championing individual liberty and property, at the same time stresses the cultural and communal context which 'provides the context for individual development, and which shapes our goals and our capacities to pursue them' (Kymlicka 1989: 253), it nevertheless seems reasonable to accept that, in some basic sense, liberalism is a doctrine in which, as Gould puts it, 'individuals count'.

It is thus no coincidence that liberal views are often associated with the promotion of the value of individual autonomy. Indeed, it has been argued by several theorists that autonomy is the central value in liberal theories – even, as John White argues, within the neutralist liberal position (i.e. the position which holds, with Dworkin, that the state should be neutral with regard to different conceptions of the good life) – which 'collapses in to a hidden perfectionism in favour of autonomy' (White 1990: 24). Kekes too notes that 'the central importance that liberalism attributes to individuals is greatly enhanced by the idea of autonomy as formulated by Kant' (Kekes 1997), while Meira Levinson goes so far as to argue that 'liberal principles depend for their justification on an appeal to the value of individual autonomy'. (Levinson 1999: 6). Thus the ideal of the autonomous individual – the person who reflects upon and freely chooses from amongst a plurality of conceptions of the good – both justifies the establishment of liberal freedoms and rights and the institutions intended to guarantee these rights, and, so the argument goes, is fostered within the framework of the liberal state. To this view is often added the insight that in exercising autonomy one is in some sense fulfilling one's essential potential as a human being, as expressed by J.S. Mill in his classic statement of liberalism:

> He who lets the world, or his own position in it, choose his plan of life for him, has no need of any other faculty than the ape-like one of imitation. He who chooses his plan for himself, employs all his faculties.
>
> (Mill 1991: 65)

It is therefore not surprising that many educational philosophers, writing within the liberal tradition, have chosen to emphasize autonomy as a central educational goal or value, relying on the argument that each person has the right to determine and pursue her own vision of the good life. This argument yields, at the policy level, the view that, in the context of a liberal state, the national system of education must refrain from laying down prescriptive programmes aimed at a particular vision of the good life. On the content level, such views often assume (whether explicitly or not) a view of human nature which puts great emphasis on the rational capacities deemed necessary for the exercise of autonomy and construct curricula designed to foster these capacities.

However, even if one accepts the position, as argued by Levinson and others, that autonomy is a necessary component of contemporary liberal theory, this does not, of course, lead to the conclusion that liberalism is the only political theory consistent with the value of autonomy. Indeed, autonomy can – and perhaps, as John White argues, should – be justified as a human value on independent grounds (e.g. from a utilitarian perspective, within a Kantian view of morality, or by reference to a notion of personal well-being). Thus one could acknowledge, with the liberals, the value of autonomy, but question the framework of the liberal democratic state and its institutions. One could, in fact, with the anarchists, argue that alternative social and political arrangements are more suited to the promotion and maintenance of autonomy. In order to examine this position, I shall, in what follows, discuss the anarchist understanding of autonomy, compare this with the liberal notion, and ascertain whether the anarchist idea of the community as the basic unit of social organization is consistent with the value of personal autonomy. Does a rejection of the framework of the liberal, democratic state yield new insights into the philosophical issues which are generally associated with the role and nature of education within a liberal framework?

Liberal education

The idea of 'liberal education', as suggested earlier, is logically connected to the idea of liberalism *per se* by virtue of the fact that the underlying values of education assumed in this context overlap with central liberal aspirations. Furthermore, the connection has obvious historical and political dimensions, for the idea of a liberal, universal education developed in conjunction with the ascendancy of liberalism as a political theory. However, it is important to refer also to the systematic work of leading philosophers of education who, particularly during the 1960s and 1970s, developed a coherent analytical account of the notion of 'liberal education'. In addition to the aforementioned points, an examination of this account yields the following insights.

Philosophers within the liberal tradition, from Richard Peters on, have focused on the idea of non-instrumentality as central to the philosophy of liberal education. As Peters puts it, 'traditionally, the demand for liberal education has been put forward as a protest against confining what has been taught to the service of some extrinsic end such as the production of material goods, obtaining a job, or making a profession' (Peters 1966: 43). Similarly, Paul Hirst, in his classic account (Hirst 1972), notes that the liberal educational ideal is essentially non-utilitarian and non-vocational. Hirst also emphasizes the idea of the mind and mental development as essential features of liberal education, involving a conception of human nature that regards human potential as consisting primarily in the development of the mind.

To talk of intrinsic aims of education is to imply that a particular aim 'would be intrinsic to what we would consider education to be. For we would not call a person "educated" who had not developed along such lines' (Peters 1966: 27). Thus, for example, an aim such as 'developing the intellect', would be intrinsic in the sense that this is arguably one aspect of what we understand education, as a normative concept, to be. In contrast, to say that it is an aim of education to contribute to the productivity of the economy is to say something that goes beyond the concept of education itself and is, therefore, 'extrinsic' to it. This classic view of liberal education has been the subject of much criticism in recent years (see, for example, Kleinig 1982). Indeed Levinson, in her recent book *The Demands of a Liberal Education*, is rather disparaging of Peters and his defence of the idea that the concept of education is logically connected with the idea of intrinsically worth-while activities. In claiming that this assertion is simply wrong (Levinson 1999: 3), however, Levinson misses the point, which is a purely analytical one: namely, that one's idea of which educational aims are worthwhile is inherently built into one's concept of education – or, more explicitly, to one's concept of what it means to be educated. It may of course be true, as John White and others have argued, that the conception of education as having intrinsic aims – a conception underlying much of the liberal educational tradition – is in conflict with the conception of education as having extrinsic – for example, economic – aims. For example, one can argue, albeit with a certain degree of simplification, that specific aims typical of the liberal educational tradition, such as autonomy, reflectiveness, a broad and critical understanding of human experience, etc. can very well conflict with typical extrinsic aims of education – specifically those construed as 'economic' aims – for example, obedience to authority, specialized training and knowledge of specific skills, and an uncritical attitude to existing socio-economic reality.

The liberal-analytical tradition in philosophy of education, as opposed to the rather more cynical Marxist view, rests, of course, as John White (White 1982) points out, on the assumption that it is possible to provide a 'neutral', logical analysis of what is involved in the concept of 'education'. Yet although this analytic enterprise has been the subject of much criticism in recent years, the analytical distinction between extrinsic and intrinsic aims of education seems to have practically achieved the status of orthodoxy in contemporary philosophy of education and is undoubtedly useful as a conceptual tool to highlight certain differences in emphasis between varying positions on the nature and role of education.

I turn now to a discussion of some key anarchist ideas, before going on to examine the implications of these ideas for education, especially in the context of the liberal tradition. My aim in this discussion, in keeping with the earlier analysis, is to establish whether the anarchist position yields a different philosophical perspective on education from that embodied in liberal thought. This will necessitate addressing the question of whether or not anarchism can arguably be construed as an extension of liberalism, or whether it is qualitatively distinct from liberalism. Consequently, we will be able to determine whether or not the anarchist position implies a challenge to the basic values underlying liberal educational ideas and whether a consideration of this tradition can yield philosophical insights which contribute to our thinking about educational issues.

2   Anarchism and human nature

As we saw in Chapter 1, many of the criticisms of anarchism as a viable political ideology and thus as a sound philosophical base for constructing ideas on education, hinge on the concept of human nature. This chapter, therefore, offers an exploration of the anarchist position on human nature, with a view to both addressing these criticisms and beginning to grasp the role of education in anarchist thought.

Many critics have dismissed anarchism as a coherent or serious political theory precisely on the basis that its view of human nature is, they argue, unrealistic or naive. Thus for example, Max Beloff (1975) states that the case for anarchism

> is based on a fundamental misunderstanding of human nature, on the unproven supposition that given total absence of constraints, or alternatively material abundance secured by communism, human societies could exist with no coercive element at all, the freedom of each being recognized as compatible with the freedom of all.

Similarly, Jonathan Wolff, in his account of anarchism in his *Introduction to Political Philosophy*, states that 'to rely on the natural goodness of human beings to such an extent seems utopian in the extreme' (Wolff 1996: 34).

As we shall see, statements such as these are based on a misconception of the anarchist view of human nature and its consequences for the anarchist social ideal. In order to proceed with this analysis, then, it is important to establish exactly what the anarchist account of human nature consists of, what its role is within anarchist theory, how it compares with connected ideas within the liberal tradition and the educational implications of this account.

In general, the focus here will be on the way the construct of human nature is put forth in order to support a particular idea. Bikhu Parekh has remarked that, although the concept of human nature 'is one of the oldest and most influential concepts in Western philosophy' (Parekh 1997: 16), there has been little agreement, throughout the history of philosophy, on what the term actually means. Parekh ultimately offers a defence of a minimalist definition of human nature, emphasizing not only the universal constants of human existence but the 'ways in which they are creatively interpreted and incorporated into the process of human self-articulation and self-understanding' (ibid.: 26). As such, his definition challenges the underlying assumption, common to all classic accounts of human nature, that there is a fairly clear distinction between nature and culture – between 'what is inherent in humans and what is created by them' (ibid.: 17). I tend to agree with Parekh that the concept of human nature is inherently problematic and that relying on it in philosophical discussions can have undesirable implications due to its tendency to assume an ahistorical position and to deny the cultural imbeddedness of human experience and character. However, what is important in the present context is the methodological role which the concept of human nature has played within philosophical positions. As Parekh notes, philosophers have used it to serve three purposes: 'to identify or demarcate human beings; to explain human behaviour; and to prescribe how human beings should live and conduct themselves.' It is the second and third purposes which are of central concern to us here.

In the context of philosophy of education, Anthony O'Hear has articulated a view similar to that of Parekh in stating that 'human nature is not something that is just given. It is something we can make something of, in the light of how we conceive ourselves and others'. Given O' Hear's understanding of philosophy of education as essentially involving a reflection on 'one's values and concept of what men [*sic*] ought to be' (O'Hear 1981: 1) and one's 'ideals for society as whole', it is thus clear that the notion of a common human nature can be a useful conceptual tool in that emphasizing particular traits, virtues or potentialities as uniquely and essentially human often plays an important methodological role in philosophically evaluating particular normative positions on education.

In anarchist theory, where the central animating ideal is that of the free society, based on mutual cooperation, decentralization and self-government, the concept of a common human nature is employed in order to demonstrate the feasibility of this social ideal. However, contrary to the opinion of many critics (see, for example, May 1994) the anarchists, in the same way as they did not believe that the future anarchist society would be free from all social conflict, did not in fact subscribe to a simplistic, naively optimistic view of human tendencies and characteristics. Nor, so I shall argue, were they unaware of the philosophical complexities involved in the idea of a common human nature.

Human nature in social-anarchist theory

In his detailed study of anarchist views on human nature, Morland (1997) notes that both Proudhon and Bakunin, two of the leading social-anarchist theorists, acknowledged human nature to be innately twofold, involving both an essentially egotistical potential and a sociable, or altruistic potential. As Bakunin picturesquely expressed this idea: 'Man has two opposed instincts, egoism and sociability. He is both more ferocious in his egoism than the most ferocious beasts and more sociable than the bees and ants' (Bakunin, in Maximoff 1953: 147).

A similar perspective arises from the work of Kropotkin, the social-anarchist theorist, who, more than any other theorist within the tradition, devoted considerable energy to developing a systematic theory of human nature. Much of Kropotkin's work – primarily his monumental treatise, *Mutual Aid*, which he wrote before becoming identified with the anarchist movement – can be interpreted as an attempt to counter the extreme version of social Darwinism often put forward by theorists such as Huxley as a justification of the capitalist system, elevating free competition amongst individuals to a positive virtue (see Hewetson 1965). Kropotkin was anxious to show that the simplistic notion of 'survival of the fittest' was a misleading interpretation of evolutionary theory, and that Darwin himself had noted man's social qualities as an essential factor in his evolutionary survival. As contemporary theorists have noted, 'for most of us, Darwinism suggests anything but communality and cooperativeness in nature' (Nisbet 1976: 364). Yet *The Origin of Species* is full of references to man's 'social nature', which, Darwin argues, has 'from the beginning prompted him to live in tightly knit communities, with the individual's communal impulse often higher indeed than his purely self-preservative instinct' and without which it is highly probable that 'the evolution of man, as we know it, would never have taken place' (ibid.: 368). By ignoring this clear emphasis in Darwin's work, the position referred to as 'social Darwinism' amounts to, as Nisbet notes, 'scarcely more than a celebration of the necessity of competition and conflict in the social sphere' (ibid.: 364). Accordingly, one can see the logic of trying to establish cooperation as a fundamental principle of nature in order to celebrate and promote the anarchist ideal of a society based on cooperation and communalism.[1]

However, it is on Darwin's earlier work, *The Descent of Man*, from which Kropotkin draws most heavily in his own work, adopting Darwin's basic account of how

> in numberless animal societies, the struggle between separate individuals for the means of existence disappears, how struggle is replaced by cooperation, and how that substitution results in the development of intellectual and moral faculties which secure to the species the best conditions for survival.
>
> (Kropotkin 1972: 28)

Kropotkin's position was based not only on his reading of Darwin but on his own extensive research into animal behaviour which he conducted with a zoologist colleague and which culminated in the publication of *Mutual Aid* in 1902. Although some critics have questioned aspects of Kropotkin's methodology, contemporary anthropological research seems to support his basic thesis that the principle of social cooperation has been a characteristic of human and other species since earliest times – predating, apparently, the primacy of the family unit. The paradigm case of the prominence of 'mutual aid' (a term derived from the biologist Karl Kessler – see Morland 1997: 132) as a factor in the evolution of animal species is that of ants. The important conclusion here is that while there may be aggressive fighting for survival between species, within the ant community, mutual aid and cooperation prevail. As Kropotkin puts it, 'The ants and termites have renounced the "Hobbesian war", and they are the better for it' (Kropotkin 1972: 36).

Kropotkin does not deny the Darwinian idea of the principle of struggle as the main impetus for evolution. But he emphasized that there are two forms which this struggle can take: the struggle of organism against organism for limited resources (the aspect of evolution emphasized by Huxley) and the kind of struggle that Darwin referred to as metaphorical: the struggle of the organism for survival in an often hostile environment. As Gould puts it,

> Organisms must struggle to keep warm, to survive the sudden and unpredictable dangers of fire and storm, to persevere through harsh periods of drought, snow, or pestilence. These forms of struggle between organism and environment are best waged by cooperation among members of the same species-by mutual aid.
>
> (Gould 1988: 4)

In terms of these two aspects of the struggle for existence, Kropotkin ultimately regards the principle of mutual aid as more important from an evolutionary point of view, as it is this principle which 'favours the development of such habits and characters as insure the maintenance and further development of the species, together with the greatest amount of welfare and enjoyment of life for the individual, with the least waste of energy' (Kropotkin 1972: 30–31). As Morland sums up Kropotkin's conclusions from the wealth of evidence collected from observations of the animal world: 'Put quite simply, life in societies ensures survival' (Morland 1997: 135).

Of course it is highly problematic to attempt to draw conclusions for human behaviour from evidence from the animal kingdom. However Darwin himself, whose methods Kropotkin obviously sought to emulate, argued that 'what is so often to be found among animals is [...] utterly universal among human beings' (Nisbet 1976: 368). Furthermore, Kropotkin assembled a wealth of evidence, which he often cited later in his various anarchist writings, of the presence of a propensity for spontaneous cooperation and mutual aid within human society. Indeed, anarchist writers today are fond of referring to cases such as that of the life-guard association, the European railway system, or the international postal service, as instances of mutual aid and voluntary cooperation in action. Even given the limitations of such examples, it seems that the point Kropotkin is making is a purely methodological one: if one wants to argue for the feasibility of an anarchist society, it is sufficient to indicate that the propensity for voluntary cooperation has some historical and evolutionary evidence in order to render such a society not completely unfeasible. Furthermore, as Barclay points out, 'Some criticise anarchism because its only cement is something of the order of moral obligation or voluntary co-operation. But democracy, too, ultimately works in part because of the same cement' (Barclay 1990: 130). I shall discuss, later, the question of the extent to which Kropotkin and other anarchist theorists relied on this 'cement' as the principal force in shaping and maintaining anarchist society, and to what extent they acknowledged the need for institutional frameworks and social reform.

The question remains as to whether Kropotkin saw the principle of mutual aid as simply an essential aspect of the human psyche. Morland suggests that, through the evolutionary process, mutual aid has indeed become a kind of 'psychological drive', basic to our consciousness of ourselves as social beings. Indeed, Kropotkin makes use of the notion of an instinct in his insistence that he is referring to something far more basic than feelings of love and sympathy in his discussion of sociability as a general principle of evolution. 'It is', he writes,

> not love to my neighbour – whom I often do not know at all – which induces me to seize a pail of water and rush towards his house when I see it on fire; it is a far wider, even though more vague feeling or instinct of human solidarity and sociability which moves me.
>
> (Kropotkin 1972: 21)

But DeHaan (1965) has argued that while Kropotkin's theory can be described as an 'instinct theory', the 'tendencies' he mentions do not have ontological status but rather should be regarded as a hypothesis. 'Natural laws', he argues, 'are not imbedded in reality; they are human constructs to help us understand nature' (DeHaan 1965: 276). It is important to bear this in mind when discussing the next step in Kropotkin's thesis, which is the argument that mutual aid is the basis for morality, and that without it, 'human society itself could not be maintained'. As Morland notes, it is only through the medium of consciousness that the propensity for mutual aid can surface and flourish – a view which clearly contradicts the Rousseauian notion of a pre-social human nature, to which Kropotkin was vehemently opposed. Indeed, in acknowledging human nature to be essentially contextualist, in the sense that they regarded it as determined not by any human essence but by social and cultural context, Kropotkin and other anarchist theorists seemed to be aware of the pitfalls of assuming what Parekh refers to as the dichotomy between culture and nature. In this sense, they were indeed far from Rousseau's romanticization of the 'state of nature' and indictment of modern civilization. Bakunin's view of human nature was also, as both Morland and Ritter note, a contextualist one, in that it rejected essentialistic notions of human nature and assumed humans to be at the same time individuals and social beings. Which of these two strands of human nature comes to the fore at any given time is, the social anarchists believed, dependent on the social and cultural environment. Bakunin puts forth this view as part of his famous critique of the state, implying at the same time an outright rejection of the religious notion of original sin, the Rousseauian view of pre-social human nature, and the idea of the social contract:

> Failing to understand the sociability of human nature, metaphysics regarded society as a mechanical and purely artificial aggregate of individuals, abruptly brought together under the blessing of some formal and secret treaty, concluded either freely or under the influence of some superior power. Before entering into society, these individuals, endowed with some sort of immortal soul, enjoyed total freedom . . .
>
> (Bakunin, in Woodcock 1977: 83)

Accepting the theoretical assumption that man is born free implies an antithesis between the free individual and society – a position which, Bakunin argues, 'utterly ignores human society, the real starting point of all human civilization and the only medium in which the personality and liberty of man can really be born and grow' (Bakunin, in Morris 1993: 87–88).

Even Godwin, an earlier anarchist thinker generally regarded as being more on the individualist than the social side of the continuum, shared this rejection of a pre-social or innate concept of human nature. 'The actions and dispositions of men', he wrote in *Enquiry Concerning Political Justice*,

> are not the off-spring of any original bias that they bring into the world in favour of one sentiment or character rather than another, but flow entirely from the operation of circumstances and events acting upon a faculty of receiving sensible impressions.
>
> (Godwin 1946: 26–27)

In the light of this discussion, it is clear that theorists who argue, with Tony Kemp-Welch, that the origins of anarchist thought 'can be traced to Rousseau's idea of man being born free and that political institutions have corrupted an otherwise innocent and pure human nature' (Kemp-Welch 1996: 26) are fundamentally mistaken, and are thereby contributing to the misconceptions surrounding anarchism.

Human nature and the capitalist state

The anarchist position, then, does not involve a simple, naive view of human nature as essentially altruistic. Kropotkin especially acknowledged, with Darwin, the presence of a drive for domination, and the theme constantly running through his thought is a dialectic conception of the tension between the principle of the struggle for existence and that of mutual aid. Unlike Proudhon and Fourier, whose economic theories clearly influenced him, Kropotkin attempts to place his anarchist ideas in a broader historical context.

He writes: 'All through the history of our civilization two contrary traditions, two trends have faced one another; the Roman tradition and the national tradition; the imperial and the federal; the authoritarian and the libertarian . . .' (quoted in Ward 1991: 85).

He goes on to identify the state with the coercive, authoritarian tradition, the antithesis of which is the kind of voluntary forms of social organization such as guilds, workers' cooperatives and parishes. Martin Buber, who had considerable sympathy for the social philosophy of anarchist thinkers such as Kropotkin and Proudhon, developed this implicit distinction between the social and political order, believing that the way forward lay in a gradual restructuring of the relationship between them. Of course, as Buber acknowledged, Kropotkin's conception of the state is too narrow, for 'in history there is not merely the State as a clamp that strangles the individuality of small associations; there is also the State as a framework within which they may consolidate' (Buber 1958: 39). Given modern conceptions such as Nozick's of the minimal, liberal democratic state, the narrowness of Kropotkin's definition is even more glaring. Yet, as Buber goes on to argue, Kropotkin was right to draw attention to the fact that the historical rise of the centralist state signalled a fundamental change in our conception of the nature of social relations – the idea of the sovereign state displacing the primacy of the idea of the free city or various forms of free contract and confederacy. Buber himself remained optimistic as to the possibility of 'a socialist rebuilding of the state as a community of communities' (ibid.: 40), but Kropotkin saw the principle of decentralization and voluntary association as fundamental to revolutionary change and any state structure as necessarily antithetical to this principle.

Kropotkin's talk of these two contrary historical 'tendencies' is intertwined with his talk of the two aspects of human nature, reflecting what Morland describes as a 'symbiotic relationship' between historical progress and human nature. Yet although, as mentioned, the position of Bakunin and Kropotkin on this issue is a contextualist one, this does not mean to say that such theorists took a neutral stance towards the two opposed aspects of human nature and the way in which they are manifested in a social context. As an examination of his arguments shows, Kropotkin assigned normative status to the altruistic strand of human nature, and seemed to regard it as in some sense dominant. In a particularly powerful piece written for *Freedom* in 1888, entitled 'Are We Good Enough?' Kropotkin sets out to counter the argument often made that 'men are not good enough to live under a communist state of things' or, rather, 'they would submit to a compulsory Communism, but they are not yet ripe for free, Anarchistic Communism' (Kropotkin, in Becker and Walter 1988). To this he answers with the question 'but are they good enough for Capitalism?'. His argument is that if people were naturally and predominantly kind, altruistic and just, there would be no danger of exploitation and oppression. It is precisely because we are not so compassionate, just and provident that the present system is intolerable and must be changed, for the present institutions allow 'slavishness' and oppression to flourish. Obviously, the point is not that people do not have a natural, instinctive propensity for justice, altruism and social cooperation but rather that they do not have *only* such propensities. If not for the opposing, egotistical streak of human nature,

> the private ownership of capital would be no danger. The capitalist would hasten to share his profits with the workers, and the best-remunerated workers with those suffering from occasional causes. If men were provident they would not produce velvet and articles of luxury while food is wanted in cottages; they would not build palaces as long as there are slums [. . .]
>
> (Ibid.)

The only way to suppress, or at least diminish, the 'slavish' and competitive instincts we are unfortunately endowed with is to change society by means of what Kropotkin refers to as 'higher instruction and equality of conditions', thereby eliminating those conditions which 'favour the growth of egotism and rapacity, of slavishness and ambition' (a state of affairs which, Kropotkin emphasizes, is damaging both to the rulers and the ruled). The principal difference, Kropotkin argues in this text, between the anarchists and those who dismiss them as unpractical, utopian dreamers, is that 'we admit the imperfections of human nature, but we make no exception for the rulers. They make it, although sometimes unconsciously . . .' (ibid.). It is this view, according to Kropotkin, which is behind the paternalistic justification of the inbuilt inequalities of the capitalist state system – that is, that, if not for a few wise rulers keeping them in check, the masses would allow their base, egotistical instincts to get out of control, leading to social and moral depravity. It is in this context that one can begin to understand the crucial and complex role of education in Kropotkin's thought.

Nurturing the propensity for mutual aid

So we see that Kropotkin believes ultimately in the power of the altruistic aspects of human nature to prevail. He contends, unlike Rousseau, that even a corrupt society cannot crush individual human goodness – that is, even the capitalist state cannot 'weed out the feeling of human solidarity, deeply lodged in men's understanding and heart' (Becker and Walter 1988: 38). Nevertheless, he acknowledges that people 'will not turn into anarchists by sudden transformation'. Thus the contextualist account of human nature can go a long way towards answering the question of why education, and schools, are necessary both to help bring about and to sustain an anarchist society.

An analysis of Bakunin's work on the subject supports this view, for Bakunin too subscribed to a contextualist view of human nature, claiming that morality derived from society – and specifically, from education. 'Every child, youth, adult, and even the most mature man', argued Bakunin, 'is wholly the product of the environment that nourished and raised him' (Maximoff 1953: 153). Thus, although there are two innate sides to human nature, the way in which different propensities develop is a function of environmental conditions. This is a key point in grasping the role assigned to education by the social anarchists, in both bringing about and sustaining a just society organized on anarchist principles. For even if the social revolution is successful, given the contextualist notion of human nature and the acknowledgement of its inherent duality, presumably an ongoing process of moral education will be necessary in order to preserve the values on which the anarchist society is constituted.

This point, albeit alongside an undeniable optimism with respect to the educative power of the revolutionary society itself in terms of suppressing the selfish aspects of human nature, is evident in the following passage from Bakunin:

> There will probably be very little brigandage and robbery in a society where each lives in full freedom to enjoy the fruits of his labour and where almost all his needs will be abundantly fulfilled. Material well-being, as well as the intellectual and moral progress which are the products of a truly humane education, available to all, will almost eliminate crimes due to perversion, brutality, and other infirmities.
>
> (Bakunin, in Dolgoff 1973: 371)

The phrase 'humane education' presumably refers both to procedural aspects of education, such as school climate and teacher–student relationships, which anarchists insisted should be non-authoritarian and based on mutual respect, as well as to the content of education, specifically its moral basis. Both of these aspects will be taken up in later chapters. It is interesting, too, to note Bakunin's demand for equal, universal educational access – a demand which must have sounded far more radical in the nineteenth-century context in which these words were written than it does to contemporary liberal theorists.

The social anarchists, then, clearly believed that an education which systematically promoted and emphasized cooperation, solidarity and mutual aid, thus undermining the values underlying the capitalist state, would both encourage the flourishing of these innate human propensities and inspire people to form social alliances and movements aimed at furthering the social revolution. Indeed, Kropotkin often anticipates the ideas expressed by Berkman and other twentieth-century anarchists concerning the 'here and now' aspect of anarchist philosophy; in other words, that it is by establishing new human values and social relationships (such as educational relationships) that the true social revolution can be achieved. At the same time, Kropotkin's underlying view of human nature also helps to emphasize the essentially educative function of the anarchist society, even once the state has been dismantled. For given the inevitable presence of slavish and selfish instincts, the opposing instincts need constant reinforcement. Kropotkin sometimes seems to suggest that it is social institutions themselves which will do this job – creating conditions of social equality and justice under which mutual aid would flourish. But, as Morland notes, he did acknowledge that 'egoism and self-assertion survive in anarchy as sociability and mutual aid endures in capitalism' (Morland 1997: 170).

Morland and other critics seem ultimately to regard this point as the downfall of Kropotkin's whole philosophical system, arguing that it leads to the inevitable use of coercion to maintain the future anarcho-communist society. However, I believe that the fact that this question arises, and the disagreements concerning it, do not detract from the force of the basic anarchist argument. I shall discuss later the ways in which various anarchist thinkers have attempted to come to terms with the problem of the inevitable presence of competition, dominance, struggles for power and conflicts of interest in the future anarchist society. In this context, meanwhile, there seems to be a fairly good case for arguing, on the basis of Kropotkin's work, that it is education, and not social and moral sanctions and rules as such, which would 'provide the glue' to hold the future anarchist society together – reinforcing the moral arguments for anarchism, and simultaneously nurturing altruistic and cooperative qualities amongst individuals. Of course one could counter to this that education, conceived in this way, is merely another form of coercion, and that we are left with something very similar to the classic view of education as cultural transmission. I will deal with this point later, in the context of the discussion of education as a means to social change.

In the light of the earlier discussion, it is important not to attach too much importance to the validity of the evolutionary aspects of the anarchist account of human nature. What is relevant, in the present context, is the methodological role which this account plays in emphasizing certain human traits deemed desirable and feasible for the transition to and maintenance of a non-hierarchical, decentralized form of social organization. In fact, many anarchist theorists, writing from an anthropological perspective have tried to defend the feasibility of such a society without recourse to a specific view of human nature. Harold Barclay, for example, in *People Without Government*, discusses a wealth of historical anthropological and ethnographic data, which, he argues, demonstrates that anarchies – defined as governmentless, stateless societies – are possible, albeit on a small scale, and, indeed, that from a historical point of view,

> anarchy is by no means unusual [...] it is a perfectly common form of polity or political organization. Not only is it common, but it is probably the oldest type of polity and one which has characterized most of human history.
>
> (Barclay 1990: 12)

Colin Ward, the contemporary British anarchist, draws similar conclusions from his analysis of contemporary experiments in non-hierarchical social organizations. The most famous example of such anarchist practice in action is that of the Paris Commune of 1871. But Ward also discusses small-scale social experiments – notably in the areas of education and health care – which support the idea of spontaneous organization based on voluntary cooperation. He quotes John Comerford, one of the initiators of the Pioneer Health Centre project in Peckam, South London, in the 1940s, as concluding that: 'A society, therefore, if left to itself in suitable circumstances to express itself, spontaneously works out its own salvation and achieves a harmony of actions which superimposed leadership cannot emulate' (Ward 1996: 33).

Thus the emphasis on the benevolent potential of human nature goes hand-in-hand with a faith in what Kropotkin called the theory of 'spontaneous order' – which holds that

> Given a common need, a collection of people will, by trial and error, by improvisation and experiment, evolve order out of the situation – this order being more durable and more closely related to their needs than any kind of externally imposed authority could provide.
>
> (Ward 1996: 32)

The ideal of rationality

Of course, such theoretical positions and principles have to be understood against the historical background of the time in which the social anarchists were developing their ideas. As is apparent from this overview, this era was, as noted by DeHaan, 'one of boundless optimism, the exaltation of science, atheism and rationalism' (DeHaan 1965: 272).

Accordingly, the anarchist view of human nature, alongside its emphasis on the human capacity for benevolence, cooperation and mutual aid, places great weight on the idea of rationality. Indeed this idea is one of the central features of the work of William Godwin, commonly regarded as the first anarchist theorist. Godwin, perhaps more than any other anarchist thinker, seems to have placed great faith in the human potential for rational thinking, believing that it was due to this potential that humans could be convinced, by means of rational argument alone, of the ultimate worth of anarchism as a superior form of social organization. Ritter has criticized Godwin's position as an extreme version of cognitivism (Ritter 1980: 92) and in fact later anarchists, especially of the socialist school, who were not, like Godwin, utilitarian thinkers, were far less dogmatic in their position on human reason, often acknowledging the role of emotion in human choice and action. Bakunin, for example, would probably have questioned Godwin's argument that 'the mind of men cannot choose falsehood and reject the truth when evidence is fairly presented' (in Ritter 1980: 95). Nevertheless, as a nineteenth-century movement, social-anarchist thought shared the Enlightenment enthusiasm for scientific method and the belief in 'the possibilities for moral and political progress through the growth of knowledge'

(Crowder 1991: 29). Thus Bakunin, like most anarchists, whether of the individualist or communist school, believed that it was through the powers of reason that humans could advance to higher, more advanced states of morality and social organization.

Although Morland argues that Bakunin ultimately rejected philosophical idealism in favour of a materialist position, other scholars question this view. Miller, for example, argues on the basis of Bakunin's writings that, in the final reckoning, he remained a Hegelian idealist in the sense that his view of historical progress involved a notion of human consciousness progressing through successive stages, each resolving the tensions and contradictions of the previous stages. Human history, on this view, is seen as a process of gradual humanization, 'whereby men emerge from their brutish condition and become, through the influence of social relations, moral beings' (Miller 1984: 71). Freedom, according to this conception, is a positive concept, involving acting in accordance with laws which one has internalized by means of the power of reason.

Accordingly, many early anarchist experiments in education assigned the concept of reason or rationality a central place in their programmes and curricula, and the international organization set up by Francisco Ferrer, an early twentieth-century anarchist educator (see Chapter 6) to coordinate such projects was called 'The Society for Rational Education'.

In their use of the term 'rational', early anarchist thinkers clearly had in mind something akin to 'scientific', in the sense of accordance with the laws of logic, empirical observation and deduction.

It is important to note that Bakunin, with his emphasis on human reason and rationality as central to moral progress, makes frequent mention of the 'ignorance of the masses'. Yet, as Ritter points out, the anarchist view is nevertheless not an elitist one. Anarchists, wary of any political programme which attempted to manipulate the masses so as to achieve social change, stressed the essential aspect of spontaneous free choice and experimentation in achieving social progress. Like Godwin, later anarchists saw this process of rational education as one 'through which rational individuals choose anarchism as the regime they create' (Godwin, quoted in Ritter 1980: 96).

From an educational point of view, this position has obvious associations with the humanistic, liberal concept of education, according to which the key to a freer society is an overall increase in education based on the principles of reason and rationality. This, perhaps, reflects a connection between the educational perspective of anarchism as a political ideology, and the liberal, Enlightenment tradition which underpins the idea of liberal education.

As mentioned earlier, most philosophers writing within the liberal education tradition place great emphasis on rationality and on the development of the mind as an essential component of the good life (see Hirst 1972). Likewise, most theorists of liberal education assume a form of epistemological realism – a view that, as Hirst puts it, 'education is based on what is true'. These points have obvious connections with the Enlightenment belief in progress and human betterment through expanding knowledge and rationality – a belief which, as we have just seen, was shared by nineteenth-century anarchist thinkers.

Human nature in liberalism

To what extent can the anarchist view of human nature be seen as overlapping with the liberal position? Although few contemporary theorists employ the term 'human nature', it is nevertheless obvious that liberal theory, and particularly liberal educational theory, makes certain assumptions about human capabilities or propensities. The question 'what characteristics of the individual does the liberal state see as important and worthy of encouragement?' (Levinson 1999: 9) is, in an important sense, a question about human nature. Anarchist theorists, as discussed earlier, choose to emphasize the human potential for benevolence, sociability and voluntary cooperation, arguing that these virtues are important and worthy of encouragement and that they are most appropriately fostered in a stateless, non-hierarchical society. Can liberalism be seen to rely on a similar methodological emphasis of particular human traits?

It is certainly true that in assigning a central position to autonomy, liberals must be assuming at the very least a human potential for benevolence, for if such a potential did not exist at all, institutions far more coercive than those of the liberal state would be needed to guarantee individual freedoms. Although it is difficult to find any systematic treatment of this idea, it seems to be supported by the literature. Leroy S. Rouner, for example, in his book on human nature, has noted that the 'positive view of human nature' – that is, the idea that humans have an inherent capacity for goodness – 'is deep-seated within the liberal tradition with which most of us identify ourselves' (Rouner 1997). Ritter, too, has noted this convergence between the liberal and the anarchist view, but he goes further, claiming that the liberal outlook is, like that of the anarchists, essentially dualistic, involving a rejection of the idea that 'malevolence is always dominant everywhere' and at the same time denying that benevolence is the universally dominant motive (Ritter 1980: 118). The contextualist view of human nature to which Proudhon, Bakunin and Kropotkin subscribed is, as Ritter puts it, 'clearly within the boundaries of liberal psychology' (ibid.).

This discussion of human nature addresses one of the main objections to anarchism which I raised in Chapter 1. It thus establishes that to characterize the anarchist view on human nature as holding simply that 'people are benign by nature and corrupted by government' (Scruton 1982: 16) is misleadingly simplistic. Accordingly, it shows that while many liberals may be sceptical about anarchism's viability, this scepticism cannot be justified on the basis of the claim that the anarchist view of human nature is 'utopian' or 'naïve'.

Nevertheless, one may still feel some cause for scepticism with regard to anarchism's feasibility. For, it could be argued, while life without the state may be theoretically possible, if we accept something like the aforementioned account of human nature, it is still dubious whether we could actually achieve and sustain it. What, in short, is to replace the state, and what, in the absence of state institutions, is to provide the 'glue' to hold such a society together? Addressing these questions means unpacking the anarchist objection to the state to see just what it consists in, and trying to ascertain what substantive values lie at the heart of anarchist theory, and what role they play in the anarchist position on social change and organization. In the course of this discussion we will also be able to develop a further understanding of the relationship between anarchism and liberalism, and of the nature and role of education in anarchist thought.

3   Anarchist values?

The preceding analysis of the anarchist view of human nature has established that the anarchist understanding of human nature is not, as often perceived, one-dimensional or naïve, an impression responsible for much liberal scepticism regarding anarchism's viability.

The fact that the anarchist account of human nature is actually a complex, anti-essentialist one, rescues anarchism, in my view, from charges of utopianism, at least as far as this point is concerned. It also goes some way towards an understanding of the role assigned to education in anarchist thought. For the fact that anarchists acknowledged human nature to be essentially twofold and subject to contextual influence, explains why they saw a crucial role for education – and specifically moral education – to foster the benevolent aspects of human nature and so create and sustain stateless societies.

Anarchists, then, are under no illusions about the continual, potentially harmful, presence of selfish and competitive aspects of human behaviour and attitudes. This both explains the need for an ongoing educational process of some kind, and indicates that simply doing away with the state will not suffice to create a new social order. Indeed, as Ritter notes,

> Anarchists show an appreciation, with which they are too seldom credited, for the insufficiency of statelessness as a setting for their system. Statelessness must in their view, be preceded and accompanied by conditions which combat the numerous causes of anarchy's internal friction that statelessness cannot defeat alone.
>
> (Ritter 1980: 138)

Education, it seems, is acknowledged by most of the social anarchists to be at least one of the major facilitators of such 'conditions'.

Yet discussion of these issues also leads to more general conclusions regarding education. In general, the anarchist view can be seen to be in contrast with the Marxist view, according to which humans attain their true essence in the post-revolutionary stage. For if one combines the above insights of anarchism regarding human nature with the anarchist insistence, discussed in Chapter 1, that the final form of human society cannot be determined in advance, it seems as if this very perspective yields a far more open-ended, creative image of education and its role in social change. On the Marxist view, education is seen as primarily the means by which the proletarian vanguard is to be educated to true (class) consciousness. Once the revolution is over, it seems, there will be no role for education, for as Lukacs writes, scientific socialism will then be established 'in a complete and definite form, then we shall see a fundamental transformation of the nature of man' (in Read 1974: 150). Anarchism, as discussed, differs from this view in maintaining, first, that the seeds of the stateless society are already present in human action, made possible by existing human moral qualities; and, second, that due to the contextualist view of human nature and the insistence that there is no one scientifically correct form of social organization, education is, and must be, constantly ongoing. Education, on this understanding, is aimed not at bringing about a fixed end-point, but at maintaining an ongoing process of creative experimentation, in keeping with moral values and principles, and in which, as Read says, 'the onus is on man to create the conditions of freedom' (ibid.: 146). This point will be taken up again in later chapters.

These points, in turn, lead one to question the exact nature of the anarchists' objection to the state. As discussed earlier, anarchism cannot be reduced to a simple rejection of the state. Furthermore, if, as this discussion suggests, the anarchist objection to the state is an instrumental one, which cannot be understood without reference to a set of substantive values, the question must then be asked: what exactly are these values and to what extent are they conceived differently from, for example, those of the liberal tradition?

As the preceding chapter suggests, the anarchist position on human nature, both in its emphasis on human rationality and in its contextualist perspective, is remarkably close to the underlying assumptions of liberalism, reflecting the common Enlightenment spirit of both these ideological movements. This sheds an interesting light on the apparent disparity between anarchists and liberals as to the ideal mode of social organization and prompts the question as to what, then, accounts for this disparity, if their assumptions about human potential are so similar. Alan Ritter brings out these political distinctions very well:

> The agreement between anarchists and liberals in psychology makes the main problem of their politics the same. By denying that malevolence is ineradicable, both rule out autocracy as a mode of organization. For only if viciousness must be widespread and rampant is autocracy needed to safeguard peace. By denying the possibility of universal benevolence, they also rule out as unworkable modes of organization which exert no cohesive force. For only if kindness is the overriding motive, can an utterly spontaneous society exist. Thus the problem of politics, for anarchists and liberals alike, is to describe a pattern of social relations that, without being autocratic, provides the required cohesive force.
>
> (Ritter 1980: 120)

The liberal solution to this problem is, of course, to accept the framework of the coercive state but to limit its power so as to guarantee maximum protection of individual liberty. The anarchists reject the state outright as a framework inconsistent with their conception of human flourishing, part of which involves a notion of individual freedom; nevertheless, they have to rely on a certain amount of public censure to ensure the cohesive force and survival of society. As Ritter points out (ibid.), it is because anarchists 'affirm the worth of communal understanding' that they can, unlike liberals, regard such censure as having a relatively benign effect on individuality.

However, this point is not as simple as Ritter suggests. For it is true that for a person engaged in the communal project of building a social-anarchist society, out of a commitment to the values of equality, solidarity and freedom from state control of social institutions, accepting a certain degree of restriction on individual freedom — for example, a demand to share one's income with the community or to take on responsibilities connected with public services such as rubbish-collecting or child-minding — may not be perceived as a great sacrifice. But if life in anarchist communities without the state becomes a reality, it is quite possible that individuals born into such communities may come to perceive such apparent external restraints, which they have not in any way chosen or instituted themselves, as an unacceptable imposition.

This problem, it seems, is at the crux of the mainstream liberal scepticism regarding the feasibility of maintaining an anarchist society. One response to it, of course, is to argue that it is precisely because of their awareness of this tension that anarchists assigned such a central place to education. In order for a social-anarchist society to work, in other words, education — both formal and informal — would have to continue to promote and support the values on which the society was founded. Furthermore, because of the anarchist view of human nature, according to which stateless, social anarchist communities would not need to change human nature but merely to draw out moral qualities and tendencies already present, this view escapes charges of 'character moulding' or coercion by means of education — processes which are inimical to the anarchist position.

Another response, however, is to argue that once stateless, decentralized anarchist communities have been established on a federalized basis and social practices and institutions have been set up to meet the needs of such communities, such institutions, and the communities themselves, being qualitatively different from those of the state, will have an important educative function. Some contemporary anarchists, such as Illich,[1] have indeed taken this position, yet most of the early social anarchists, as discussed earlier, and as will be explored in the following chapters, explicitly acknowledged the need for a formal education system of some kind after the revolutionary period.

There is considerable confusion in the anarchist literature surrounding this point — confusion which I believe is largely a result of the failure of anarchist theorists to distinguish between life within the state and life beyond the state. This issue is explored further in the course of the following discussion.

Autonomy in anarchism and liberalism

A great deal of criticism of the anarchist position hinges on the claim that there is an internal inconsistency in the belief that one can sustain a stateless society characterized by solidarity, social equality and mutual aid and at the same time preserve individual autonomy. In order to understand more fully the anarchist response to this criticism, it is important to examine the role assigned to autonomy and individual freedom within anarchist thought. Furthermore, a discussion of these notions is an essential aspect of the analysis of the anarchist position on education, particularly in the context of liberal education, where autonomy plays a central role.

As mentioned earlier, most liberal theorists on education cite autonomy as a, if not the, central value in education. Indeed, as Carr and Hartnett put it (1996: 47), 'in many ways, the mobilizing principle behind most theoretical justifications for liberal education has been a commitment to the aims and values of "rational autonomy"'. Some writers in this tradition, like Meira Levinson, specifically link the value of autonomy to the goal of sustaining the liberal state. Patricia White, while not specifically focusing on the educational implications of liberalism as a political doctrine, makes a similar point when she argues that the rationale for our current political arrangements (i.e. those of the democratic, liberal state) is 'to provide a context in which morally autonomous people can live' (White 1983: 140) and that therefore 'educational arrangements must provide the conditions for the development and flourishing of autonomous persons' (ibid.). Other theorists – most notably R.S. Peters and Paul Hirst – refer to a supposedly neutral, analytical account of education defined as initiation into worthwhile activities, or development of the mind. Yet even in this second case, it is liberal values which underlie the account. Furthermore, in both cases, these theorists usually assume something like a Kantian account of autonomy.

R.S. Peters, in summing up the notion of autonomy in the context of his discussion on education, notes two main factors as central to the Kantian conception of autonomy:

1 The idea of adopting a 'code or way of life that is one's own as distinct from one dictated by others' – this can be understood as the condition of authenticity;
2 Rational reflection on rules in light of universal principles.

(Peters 1998: 16)

Another way of grasping this view of autonomy is by means of the idea of the self-legislating person. This notion, which is central to the Kantian view, is, likewise, connected to the idea of the human capacity for reason.

Wolff (1998) links this account with the similarly Kantian idea of moral responsibility, arguing that 'every man who possesses free will and reason has an obligation to take responsibility for his actions' (Wolff 1998: 13) and that it is only the person acting in this way who can be described as an autonomous person (ibid.).

Peters comments that the idea of autonomy as involving acting in accordance with a code which one has adopted as a result of rational reflection on intrinsic considerations (as opposed to rewards, punishments, etc.) implies that the individual be 'sensitive to considerations which are to act as principles to back rules' (Peters 1998: 23) and to regard these considerations as reasons for doing things. Peters leaves the question as to how children acquire such sensitivity open, but it is worth noting that the original Kantian formulation is even stronger in its emphasis on this idea, insisting that for an action to be fully autonomous it must be done for duty's sake and not from inclination or from any empirical motive such as fear (see Ritter 1980: 114).

Yet even if one accepts the arguments of Levinson and others who identify autonomy as a necessary condition for maintaining the liberal state and, therefore, the development of autonomy as a central component of liberal education, it does not of course follow that the liberal state is the only, or even the best, framework in which to realize and promote the value of personal autonomy.

As suggested here, autonomy can be defended as a value in and of itself, for example within a Kantian framework of morality. From an educational perspective, then, the question becomes whether, given the value of autonomy (along with other liberal ideas), one can in fact support a radically different idea of education and schooling – one more compatible, for example, with the anarchist idea. From a political point of view, the anarchist commentator Paul Wolff has argued that, if one takes the value of autonomy seriously, 'there can be no resolution of the conflict between the autonomy of the individual and the putative authority of the state' and that therefore 'anarchism is the only political doctrine consistent with the virtue of autonomy' (Wolff 1998: 12–13). I shall look at Wolff's argument in greater detail later, but in the present context, it is worth noting that if one accepts it, one can then go on to challenge the analogous assumption that liberal education, conceived as universal, compulsory education by and in a liberal state, is the best educational framework in which to pursue and promote the central liberal value of autonomy.

The question that concerns us in this context is whether the understanding of autonomy, and the role assigned to it, within anarchist thought, is similar to that within the liberal tradition and what bearing this has on the anarchist position on education.

There is no doubt that anarchist theorists in the tradition which we have been considering here, while not perhaps providing a systematic account of the notion of autonomy, nevertheless subscribed to something very like the notion described earlier. Indeed, one commentator has argued that for many anarchists, freedom is conceived of as moral autonomy (De George 1978: 92).

Of all the anarchist theorists to write on the subject, it is Godwin whose account of freedom and autonomy most obviously resembles the liberal, Kantian account outlined earlier. For Godwin, the free person is not simply one whose actions are not constrained by external forces, but one who, prior to acting, 'consults his own reason, draws his own conclusions and exercises the powers of his understanding' (Godwin, in Ritter 1980: 11). Furthermore, this formulation presupposes a faith in the human capacity for rationality, which was basic to Godwin's position. As Ritter points out, it follows, from this and similar accounts by other anarchist thinkers, that the only acceptable restraints on individual liberty are those which are the result of rational deliberation.

Other, later anarchist thinkers also seem often to be subscribing to something like the liberal notion of autonomy in their discussions of freedom. Stanley Benn's account of the autonomous person as someone who does not simply accept 'the roles society thrusts on him, uncritically internalizing the received mores, but is committed to a critical and creative search for coherence' (Benn 1975: 109) seems to be in keeping with views expressed by anarchist thinkers such as Bakunin, who states:

> Freedom is the absolute right of every human being to seek no other sanction for his actions but his own conscience, to determine these actions solely by his own will, and consequently to owe his first responsibility to himself alone.
>
> (Guerin 1970: 31)

Yet, as Guerin notes, Bakunin held that this individual freedom could be fully realized 'only by complementing it through all the individuals around him, and only through work and the collective force of society' (ibid.). Although insisting that membership in society or any of its associations is voluntary, Bakunin was convinced that people would choose freely to belong to a society that was organized on the basis of equality and social justice.

So although autonomy is clearly a value within anarchist thought, it would be misleading to imply, as De George does (De George 1978) that the anarchist understanding of freedom – especially for the social anarchists – can be reduced to something like the liberal notion of individual autonomy. Crucially, most of these thinkers tried to develop an account of freedom as bound with a notion of social justice, in the sense that the notion of individual freedom which they defended only made sense in the context of an account of political and social freedom. This position is particularly evident in the work of Bakunin, who argued:

> I can feel free only in the presence of and in relationship with other men. In the presence of an inferior species of animal I am neither free nor a man, because this animal is incapable of conceiving and consequently of

recognizing my humanity. I am not myself free or human until or unless I recognize the freedom and humanity of all my fellow men.

(Bakunin, in Dolgoff 1973: 76)

As suggested in the earlier discussion on human nature, Bakunin is making an anti-metaphysical point about freedom, focusing on the subjective experience of individual freedom rather than suggesting any essentialist notion. Thus, in a passage clearly intended to contrast with Rousseau's famous statement that 'man is born free...', he writes:

> The primitive, natural man becomes a free man, becomes humanized, and rises to the status of a moral being [...] only to the degree that he becomes aware of this form and these rights in all his fellow-beings.

(Bakunin, in Dolgoff 1973: 156)

For most anarchists, then, autonomy, although an important value within their ideology, did not enjoy any privileged status. Furthermore, this notion is, as shall be discussed later (see Chapter 4), conceptually linked with the equally important social values of solidarity and fraternity. This conceptual connection allows anarchist theorists to go on to draw further, important connections between freedom and equality.

Reciprocal awareness

Some theorists in fact, amongst them Walter and Ritter, have argued that individual freedom, or autonomy, is of instrumental value in anarchist theory, the chief goal of which is what Ritter (1980) calls 'communal individuality'. Ritter bases his account of this notion primarily on Godwin's idea of 'reciprocal awareness', which, it is argued, provides the moral underpinnings of the social-anarchist society. The idea of 'reciprocal awareness' implies a normative view of social relationships based on cooperation and trust, in which each individual perceives her freedom as necessarily bound up with the good of the community. Such an awareness, which seems to be referring primarily to psychological and emotional processes, is obviously one of the qualities to be fostered and encouraged by means of education. This psychological, or emotional attitude, in turn, forms the basis for the moral ideal which Ritter refers to as 'communal individuality'.

This view that it is community, or what Ritter calls 'communal individuality', and not freedom, which is the main goal of social anarchism, finds further support in Bakunin's writings. Bakunin, like other social anarchists, was keen to refute what he regarded as the guiding premise of Enlightenment thinkers such as Locke, Montesquieu and Rousseau; namely that individuality and the common good represent opposing interests. Bakunin writes, 'freedom is not the negation of solidarity. Social solidarity is the first human law; freedom is the second law. Both laws interpenetrate each other, and, being inseparable, constitute the essence of humanity' (Bakunin, in Maximoff 1953: 156).

This passage is a typically confusing piece of writing on Bakunin's part, and he seems to offer no explanation as to what he means by 'the first human law'. However, it does seem to be clear that Bakunin, like most social-anarchist thinkers, regards individual freedom as constituted by and in social interaction. Bakunin insisted that it is society which creates individual freedom: 'Society is the root, the tree of freedom, and liberty is its fruit.' (Maximoff 1953: 165).

Significantly, it is this position which enables thinkers like Bakunin to go on to draw conceptual connections between freedom, solidarity – or what Ritter calls 'communal individuality' – and equality, as follows: 'Since freedom is the result and the clearest expression of solidarity, that is of mutuality of interests, it can be realized only under conditions of equality [by which Bakunin means, as discussed later, economic and social equality]' (ibid.).

Yet it is still not entirely clear what status Bakunin is assigning to the connections between freedom and equality. Morland suggests that Bakunin was in fact a Hegelian in this respect, and that his argument that the individual is only truly free when all around him are free implies a notion of liberty as omnipresent in a Hegelian sense, in which 'all duality between the individual and society, between society and nature, is dialectically overcome' (Marshall, quoted in Morland 1997: 81).

Yet I am inclined to think that the justification for Bakunin's arguments for the important connections between social equality and liberty stems more from a psychological account than from a Hegelian dialectic. This seems apparent in the aforementioned passage from Bakunin, in which he argues that

> The liberty of every human individual is only the reflection of his own humanity, or his human right through the conscience of all free men, his brothers and his equals. I can feel free only in the presence of and in relationship with other men.
>
> (Bakunin, in Dolgoff 1973: 237)

Godwin, too, seems to be making a psychological observation in describing individual autonomy as a form of mental and moral independence and noting that this kind of freedom 'supports community by drawing people toward each other leading to a kind of reciprocal awareness which promotes mutual trust, solidarity, and emotional and intellectual growth' (Ritter 1980: 29).

It sounds as if what Godwin has in mind here is something like the point commonly made by individualist anarchists, that 'only he who is strong enough to stand alone is capable of forming a genuinely free association with others' (Parker 1965: 3).

The social anarchists, although explicitly anti-individualistic in their views, seemed to subscribe to a similar psychological view of the connections between individual freedom and the kinds of social values necessary to ensure life in communities. Alongside this position, they invariably tied their discussion of freedom into their insistence on the immediate improvement of the material conditions of society. As Goodwin and Taylor put it: 'While liberals traditionally see the progress towards greater freedom and rationality in terms of "the progress of the human mind", the early socialists conceived of progress as situated in the context of real material circumstances' (Goodwin and Taylor 1982: 147). Of course, in the same way as autonomy is clearly not conceptually prior to other values within anarchist thought, it is important here to note that neither are all liberals committed to assigning autonomy a position of primary importance. Hocking, for example (1926), has argued that anarchist and liberal aims overlap because both regard liberty (understood as the absence of coercion by the state) as the chief political good. Yet as Ritter (1980) points out, this position is misleading not only because it ignores the view that, for many anarchists, individual freedom in this sense is actually only a means to the conceptually prior value of communal individuality, but because it overlooks strands of liberal thought in which freedom is instrumental (e.g. utilitarian liberalism).

Liberal paternalism and libertarianism

The social anarchists' rejection of the abstract, Rousseauian idea of pre-social freedom, and their insistence that autonomy is not a natural, essential aspect of human nature, but something to be developed and nurtured within the context of social relationships, not only distinguishes them from early Enlightenment liberal thinkers, but also partly explains why, from an educational perspective, they do not adopt an extreme libertarian position – that is, a philosophical objection to all educational intervention in children's lives. Acknowledging, along with later liberal thinkers such as J.S. Mill, that individual freedom is restrained by deliberative rationality, and ever-conscious of the social context of developing human freedom, most anarchist thinkers have no problem in endorsing rational restraints on individual freedom even in the context of a post-state, anarchist society. From an educational point of view, the implication of this position is that anarchists agree with liberals in accepting something like the paternalistic exception to Mill's harm principle in the case of children. In other words, they do not take the extreme libertarian position that educational intervention constitutes a violation of children's autonomy.

This position can be seen most clearly in the work of Bakunin who, dealing with the question of children's rights and the provision of education, expresses views that are strikingly similar to the liberal, humanist tradition. The following passage in particular reflects the development of Bakunin's thought from the Enlightenment tradition:

> It is the right of every man and woman, from birth to childhood, to complete upkeep, clothes, food, shelter, care, guidance, education (public schools, primary, secondary, higher education, artistic, industrial, and

scientific), all at the expense of society [....] Parents shall have the right to care for and guide the education of their children, under the ultimate control of the commune which retains the right and the obligation to take children away from parents who, by example or by cruel and inhuman treatment, demoralize or otherwise hinder the physical and mental development of their children.[2]

(Bakunin, in Dolgoff 1973: 112)

Even when he acknowledges that children themselves have rights and can in some sense be regarded as moral agents, it is nevertheless quite clear from these writings that Bakunin is far from adopting an extreme libertarian view of children as autonomous beings responsible for determining their own educational aims and processes:

We do not claim that the child should be treated as an adult, that all his caprices should be respected, that when his childish will stubbornly flouts the elementary rules of science and common sense we should avoid making him feel that he is wrong. We say, on the contrary, that the child must be trained and guided, but that the direction of his first years must not be exclusively exercised by his parents, who are all too often incompetent and who generally abuse their authority. The aim of education is to develop the latent capacities of the child to the fullest possible extent and enable him to take care of himself as quickly as possible.[...]

Today, parents not only support their children [i.e. providing food, clothes, etc.] but also supervise their education. This is a custom based on a false principle, a principle that regards the child as the personal property of the parents. The child belongs to no one, he belongs only to himself; and during the period when he is unable to protect himself and is thereby exposed to exploitation, it is society that must protect him and guarantee his free development. It is society that must support him and supervise his education. In supporting him and paying for his education society is only making an advance 'loan' which the child will repay when he becomes an adult proper.

(Ibid.)

So although one can find some echoes of the liberal ideal of autonomy within the anarchist tradition, this notion does not play such a central role within social-anarchist thought as it does within liberal theory and, connectedly, liberal ideas on education.

Autonomy and community – tensions and questions

Nevertheless, even if autonomy is only one of several connected goals within anarchist thought, it is still important to try and answer the question of its role within the anarchist position on education. Specifically, if education for personal autonomy is a common educational goal for both liberal and anarchist theorists, would the same liberal restrictions and principles that apply to the state as an educating body apply to the community within the framework of a stateless, anarchist society? For although anarchists reject the state and the associated centralist control of social institutions, they do nevertheless acknowledge, as we have seen, the need for some kind of educational process which, in the absence of a centralist state, would presumably be run on a community level. Thus, given the anarchist acceptance of the value of individual autonomy, understood as the ability to make and implement choices on the basis of rational deliberation, without external constraints, one could still argue, based on the classic liberal argument for neutrality (see Dworkin 1978), that the community has no right to impose particular versions of the good life on any of its members.

For the social anarchists, the basic unit of social organization is the commune, association within and amongst communes being conducted on an essentially federalist basis. One important element of this federalism is the right to secession – a point which Bakunin made on several occasions:

> Every individual, every association, every commune, every region, every nation has the absolute right to self-determination, to associate or not to associate, to ally themselves with whomever they wish and repudiate their alliances without regard to so-called historic rights...The right of free reunion, as well as the right of secession, is the first and most important of all political rights.
>
> (in Morland 1997: 102)

However, even if secession is a real option, it is quite conceivable that various communities would be organized around particular ideologies and would therefore choose to educate their members according to a substantive vision of the good life as reflected in the organization and ethos of that community. In the absence of any other restriction, it is quite possible that certain such communities would undermine the value of autonomy.

Michael Taylor, in his book *Anarchy, Liberty and Community* (Taylor 1982), has examined this potential tension within anarchist theory in considerable detail. Taylor restates the classic liberal argument that in order for an individual to be autonomous, she must be able to critically choose from amongst genuinely available values, norms and ways of life, and that such possibility for choice only exists within a pluralistic society. Thus, in 'primitive and peasant communities', with strong traditions and considerable homogeneity in terms of lifestyles and values, individual autonomy cannot be said to exist. But Taylor goes on to make the point that, in fact, for members of such communities, autonomy is simply not an issue (and, indeed, not the problem it often becomes in pluralistic societies) for such people 'feel at home in a coherent world' (Taylor 1982: 161). This view seems to support Joseph Raz's argument

(Raz 1986) that individual well-being does not depend on the presence of autonomy. Nevertheless, given that for anarchist theorists, autonomy, in the sense of individual freedom of choice, does seem to have been a central value, one must ask whether the types of communities they sought to create were supportive of this value.

Taylor argues that as utopian communities are always islands within the greater society, and as their members are recruited from that society, the values of the 'outside' world will always, in a sense, be present as real options, as will the possibility of leaving the community – thus ensuring the autonomy of the individuals within it. But if the anarchist–socialist revolution is successful and the state is completely dismantled, the picture one gets is of a future society composed of several federated communities which will not be radically different in terms of their values. The particular social practices and lifestyles may differ from commune to commune, but as all practices are expected to conform to principles of equality and justice, as conceived by theorists such as Bakunin, it is hard to see how any commune could present a radically challenging alternative to an individual in another commune. As an example, one may cite the *kibbutzim* in Israel which, although superficially different from one another (e.g. in terms of the cultural origins and customs of their members, their physical characteristics, their main source of livelihood, etc.), are nevertheless all instantly recognizable as *kibbutzim* in that they clearly exhibit common basic features of social organization and underlying values which distinguish them from the surrounding society.

Can one, then, argue that a child growing up in an anarchist commune after the demise of the nation state, would be less autonomous than a child growing up in a liberal-democratic state? I think there are two possible responses to this. One is to take the line that children growing up in a pluralistic, democratic society are not genuinely autonomous as their choices are restricted by their environment and upbringing. Thus, for example, a child growing up in a thoroughly secular environment could never really have the option of autonomously choosing a religious way of life. Yet this argument does not seem very serious to me. The fact is, it does sometimes happen that such children break away from their backgrounds and choose radically different lifestyles, adopting values which are completely at odds with those of their upbringing. And there seems to be some grounds for the claim that it is the very presence of the alternative, 'somewhere out there' that creates this possibility of choice.

A more promising line of argument is that which connects the discussion to the idea of the conditions of freedom. It makes no sense to talk of someone being able to exercise freedom, either in the sense of negative liberty, or in the sense of autonomy, without the satisfaction of basic material conditions. It seems to me that this is the key to understanding the apparent problem of autonomy within anarchist communes. For, as argued earlier, the autonomy of individual members of a commune may seem to be severely restricted by the absence of genuine alternative versions of the good life from which to choose, either within the commune or amongst other communes. Yet the very values which create a high degree of similarity between communes and amongst members of the same commune – that is, values of economic and social equality – are those values that constitute prerequisites for the exercise of any form of freedom. Thus although one could argue that the autonomy of a particular individual may be limited in a commune, as opposed to a pluralist, democratic state, there would be fewer members of society lacking in effective freedom than there would, in this view, in less equitable societies. This seems to support the essentially anti-individualistic tendencies of the social anarchists, as well as their insistence on immediate improvement of the material conditions of society. As Goodwin and Taylor emphasize, for the anarchists,

> [...] the values of harmony, association, community, and co-operation were not vague ethical ideals to be realized at some indeterminate point in the future through the loosening of legal restraints, the establishing of declarations of the rights of man, and the winning of constitutional-institutional reforms. Rather the future utopia required quite specific – objective rather than subjective – changes in the material basis of society, changes which could only be brought about through the implementation of an overall, collective plan – a fairly detailed blueprint – of some description. It was in this respect that the very term 'socialism' emerged in the 1830's as the antithesis of liberal 'individualism'.
>
> (Goodwin and Taylor 1982: 147)

All the same, I am inclined to agree with those critics of anarchism who argue that this tension between personal autonomy and the possible coercive effects of public censure is the most worrying aspect of anarchist ideology, and one to which most anarchists have not provided a very satisfactory answer, other than the faith that such conflicts can and simply will be resolved justly in the moral climate and free experimentation that will prevail in the stateless society.

Robert Wolff and the argument from autonomy

It is important to understand that, in advocating autonomy as a central value – albeit with different emphases than those of the liberal tradition – anarchists are not simply going one step further than liberals in objecting to all forms of coercion. It is not a variant of this position which constitutes the philosophical explanation for their principled objection to the state. It is, in fact, this mistaken interpretation of anarchism that, I would argue, lies behind Robert Wolff's attempt to offer a philosophical defence of the anarchist position (Wolff 1998).

It is worth looking into Wolff's argument here, for I believe its very construction helps to highlight some of the points I want to make in this discussion about the difference in perspective between anarchism and liberalism.

Wolff sets out to establish that there is a philosophical contradiction between individual autonomy and the *de jure* state – defined as an entity instantiating *de jure* authority – and that anarchism is thus the only political position compatible with the value of personal autonomy. The anarchist understanding of authority also has bearings on Wolff's argument, as will be discussed later. But the essential point here is that, as Miller notes, Wolff's argument rests on the premise that 'autonomy is the primary moral desideratum' (Miller 1984: 27). Yet, as the foregoing discussion suggests, this premise is questionable, not only within liberalism, but also within anarchist theory itself. However, most commentators on Wolff have not questioned this premise, but have tried, instead, to find fault in his argument (see, for example, the discussions in *American Philosophical Quarterly*, IX, (4), 1972). Without going into the philosophical details of Wolff's argument, the point I wish to make here is that whether or not it is valid, it suggests a misleading interpretation of anarchism and, in fact, obscures the difference of perspective which distinguishes anarchists from liberals.

In a sense, Wolff's argument, if valid, proves too much. Anarchists are not concerned with refuting the validity of the *de jure* state from a philosophical point of view; their objection to the state, as will be discussed below, is based on a more complex and concrete analysis than the conceptual argument that it conflicts with individual autonomy. Similarly, many anarchists – particularly the social anarchists – would not agree with Wolff that 'the defining mark of the state is authority, the right to rule' (Wolff 1998: 18). I shall discuss the anarchist objection to the state in greater detail later. However, at this point, it is important to understand how Wolff's apparent attempt to reduce anarchism to a defensible philosophical argument is connected to the above discussion of the multiplicity of values within anarchist thought.

While attempting to reduce any ideology to a single, logically prior value is, of course, problematic, in the case of anarchism this would seem especially so, for anarchism is in principle opposed to hierarchical thinking. As Todd May points out, anarchist thought involves a 'rejection of strategic political philosophy', and the social-anarchist struggle is conceived 'in terms of getting rid of hierarchic thinking and action altogether' (May 1994: 51). Thus, the anarchist vision of the future ideal society as a decentralized network, in which 'certain points and certain lines may be bolder than others, but none of them functions as a centre from which the others emerge or to which they return' (ibid.: 53) is, I would suggest, reflected in the philosophical position that no one value or goal can be regarded as logically prior or ultimate. This is not to claim that there is no conflict between values within anarchist thought; indeed, as we have seen earlier, the two interrelated anarchist goals of individual freedom and communality may well be in tension under certain circumstances. These conflicts are not conceptual dilemmas to be resolved by philosophical arguments but concrete social problems to be creatively solved as the situation demands. It seems to me that Bakunin's attempts to paint a picture of such a network of interconnected values as one coherent whole could be read not just as a philosophically confused argument but as a reflection of this anti-hierarchical stance.

Interestingly, after claiming that personal autonomy is logically incompatible with the *de jure* state, Wolff then goes on to suggest that unanimous direct democracy 'is a genuine solution to the problem of autonomy and authority' (Wolff 1998: 27). As Grenville Wall points out (Wall 1978: 276); this move in itself is puzzling as it seems to contradict the premise that this conflict is *logically* irreconcilable. Yet, aside from this methodological problem, this aspect of Wolff's argument also reveals a similar misconception of anarchism. Wolff describes the ideal of unanimous direct democracy as one in which 'every member of the society wills freely every law which is actually passed' (Wolff 1998: 23). As the autonomous person, on both the liberal and the anarchist account, is one whose actions are restrained only by the dictates of his own will and reason, it follows that in a direct democracy, there need be no conflict between 'the duty of autonomy' and the 'commands of authority' (ibid.). Wolff's use of the phrase 'the duty of autonomy' reveals his strong Kantian orientation and, again, is an inaccurate representation of the anarchist view, according to which autonomy is less a 'duty' than a quality of life to be created, aspired to and dynamically forged in a social context along with other social values.

Wolff's picture of a unanimous direct democracy, although described in purely procedural terms, may be quite in keeping with the social-anarchist ideal. Yet interestingly, when discussing the possibility of this theoretical solution to his proposed dilemma (a solution which, as Wall remarks, Wolff seems to regard as unworkable for empirical, rather than philosophical reasons), the basic unit under consideration, for Wolff, is still that of the state. He acknowledges, apparently, the assumption that unanimous democracy 'creates a *de jure* state'. But the point is that anarchists object to the state for other reasons than that it embodies *de jure* authority, so even a state founded on unanimous direct democracy, in which personal autonomy, if we accept Wolff's argument, could flourish, would still be a *state* and would be objectionable for other important reasons. In addition to their positive commitment to specific values, to be discussed later, crucially, the anarchists' objection to the state stems, in large part, from their anti-hierarchical stance. Basic to this stance is the view that, as Woodcock puts it,

> What characterizes the State, apart from its foundation on authority and coercion, is the way in which it cumulatively centralizes all social and political functions, and in doing so puts them out of the reach of the citizens whose lives they shape.
>
> (Woodcock 1977: 21)

Accordingly, all anarchists refer in their discussion of social organization to a basic unit of direct cooperation. This unit, whether a commune, a workshop or a school, is, crucially, something qualitatively distinct from, and inevitably far smaller than, the state.

It is for this same reason that Wolff's creative suggestions towards overcoming the practical obstacles in the way of direct democracy in contemporary societies undermine the very anarchist idea that his argument is ostensibly intended to support. Wolff's picture of a society, the size of the United States equipped with 'in-the-home voting machines' transmitting 'to a computer in Washington', 'committees of experts' gathering data, and the establishment of a position of 'Public Dissenter in order to guarantee that dissident and unusual points of view were heard' (Wolff 1998: 34–35) could not be further removed from the social-anarchist ideal in which social functions are organized from the bottom-up, in cooperative networks based at the level of the smallest possible scale, and where 'face-to-face contacts can take the place of remote commands' (Woodcock 1977: 21).

To sum up the discussion so far, it seems that anarchism overlaps liberalism in its emphasis on personal autonomy – although it does not assign the value of personal autonomy any priority – and in its acknowledgement of the benevolent potential of human beings; furthermore, it shares the essentially rationalistic stance of liberal education and the faith in human reason as the key to progress. Although several commentators (e.g., Bellamy, Ritter and Walter) have argued that anarchism cannot be regarded as an extension of liberalism due to its emphasis on community, this point could be countered with the argument that an emphasis on the value of community is perfectly consistent with the brand of liberalism defended by theorists such as Kymlicka and Raz.

The essential points on which anarchist and liberal aims diverge seem to be firstly in anarchism's rejection of the framework of the state and, connectedly, in its perspective on the possibility of achieving the desired social change. The essence of this distinct perspective is, it seems to me, captured in Ritter's remark that: 'To redeem society on the strength of rational, spontaneous relations, while slaying the leviathan who offers minimal protection – this is the anarchists' daring choice' (Ritter 1980: 133).

4   Authority, the state and education

Anarchism and liberalism, as we have seen, share certain important underlying values. We now have to ask whether this means that the philosophical and moral underpinnings of the anarchist conception of education are not essentially different from those that form the basis of the idea of liberal education.

Once again, the difference would seem to turn not on the question of the adherence to certain values and virtues, such as autonomy, rationality or equality, but on the different scope and perspective on social change within which such values are understood, and the role of education in achieving this change.

Crucially, in spite of their emphasis on the inherent human propensity for benevolence and voluntary cooperation, and in spite of their rationalist convictions, it would appear that the social anarchists, with their critical analysis of capitalist society and its social institutions, alongside their pragmatic view of the innate lust for power potentially present in everyone, could not, like Mill, or indeed Godwin, put all their faith in the Enlightenment ideal of the ultimate triumph of human reason over oppressive forms of social organization.

Thus Bakunin, a thinker typical of this tradition, did not stop at the liberal idea of achieving social change – or even the overthrow of oppressive regimes – by means of rational education. As a revolutionary thinker, he insisted on the ultimate abolishment of all structural forms of authority which he saw as hostile to individual freedom. 'The revolution, instead of modifying institutions, will do away with them altogether. Therefore, the government will be uprooted, along with the church, the army, the courts, the schools, the banks and all their subservient institutions' (Bakunin, in Dolgoff 1973: 358).

Yet as we shall see, experiments in implementing social-anarchist principles on a community level did not involve abolishing schools altogether, but, on the contrary, often centred around the establishment of schools – albeit schools that were radically different from the typical public schools of the time. Crucially, these schools were seen not just as a means for promoting rational education and thus encouraging children to develop a critical attitude to the capitalist state, and, hopefully, to eventually undermine it; rather, the schools themselves were regarded as experimental instances of the social-anarchist society in action. They were, then, not merely a means to social revolution but a crucial part of the revolutionary process itself.

So Bakunin and other nineteenth-century social-anarchist thinkers shared certain liberal assumptions about human nature and a liberal faith in the educative power of social institutions, as reflected in Bakunin's claim that: 'it is certain that in a society based on reason, justice, and freedom, on respect for humanity and on complete equality, the good will prevail and the evil will be a morbid exception' (Bakunin, in Dolgoff 1973: 95).

Yet such thinkers did not believe that such a society was possible within the framework of the state — however liberal. The focus of their educational thought and experimentation, therefore, was on developing active forms of social interaction which would constitute an alternative to the state. In so doing, however, the conceptualization of education which informed their views, as I shall argue further later, was not one of education as a means to an end but a more complex one of education as one of the many aspects of social interaction which, if engaged in in a certain spirit, could itself be part of the revolutionary process of undermining the state and reforming society on a communal basis.

This reflects the crucial aspect of social anarchism expressed by Paul Goodman as follows: 'A free society cannot be the substitution of a "new order" for the old order; it is the extension of spheres of free action until they make up most of social life' (quoted in Ward 1996: 18).

The anarchist objection to the state

The earlier discussion notwithstanding, the anarchists' rejection of the state as a mode of social organization which they regarded as inimical to human freedom and flourishing raises two important questions: first, is the anarchist rejection of the state a principled rejection of states *qua* states or is it a contingent rejection, based on the fact that the modern nation state typically has properties which the anarchists regard as objectionable? Second, even if Wolff and other commentators are mistaken in implying that it is the notion of authority which constitutes the core of the anarchist objection to the state as a form of social organization, suspicion of authority is nevertheless a central aspect of all anarchist thought. It is important, then, particularly in the context of education, to ascertain what anarchists understand by the notion of authority and connected notions, and whether their objection to it is philosophically coherent and defensible.

Although certain commentators, such as Miller and Reichert, talk of anarchism's 'hostility to the state' (Miller 1984: 5) as its defining characteristic, often implying that this hostility is a principled one towards the state as such, many theorists have acknowledged the nuances involved in this hostility. Thus, Richard Sylvan notes (Sylvan 1993: 216) that, although it may be true that anarchists oppose all existing systems of government, this is 'crucially contingent upon the character of prevailing state systems.' One can in fact find support for this interpretation in the writings of the social anarchists themselves. Kropotkin, for example, made the claim, late in his life (quoted in Buber 1958), that what the anarchists were calling for was 'less representation and more self-government' – suggesting a willingness to compromise with certain elements of the democratic state.

Bakunin, too, devoted much of his writings against the state to a detailed account of what he regarded as the characteristics of the modern state. In 'The Modern State Surveyed' (Dolgoff 1973: 210–217), which very title lends itself to the interpretation suggested by Sylvan, Bakunin outlines a list of what he regards as the principal faults of the state. Chief amongst these are capitalism, militarism and bureaucratic centralization. This analysis, along with the considerable space Bakunin and other nineteenth-century anarchists devoted to attacking the association between the state and the Church, suggests that their objection to the state was, indeed, an objection to particular features which they regarded as inherent properties of the state. Yet most of these features are, arguably, contingent on particular historical forms of the state – and were particularly salient in the evolving nineteenth-century model of the powerful nation state in the context of which the social anarchists were developing their position.

It is therefore apparently not logically inconceivable that a political system calling itself a state could be compatible with anarchist principles. Some contemporary anarchists, in fact, have suggested that the Swiss cantons are a close approximation of anarchist political principles, although the social anarchists would probably have criticized them for their inequitable economic policies. The point that Sylvan is making is that the modern state *as we know it* has come to constitute 'the paradigmatic archist form' (Sylvan 1993: 217) and as such, it is incompatible with anarchist principles.

I would therefore disagree with the argument made by Miller and others that perhaps the central defining feature of anarchism is its 'hostility to the state'. This hostility, in fact, as discussed earlier, and as I shall argue further in what follows, is an instrumental one; the crucial core of anarchism is, rather, the positive values which it espouses, and it is the state as inimical to these values, not the state as such, to which anarchists object. Miller argues that anarchists 'make two charges against the state – they claim that it has no right to exist, and they also claim that it brings a whole series of social evils in its train' (Miller 1984: 5). But I would argue that this formulation is misleading: the claim that the state has no right to exist is not an independent, *a priori* claim. It is because of its 'social evils' that the state, under a particular definition, has no right to exist. These are, then, not two charges, but one and the same charge.

Nevertheless, even if anarchism's hostility to the state is 'contingent and consequential [...], derived from the conjunction of anarchism's defining features together with a particular standard theoretical characterization of "the state" ' (Sylvan 1993: 218), one must ask what exactly this characterization consists of.

Most political theorists writing on this topic accept something like Weber's classic definition of the state as an association that 'successfully claims the monopoly of legitimate use of physical force within a given territory' (see Taylor 1982: 4–5).

Many social anarchists seem to have had something like this notion in mind in formulating their rejection of the state. However, as suggested here, this rejection derived more from what Sylvan refers to as 'anarchism's defining features' than from any coherent theoretical characterization. This point is perhaps most apparent in the writings of Bakunin, who devoted considerable space (see Dolgoff 1973: 206–208) to a rejection of what he calls the 'theology of the state' – namely, the defence of the idea of the state by social contract theorists such as Rousseau. Yet in fact, most of Bakunin's objection centres on specific features which he claims to be logically associated with the state. First, he argues, the state 'could not exist without a privileged body' (ibid.). Here, Bakunin's objection stems from his socialist-egalitarian commitments, his conviction being that the state 'has always been the patrimony of some privileged class' (ibid.). Yet this, of course, is an empirical point. Furthermore, he argues, the modern state is 'necessarily a military state', and thus 'if it does not conquer it will be conquered by others' (ibid.). Yet this, again, seems to be an empirical point and, as cases like Switzerland suggest, it is highly contentious.

In short, it seems to be modern capitalism and its resulting inequalities which constitute the basis for Bakunin's objection to the state. Although there are obvious connections between capitalist production and the structure of the nation state, it is arguable whether the former is a necessary feature of the latter. Thus, once again, it would seem that the anarchist objection to the state, on this point, is an instrumental one.

Authority

Of course, as Taylor (1982) notes, even if anarchists implicitly accepted something like Weber's (albeit problematic) definition of the state, there is no logical reason why rejecting the state should entail a complete rejection of authority or censure. Yet the idea of authority is clearly conceptually linked to this idea of the state. Wolff, for example, suggests a revision of Weber's definition as follows: 'The state is a group of persons who have and exercise supreme authority within a given territory or over a certain population', arguing that 'the defining mark of the state is authority, the right to rule' (Wolff 1998: 18).

Indeed, the impression that what the anarchists object to in the state is the idea of authority itself is reinforced by some early anarchist writers. Sebastien Faure, for example, writing in the nineteenth-century *Encyclopedie Anarchist* (quoted in Woodcock 1977: 62) claimed that what unites anarchists of all varieties is 'the negation of the principle of authority in social organizations and the hatred of all constraints that originate in institutions founded on this principle'.

Yet although individualist anarchists such as Stirner do at times seem to be defending a philosophical objection to authority *per se*, a reading of the social anarchists, along with other anarchist theorists who developed a more careful account of authority, suggests that it is not authority *per se* but certain kinds of authority to which the anarchists object, and which they regard as instantiated in the modern state and its institutions.

One of the most comprehensive philosophical accounts of the anarchist position on authority is that provided by De George (1978), who argues that most anarchist theorists were well aware of the fact that some kind of authority is necessary for social organization to function. But in rejecting the type of authority characteristic of the state and its institutions, what the anarchists were asserting, according to De George, was that

> The only justifiable form of authority comes ultimately from below, not from above. The autonomy of each individual and lower group should be respected by each higher group. The higher groups are formed to achieve the will of the lower groups and remain responsible to them and responsive to their will.
>
> (De George 1978: 97)

De George's choice of imagery here may look odd in the light of the anarchist opposition to hierarchies. But I think that the use of the terms 'higher' and 'lower' in the aforementioned passage serves to illustrate the purely functional nature of authority in a social-anarchist society. A more appropriate image, in fact, may be that of concentric circles; the 'lower' group, in other words, would be the most basic, inner circle – that of the self-governing, face-to-face community, where social arrangements would be established to meet the needs of this community. In the event of needs arising which could not be met by the community itself, an outer circle would come into being, representing the federated coordination with another community – for purposes of trade, for example, or common interests such as transport. This outer circle would then have functional authority, purely for the purposes of the function it was set up to fulfil, towards those in the inner circle. There could, in theory, be an infinite, elaborate network of such circles, the crucial point being that none of them would have absolute authority; all could be dismantled or rearranged if they failed to perform their functions, and all would be ultimately justifiable in terms of the needs of the basic unit of community.

The point De George is leading up to in his analysis is that, in fact, what the anarchists were rejecting was not authority but authoritarianism which, as De George points out, 'starts at the top and directs those below for the benefit of those above' (De George 1978: 98).

In short, the anarchist, De George argues, 'is a sceptic in the political arena. He insists on the complete justification for any political or legal system prior to accepting it' (ibid.: 91). This demand for 'justification' is in fact a demand for accountability to the smallest possible unit of social organization, to whom any such system of moral or legal rules must be responsive.

This analysis is supported by Richard Sennet's discussion of nineteenth-century anarchist thinkers who, he says, 'recognized the positive value of authority' (Sennet 1980: 187). In fact, Sennet argues, what thinkers like Kropotkin and Bakunin were aiming at was to create 'the conditions of power in which it was possible for a person in authority to be made fallible' (Sennet 1980: 188).

The above points also illustrate how the anarchist understanding of what constitutes legitimate authority is linked to the anarchist faith in human rationality – a faith which, in turn, is reflected in the call for 'rational education'; in other words, an education which was not only anti-authoritarian, but which encouraged children to accept the kind of authority which was rational in nature (see Chapter 6). Perhaps the philosophical account of authority which comes closest to what the social anarchists had in mind in this context is that suggested by Gerald Dworkin in his notion of 'epistemological authority' (Dworkin 1988: 45), namely, the practice of accepting or consulting the authority of others in non-moral matters. This practice, Dworkin explains, is essentially rational, for a variety of practical and social reasons.

In the light of the earlier discussion, one can begin to understand the role of authority within anarchist thought, and to appreciate the claim that anarchists are not, in fact, opposed to authority *per se*, but to 'any exercise of authority which carries with it the right to require individuals to do what they do not choose to do' (Wasserstrom 1978: 113). In fact, even this formulation is unnecessarily strong. As we have seen, what the anarchists objected to was the idea of an *absolute right* to command authority. They have no problem in acknowledging that individuals or organizations may have a right to command others, but such a right must always be temporary, and always justifiable in terms of the needs of the community in question.

So as anarchists recognize that some form of social organization will always be necessary, they also recognize that some form of authority must be accepted in order for social arrangements to function. The types of authority which would be acceptable – and perhaps necessary – in an anarchist society are what De George calls 'the authority of competence', 'epistemic authority', or 'operative authority'. Miller (1984) makes a similar distinction in discussing the anarchist acknowledgement of what he calls 'authority in matters of belief' , and indeed this point is reflected in the analytic literature on the subject, namely in the distinction, noted by Richard Peters, between authority *de jure* and authority *de facto* (Peters 1967: 84–85). The point of this distinction is that a person can possess authority by virtue of 'personal history, personal credentials and personal achievements', including, in certain cases, the kind of charisma associated with authoritative figures. However this is different from having or claiming authority by virtue of one's position within a recognized normative structure. The anarchists, of course, reject the kind of authority that is derived solely from one's position in a preordained social system – this is the kind of authority which they refer to as 'irrational'. However, if De George is right in emphasizing that the anarchists' chief objection was to authority imposed from above, presumably anarchists would have to acknowledge that certain forms of authority which are determined by defined roles within social or political systems would be legitimate, provided the system in question was one which had developed organically, in other words, from below, in response to and in accordance with the needs of people and communities. Indeed, most anarchists recognize that there can be people who are *authorities* in various realms and are accepted as such. To connect this point back to the previous discussion of rationality as a key aspect of moral autonomy, it seems that rationality is the overriding criterion for the anarchists in judging which types and instances of authority are legitimate. Bakunin expressed this idea when he stated: 'We recognize, then, the absolute authority of science. Outside of this only legitimate authority, legitimate because it is rational and is in harmony with human liberty, we declare all other authorities false, arbitrary and fatal' (in Maximoff 1953: 254).

One might well question this idea, however, as it is all too obvious that it could lead one to the dangerous position of blindly revering everything 'scientific', thereby elevating science, *qua* science, to the position of an unquestionable authority. However Bakunin himself seems to have been well aware of this danger, and explicitly warned against the idea of what he referred to as 'dictatorship by scientists' (Bakunin, in Maximoff 1953: 250), in which all legislation would be entrusted to a learned academy of scientists. Such systems would, Bakunin argues, be 'monstrosities' (ibid.), first due to the fact that 'human science is always and necessarily imperfect', and second because

> a society obeying legislation emanating from a scientific academy, not because it understood the reasonableness of this legislation (in which case the existence of that academy would become useless) but because the legislation emanated from the academy and was imposed in the name of science, which was venerated without being understood – that society would be a society of brutes and not of men.
>
> (Ibid.)

Furthermore, a scientific academy, like any similar body invested with 'absolute, sovereign power', would inevitably become 'morally and intellectually corrupted' (ibid.).

These remarks of Bakunin's are indicative of the essence of the anarchist objection to certain kinds of authority, which has echoes in Erich Fromm's distinction between 'rational' and 'irrational' authority. The key feature of rational authority is that, while it is based on competence, it must be subjected to constant scrutiny and criticism and, above all, is always temporary.

This notion is particularly salient in Bakunin's critique of Marx, and has important connections with the anarchist insistence on the commensurability of the means and the ends of the revolution. For if the ultimate objective is a society free from authoritarian, hierarchical structures, then, as Bakunin argued, the revolutionary movement itself has to avoid such structures and processes. Indeed, it was this point that led to the bitter dispute between the anarchists and the Marxists after the First International. Bakunin argued, with depressing accuracy, that the Marxist idea of the working class seizing political power would lead to a dictatorship of the proletariat which would be only superficially different from that of the state, and was sceptical regarding the Marxist claim that such an arrangement would be only transitional. In Bakunin's view, the International as an 'embryo of future society' must, according to the anarchist position, reject all principles associated with authoritarianism and dictatorship. Bakunin, as Morland notes, was not so naive as to overlook the natural tendency of people in revolutionary movements to take on different roles according to different propensities and talents, some inevitably commanding, initiating and leading, while others follow. But the crucial point in anarchist thought is that

> no function must be allowed to petrify and become fixed, and it will not remain irrevocably attached to any one person. Hierarchical order and promotion do not exist, so that the commander of yesterday can become a subordinate tomorrow. No-one rises above the others, or if he does rise, it is only to fall back a moment later, like the waves of the sea forever returning to the salutary level of equality.
>
> (Bakunin, in Joll 1979: 91–92)

It is, then, this notion of what Miller refers to as 'functionally specific authority' (Miller 1984: 57), that underlies most anarchist thinking on social structures.

This acceptance, by anarchist thinkers, of certain kinds of rational authority explains how they can, while rejecting the state, nevertheless coherently acknowledge the legitimacy of certain rules of social organization. The members of an anarchist community may well, in this view, come to accept the need for social rules of some kind, but such rules or sanctions would not constitute an infringement of one's personal freedom, for this freedom, as Bakunin puts it, 'consists precisely in this: he does what is good not because he is commanded to, but because he understands it, wants it and loves it' (Ritter 1980: 23). The distinction which Bakunin makes between social sanctions – which may have a legitimate role in the stateless society – and government, which 'coerces its subjects with commands instead of persuading them with reasons' (ibid.) is arguably, as Ritter suggests, the only plausible defence of the reconciliation between freedom and censure.

There are obviously several ways in which the anarchist position on authority, and the connected ideas discussed here, can have bearings on educational issues. In the present context, the important point to note is that the anarchist acceptance of certain kinds of authority as legitimate is sufficient to reject the extreme libertarian claim that education *per se*, as conceived as a form of human interaction necessarily involving some kind of authority, is morally illegitimate.

5   The positive core of anarchism

The preceding discussion suggests the following conclusions:

First, what the social anarchists object to is not the state as such but the state as instantiating a number of features which they regard as objectionable because of their infringement on human development and flourishing, understood as involving freedom, solidarity and reciprocal awareness – values that are inherently interconnected and interdependent.

Second, and connectedly, the anarchist stance is, above all, not anti-state or anti-authority, but anti-hierarchy, in the sense that all centralized, top-down structures are to be regarded with suspicion, and small communities favoured as basic units of social organization. As Woodcock remarks:

> Instead of attempting to concentrate social functions on the largest possible scale, which progressively increases the distance between the individual and the source of responsibility even in modern democracies, we should begin again from the smallest possible unit of organization, so that face-to-face contacts can take the place of remote commands, and everyone involved in an operation can not only know how and why it is going on, but can also share directly in decisions regarding anything that affects him directly, either as a worker or as a citizen.
>
> (Woodcock 1977: 21)

This perspective is supported by J.P. Clark who, in his analysis (Clark 1978: 6) argues that 'anarchism might also be defined as a theory of decentralization'. One of the implications of these points is that the normative core of anarchism is not a negative one but a positive one. I have already discussed the anarchist conception of mutual aid, which is essential for the flourishing of the kind of communities envisaged by social anarchists. This notion is, perhaps, the most important element of this positive core. As Ritter points out, for the social anarchists, notably Kropotkin, who developed the theory of mutual aid from a historical and anthropological perspective, benevolence, understood as 'a generous reciprocity that makes us one with each other, sharing and equal' (Ritter 1980: 57) is the 'mediating attitude of anarchy' (ibid.).

Ritter notes that the notion of mutual aid – a notion to some extent anticipated by Godwin's ideal of 'reciprocal awareness', discussed earlier – supports not only the ideal of the equitable, cooperative society so central to the social anarchists but also the notion of creative individualism which is a common theme in anarchist literature, most notably – although not exclusively – amongst the more individualist anarchist thinkers. The attempt to combine, in an educational setting, attitudes of mutual respect and cooperation, with the pursuit of individual creativity and freedom of expression, is apparent in the American anarchist educational experiments discussed in Chapter 6. The theoretical basis for this connection between the notion of mutual aid and that of creative individualism is summed up by Ritter in his argument that 'the knowledge that one can rely on this reciprocal support from others gives one courage to pursue unique and creative paths in self-becoming' (Ritter, ibid.) – suggesting a primarily psychological basis for this connection.

But, as Bakunin's instrumental rejection of the state suggests, there are other connected, substantive values which form the positive core of the anarchist position, and which have not been discussed in detail in the preceding analysis. The central such values are: equality and fraternity.

Equality

In general, most anarchist thinkers seem to have understood the notion of equality in terms of distributive social justice, emphasizing the social and economic implications of this notion, rather than the legalistic aspects. Indeed, the nineteenth-century social anarchists – like all early socialists – were highly critical of the theorists of the French Revolution who, they argued, promised equal rights in terms of equality before the law but neglected to deal with the material aspects of social inequality.

Even Godwin, who, as discussed earlier, was an anarchist thinker closer to the individualist than the socialist end of the spectrum, was adamant on the evils of social and economic inequality. As Ritter explains, Godwin saw unequal distribution of wealth, and its negative effects on human character and communal relations, as the principal reason for the imposition of legal government and the establishment of the state (Ritter 1980: 76). Alongside the fundamental argument that economic inequality is unjust because it denies some people the means of a happy and respectable life (ibid.: 77) and gives the advantaged 'a hundred times more food than you can eat and a hundred times more clothes than you can wear' (ibid.), Godwin also argues that inequality damages human character, particularly from the point of view of the rational independence which he regarded as a supreme value. Both the poor and the rich, in a stratified society, have their rational capacities sapped by servility on the one hand and arrogance on the other (ibid.).

Godwin talks in terms of a floor of basic goods to which all members of society are entitled on the basis of a conception of the basic needs of individuals.

Beyond this, he is prepared to accept a certain amount of inequality, based on merit. 'The thing really to be desired is the removing as much as possible of arbitrary distinctions, and leaving to talents and virtue the field of exertion unimpaired' (Ritter 1980: 78).

Thus Godwin, while aware of the damaging effects of inequality for the ideal of communal individuality, was far from endorsing the social anarchists' ideal of 'to each according to his need' – which, according to Guerin (Guerin 1970: 50) 'should be the motto of libertarian communism'.

As Ritter notes, the social anarchists who succeeded Godwin gradually tried to rid anarchism of its 'anti-egalitarian, meritocratic elements' (Ritter 1980: 79). Kropotkin went furthest in this respect, advocating a redistribution of wealth based entirely on the conception of needs and not contribution or merit. Indeed, in arguing for a floor of basic needs as the basis for social-economic policy, the social anarchists were clearly closer to Marxism than to classical liberalism. Kropotkin's form of communal anarchism demanded 'the right of all to wealth – whatever share they may have taken in producing it' (Ritter 1980: 81). Similarly, twentieth-century social anarchists were highly critical of the Bolshevik revolution precisely concerning this issue. One of the greatest mistakes of the Bolsheviks, argued Alexander Berkman in *An ABC of Anarchism* in 1929, was to introduce a differential scale of rationing in the immediate post-revolutionary period. 'At one time', Berkman claims, 'they had as many as fourteen different food rations' (Berkman 1995: 89), the best rations being for Party members and officials. The inevitable material inequality and political tensions that this situation created were, according to anarchist critics, just one symptom of the Bolshevik failure to base their political programme on an understanding of 'the needs of the situation' (ibid.). Berkman, like Guerin, argues that the principle of 'to each according to his needs' must be the guiding principle behind socio-economic organization in the anarchist society.

In this context, it is important to keep in mind, as Ritter points out, that none of the anarchists can be seen to hold the radical egalitarian thesis – that is, the thesis that everybody should be treated alike. Ritter cites Kropotkin's commitment to need as the criterion of distribution as an example of this: 'needs', the argument goes, 'cannot be satisfied without treating people differently' (Ritter 1980: 82). Thus, as Ritter argues, while the social anarchists seek to eliminate inequalities of rank and hierarchy, they seek to increase those of kind, which support the kind of social diversity which they regard as highly valuable and desirable.

It seems, then, that the anarchist understanding of equality is fairly close to that developed within egalitarian liberalism. Specifically, Bakunin and other social anarchists seem to have adopted a view akin to Rawls' notion of 'primary social goods'. Bakunin talks of the need 'to organize society in such a manner that every individual, man or woman, should, at birth, find almost equal means for the development of his or her various faculties and the full utilization of his or her work' (Bakunin, in Maximoff 1953: 156). Although the emphasis in this conception may be different from that of Rawls, the basic perspective on social justice makes the anarchists far closer, here, to egalitarian liberals than, say, to utilitarians – given, of course, that the social anarchists may interpret Rawls' notion of 'primary social goods' somewhat differently.

Some theorists have criticized Rawlsian liberalism for failing to offer guidelines for moral and just action on an interpersonal level. Thus G.A. Cohen, for example, argues that Rawls' contention that he has provided, in *A Theory of Justice*, a comprehensive conception of justice, is questionable, for 'a society that is just within the terms of the difference principle [...] requires not simply just coercive *rules*, but also an ethos of justice that informs individual choices' (Cohen 2001: 128). It is thus questionable, Cohen argues, whether 'the ideals of dignity, fraternity, and full realization of people's moral natures' are actually delivered by the Rawlsian account of justice (ibid.: 136). This point has important connections with the anarchist perspective, as will be discussed later. However, it seems an unfair criticism of Rawls who, in *Justice as Fairness, a Restatement*, clearly states that his theory of justice is intended 'not as a comprehensive moral doctrine but as a political conception to apply to that structure of political and social institutions' (Rawls 2001: 12). Crucial, indeed, to Rawls' argument, is the distinction between the political and the moral. He insists on preserving the narrow focus of his conception of justice which, although it will hopefully gain the support of a broad overlapping consensus, cannot, on this understanding, have anything to say about the 'transcendent values – religious, philosophical or moral' with which it may conflict. It cannot, in other words, 'go beyond the political' (ibid.: 37).

The anarchists, however, would, I believe, reject this distinction between the political and the moral, partly because they do not start from an acceptance of an institutional framework – that of constitutional democracy – as Rawls and many other liberal theorists do. Furthermore, most anarchists, as May notes (May 1994: 85), 'regard the political as investing the entire field of social relationships' – in other words, they would not accept Rawls' focus on the 'basic structure' of society as the sole subject for political deliberation.

The anarchist account, which can by no means be regarded as a comprehensive account of distributive justice, does seem to place less emphasis on procedural rules and principles for the just management of social affairs and more on the moral qualities needed, as Cohen suggests, to sustain human relationships conducive to social justice. It is indeed partly for this reason that education plays such an important role in anarchist thought.

The anarchist conception of the value of equality has obvious conceptual connections both with the idea of community and with the view of human nature. Michael Taylor (Taylor 1982) argues that equality is perceived as an important value for the anarchists but is secondary to the basic good of community. Following on from his central argument that it is only in community that social order without the state can be maintained, Taylor points out that community requires a considerable degree of basic material equality in order to flourish. For 'as the gap increases between rich and poor, so their values diverge, relations between them are likely to become less direct and many-sided, and the sense of interdependence which supports a system of reciprocity is weakened' (ibid.: 95). Yet, as he points out – and this seems to be supported by the writings of the social anarchists – it is only gross inequality which undermines community.

As Taylor notes, this argument runs counter to the prevailing liberal argument that the state is necessary to ensure even approximate equality – specifically, that as 'the voluntary actions of individuals' inevitably disrupt material equality, even approximate equality can only be maintained by 'continuous interference by the state in people's lives' (ibid.: 96). The neo-liberal development of this argument is the claim that, as such interference is clearly in violation of individual rights (primarily property rights), then any pursuit of economic equality must be secondary to the defence of the basic value of individual liberty. But as Taylor argues, this argument rests on certain assumptions about human nature, or at the very least, about what people will voluntarily do in a given kind of society. The anarchist position on human nature, combined with their faith in the potential of rational education in a climate of solidarity and mutual aid, leads to far less pessimistic conclusions regarding the possibility of maintaining relatively equitable socio-economic arrangements in a stateless, self-governing community, than those, for example, of Nozick, in his famous 'Wilt Chamberlain' thought experiment[1] (Nozick 1974: 161–164). Furthermore, as Taylor points out, in a society unlike the modern, industrialized one which Nozick assumes, 'where wealth and power are already unevenly distributed', people may voluntarily choose to act in ways which maintain equal distribution of wealth (ibid.: 100). Taylor acknowledges that even in equality-valuing communities, no actions undertaken to maintain equality can be described as absolutely 'voluntary', for, in the absence of interference by the state, there are always some kind of sanctions in place to ensure the survival of relative equality and, therefore, of the community. In short, although Taylor concedes that approximate economic equality is unlikely to last without some form of counteractive influence, that does not necessarily have to be provided by the state.

The social anarchists, in conclusion, seem to have genuinely believed that the natural human propensity for mutual aid and benevolence, if encouraged and promoted by social relationships and institutions, would go a long way towards ensuring the survival of a relative degree of material equality. Both this argument and Taylor's moderate version of it reveal, once again, the important role of education in anarchist society. For education must systematically promote the values which support the flourishing of community, and, as Taylor argues, community both needs equality and provides the conditions for it to survive.

It is important to keep in mind here the point which I made earlier in discussing the multiplicity of values within anarchist thought. It is in keeping with anarchism's anti-hierarchical stance that no single value can be regarded as conceptually prior within this system of thought – in spite of attempts by theorists, both within and outside the anarchist tradition, to defend such accounts. Thus while equality plays an important role in the social critique of the social anarchists, its full significance cannot be grasped without an understanding of its conceptual links with other, equally important values, notably that of fraternity. Thus while many social anarchists talk of needs as a basis for distributive justice, it would be misleading to conclude that their conception of the just society or human flourishing is basically a needs-based one. In this, perhaps, they would have agreed with Michael Ignatieff's comment that:

> To define what it means to be human in terms of needs is to begin, neither with the best, nor with the worst, but only with the body and what it lacks. It is to define what we have in common, not by what we have, but by what we are missing. A language of human needs understands human beings as being naturally insufficient, incomplete, at the mercy of nature and of each other. It is an account that begins with what is absent.
>
> (Ignatieff 1994: 57)

Far from assuming that something was absent, the social anarchists, as is apparent from the earlier discussion of human nature, worked on the assumption that human beings have a great capacity for fraternal, benevolent sensibilities and action, and that the just society must be – and can be – underpinned by such values.

Fraternity

The relatively under-theorized concept of fraternity – a concept which Adam Swift describes as 'quaint and politically incorrect' (Swift 2001: 133) has, of course, conceptual links with that of equality. In fact Swift himself acknowledges that 'economic inequality may be inimical to fraternal relations in a society' due to the fragmentation and stratification associated with high levels of socio-economic inequality (ibid.: 113–114). As Patricia White defines it in *Beyond Domination*, fraternity consists in 'feeling a bond between oneself and others as equals, as moral beings with the same basic needs and an interest in leading a life of one's own' (White 1983: 72). White argues that this attitude is necessary amongst citizens of a participatory democracy (contrasted with servility and patronage), but she also goes further than this and makes the educationally important point that the attitude of fraternity can be a motivating force.

If one adopts the view that fraternity is an 'attitude', then presumably, like other moral dispositions such as gratitude, it is something which can be learned. White indeed seems to take this view. In other words, people develop fraternal feelings by coming to hold certain beliefs and attitudes about others. Developing such beliefs and attitudes, then, is clearly a task for education. Furthermore, as White notes,

> in a fully-fledged participatory democracy, fraternal attitudes will both underpin the institutions of the society and also be themselves under-girded by the social structure which does not permit gross discrepancies in the share of primary goods between citizens.
>
> (Ibid.)

This suggests that the conceptual connection between fraternity and equality can work both ways: not only does a relatively high degree of socio-economic equality foster and support fraternal attitudes, but the institutional mainte-nance of such equality may depend on a degree of fraternal feeling. Some social-anarchist theorists may well have endorsed this view, although they would obviously understand the notion of 'participatory democracy' in a narrower sense than that in which White seems to be using it. For the anar-chists, any form of participatory democracy which was institutionally depen-dent on a centralized, hierarchical state, was to be viewed with suspicion. A 'fully fledged' participatory democracy could only, so the social-anarchist view seems to imply, exist at the level of the workshop, the community, or the school. It is at these levels, in fact, as the foregoing discussion suggests, that we should focus our analysis of desirable educational qualities. And indeed, the anarchist insistence that the schools they founded be run as com-munities (see Chapter 6), in which solidarity and mutual respect prevailed, supports the view that fraternal attitudes were both 'taught', in such educa-tional settings, by means of the prevailing climate, and helped to sustain and foster the kinds of experimental communities that were being created as an alternative to the state.

But White's comments also draw attention to another important aspect of fraternity in an educational context. Part of the anarchist objection to the state is precisely that, as Kropotkin argues in his discussion of mutual aid (see Chapter 2), the capitalist state system undermines precisely those fraternal attitudes which should ideally underpin social institutions. Thus, in disagreeing with White that the state itself could underpin the kinds of fraternal attitudes essential to a genuine democracy, the anarchists are tacitly admitting that social processes at the community level – primarily education – must take on even more of a responsibility for promoting these attitudes.

White also notes, in reply to critiques from the individualistic liberal tra-dition, that this notion of fraternity is in no way a threat to individuality and freedom, as it goes hand-in-hand with a tolerance for diversity (something much championed by anarchists), and 'carries no demands that people should engage in communal projects or should enjoy spending the major part of their time in the company of their fellows' (White 1983: 74).

Another interesting theoretical perspective on the notion of fraternity comes from the work of Eric Hobsbawm. In his article 'Fraternity' (Hobsbawm 1975), Hobsbawm argues that the reason fraternity has been the most neglected by theorists of the revolutionary triad is largely due to the fact that 'While parts of what may be defined as liberty [. . .] and parts of equality may be achieved by means of laws or other specific measures of polit-ical reform, fraternity cannot be so conveniently translated into even partial practice' (ibid.: 471), being rather 'a function of certain types of society or movement' (ibid.).

Hobsbawm argues that the notion of fraternity implies both 'an ideal of society as a whole, and an ideal relationship between people for particular purposes: a programme and a technique' (ibid.: 472). Yet this distinction between the 'programme' and the 'technique' reflects precisely the kind of crude distinction between 'means' and 'ends' which the anarchists were so opposed to, as is evident in their critique of Marxism (see Chapter 4). For the social anarchists, in conceptualizing revolutionary social change, the 'programme' and the 'technique' were one and the same thing. The social-anarchist vision of the good society is, then, arguably precisely the conjunction of both aspects of fraternity which Hobsbawm mentions – the social ideal and the ideal form of relationships – and, perhaps, the insistence that they are one and the same; the fraternal relationships which are so essential to building func-tional communities for a common purpose, are exactly those which should underpin the ideal of the good society, on the social-anarchist view. It is in this respect, indeed, that fraternity can be regarded as a core educational value – implying both the ideal and the practice necessary to promote and underpin it.

Hobsbawm offers a historical account of the development of the notion of fraternity, suggesting that 'middle–class liberal political thought has always been essentially individualist' (ibid.), regarding fraternity therefore as only 'a by-product of individual impulses' or the result of functionalist systems.

Furthermore, he argues, 'The people who have used and needed fraternity most in modern societies, are least likely to write books about it; or if they do, they tend to be esoteric, like most Masonic literature' (ibid.). Illustrative of this point is the fact that fraternity has always been regarded as a basic value of the labour movement, but is not, as such, an articulated aspect of political theory.

Hobsbawm in fact makes the claim that the revolutionary triad – 'Equality, Liberty, Fraternity' – was almost certainly historically derived from the Freemasons. The Masonic notion of fraternity embodied, according to Hobsbawm, the idea of 'a relation of voluntary mutual aid and dependence, which implies that each member can expect the unlimited help of every other when in need' (Hobsbawm 1975: 472), and thus implied a 'certain type of social cooperation' (ibid.). This notion is remarkably close to Kropotkin's notion of mutual aid, although without Kropotkin's historical and evolution-ary perspective on its political manifestations and its conceptual connections to different types of social organization. As Hobsbawm points out, it is essential to this idea of mutual help that it is 'not measured in terms of money or mechanical equality or reciprocal exchange' (ibid.) and thus has the notion of kinship built into it. More pertinently, he argues that this notion invariably has 'overtones of communism', as 'the obligations of artificial brotherhood frequently implied the sharing, or at least the free use, of all property between "brothers"' (ibid.).

Both White's and Hobsbawm's analyses draw attention to the strong ethical aspect of fraternity, and also to its emotional aspect – an aspect which seems somewhat neglected in the anarchist treatment of the notion.

Hobsbawm notes that, although theoretically neglected, the fraternal code has survived to some extent in revolutionary organizations, unions, and some political parties, where it has an essential function. As part of a political programme, however, it is, as he remarks, 'less clear and codified', and has played a generally minor role in political programmes, where it is most often used to propagate the idea of the 'brotherhood of man' as opposed to the narrower bonds of nationalism and patriotism. Interestingly, Hobsbawm barely mentions social-anarchist progammes in his historical account. This omission is particularly surprising given Hobsbawm's general remarks on the role played by the notion of fraternity after the French Revolution, when it expressed, as he puts it, 'part of what men expected to find in a new society' (Hobsbawm 1975: 472). A fraternal society, Hobsbawm writes, in a description which sounds like a paraphrase of Kropotkin,

> was not merely one in which men treated each other as friends, but one which excluded exploitation and rivalry; which did not organize human relations through the mechanism of a market – or perhaps of superior authorities. Just as slavery is the opposite of liberty, and inequality of equality, so the competitive system of capitalism was the opposite of fraternity.
>
> (Ibid.)

So for the social anarchists, fraternity and the connected notions of mutual aid, benevolence and solidarity were not only argued to be real and salient features of human life in society but were assigned normative status as the basis for the ideal, stateless society. In this context one can also see the further significance of the anarchist insistence on small, face-to-face communities as the basic units of social organization. Keeping social units and institutions as small as possible not only has the function of facilitating non-hierarchical, decentralized forms of social organization and avoiding oppressive bureaucratic structures but is also clearly essential to ensure the flourishing of fraternity. For only in small communities can the basic sense of solidarity with and fraternity towards others be maintained. It is anonymity and lack of interpersonal understanding which not only exacerbates socio-economic injustice but also facilitates the phenomenon of free-riders which many theorists cite as an inevitable problem of stateless societies.

Interestingly, in this connection, many liberal theorists – most notably Rawls – seem to start from the assumption of a community of rational individuals not characterized by fraternal feelings. Rawls' 'circumstances of justice', in fact, are necessarily defined in this way, leading some critics of Rawlsian liberalism, like Michael Sandel (1982), to point out that justice only becomes relevant in the absence of feelings such as fraternity and benevolence. Sandel quotes Hume, who remarked: 'Increase to a sufficient degree the benevolence of men, or the bounty of nature, and you render justice useless, by supplying in its place much nobler virtues, and more favourable blessings' (ibid.: 32). Perhaps the most outspoken exponent of the view that such 'nobler virtues' have a basis in human nature, and accordingly can underpin a well-functioning, equitable stateless society, was Joseph Proudhon, who anticipated Kropotkin in arguing for a 'social instinct' which is prior to any formal account of social justice:

> To practice justice is to obey the social instinct; to do an act of justice is to do a social act . . . man is moved by an internal attraction towards his fellow, by a secret sympathy which causes him to love, congratulate, condole; so that, to resist this attraction, his will must struggle against his nature.
>
> (Proudhon, in Edwards 1969: 226–227)

This sense of the social virtues as constituting the foundation for social organization and, if not undermining the priority of justice altogether, at least giving rise to a different understanding of what justice may mean, is captured by Kropotkin in the following passage:

> It is not love and not even sympathy upon which society is based in mankind; it is the conscience – be it only at the stage of an instinct of human solidarity. It is the unconscious recognition of the force that is borrowed by each man from the practice of mutual aid; of the close dependency of everyone's happiness upon the happiness of all; and of the sense of justice, or equity, which brings the individual to consider the rights of every other individual as equal to his own. Upon this broad and necessary foundation the still higher moral feelings are developed.
>
> (Kropotkin 1972: 22)

This passage also reflects the anarchist view that life in cooperative communities is not only underpinned by the social virtues, but itself constitutes an important educative force in fostering and maintaining these virtues.

Sandel, in his critique of Rawls, provides further support for the argument that the anarchist insistence on small communities implies normative moral, as well as functional considerations pertaining to the priority of social values. As he notes, we can easily imagine large-scale organizations like the modern state meeting the requirements of the circumstances of justice, but 'we can readily imagine a range of more intimate or solidaristic associations in which the values and aims of the participants coincide closely enough that the circumstances of justice prevail to a relatively small degree' (Sandel 1982: 30–31).

Although Rawls, of course, acknowledges the social significance of inter-personal ties and sentiments of affection, solidarity and so on, he does not include such sentiments as part of the motivations of the people in the orig-inal position, who are, as Sandel remarks, 'theoretically defined individuals' (Sandel 1982: 147). One would expect to find people with a sense of justice acting in accordance with such sentiments 'once the veil of ignorance is lifted', as Sandel comments, but they cannot form part of the theoretical foundations on which the just society is constructed. Yet as Hume pointed out, the 'nobler virtues' of benevolence and fraternity, if increased, would render justice, if not totally irrelevant, at least theoretically less central.

On the anarchist view, fraternity and the connected social virtues are not just fostered by life in small, face-to-face communities, but are at the same time necessary for the stability of such communities, as Michael Taylor has discussed. Obviously, as McKenna points out, 'one is less likely to fight within a community, or to wage war with another community, if they view people of that community as connected to themselves' (McKenna 2001: 61). Similarly, it makes no sense, as the member of such a community, to under-mine other people's projects, or to produce something of inferior quality, because 'at some point the inferior product will come back to you' (ibid.).

Liberal values? Anarchist values?

Both the discussion of human nature and the earlier discussion of the core values of social anarchism seem to suggest that anarchism, as an ideology, is not as far removed from liberalism as may have first appeared, and in fact overlaps with liberal values in important respects. The difference seems to lie primarily in what Ritter refers to as the anarchists' 'daring leap' of supposing that a society which embodies, as fully as possible, the virtues of individual autonomy, social equality and mutual aid, can be sustained without the institutional mediation of the state.

Yet another, important, conclusion is also emerging from this discussion, namely, if the stability of a social-anarchist society rests so clearly on the pres-ence of these social virtues, and if there is to be no state structure to maintain it, it seems as if education, and particularly moral education, has an impor-tant role to play. What form, then, is such an education to take in an anarchist society? There are two ways of approaching this question. One is to construct, on the basis of anarchist theory, a philosophical argument for an educational process designed to foster and maintain the types of ideal communities envis-aged by the social anarchists. Another approach is to look at actual accounts of educational experiments conducted by anarchists over the years and to ascertain whether such practice is consistent with anarchist principles and in what way – if at all – it was conceived as playing a role in achieving the desired social change. In the following chapters, I shall employ both these approaches in an attempt both to illustrate instances of educational practice by anarchists and to discuss the philosophical perspective on education behind such practice.

Education for the social virtues

Given the central importance assigned to the social virtues in sustaining an anarchist society, it follows that a moral education which fosters this attitude must surely form the basis of all anarchist education. I suspect, too, that most anarchist thinkers were aware of the fact, mentioned in the preceding chapter, that the problem of how to maintain a stateless, decentralized community without resorting to a certain degree of public censure, remains one of anarchism's chief theoretical stumbling blocks. The central role played by educational programmes in so much of the anarchist literature seems to be, amongst other things, an implicit acknowledgement of the need to surmount this problem, although it also, of course, results from the anarchists' contextualist perspective on human nature, as discussed in Chapter 2. And of course, as Goodwin and Taylor note, ideals such as the social anarchists' ideal of a society based on the principles of self-government and participatory democracy, in which there were very few rules for adults, often rested on the assumption of there being 'massive moral education of children' (Goodwin and Taylor 1982: 45).

The clearest expression of this idea in the anarchist literature is in Kropotkin's essay, 'Anarchism: Its Philosophy and Ideal' (Kropotkin 1897), in which he states: 'When we ask ourselves by what means a certain moral level can be maintained in a human or animal society, we find only such means: the repression of anti-social acts; moral teaching, and the practice of mutual help itself' (ibid.: 23).

Following a similar line of thought, Kropotkin goes on to write of the importance of 'moral teaching':

> especially that which is unconsciously transmitted in society and results from the whole of the ideas and comments emitted by each of us on facts and events of everyday life. But this force can only act on society under one condition: that of not being crossed by a mass of contradictory immoral teachings resulting from the practice of institutions.
>
> (Ibid.)

These passages reveal both the central role assigned to moral education in anarchist thought and the anarchist view that if social institutions are to fulfil their educational role both before and after the dismantling of the state, they must themselves embody anarchist principles. On a more sinister note, the aforementioned passage also hints, in its reference to 'the repression of anti-social acts' at an acknowledgement of the need for some form of what Ritter refers to as 'public censure'. Of course, one can imagine certain relatively benign versions of 'public censure', such as the practice of 'shaming' – which has recently aroused renewed theoretical interest through the development of theories of reintegrative justice. Nevertheless, one cannot help feeling that, given this choice of phrase, Ritter and others may be justified in fearing that the value of individual autonomy may be under serious threat in a social-anarchist community.

I have argued here that not only does an attempt to take the anarchist perspective on social change seriously prod us to think about education in a different way, but also that there is a substantive, primarily moral core to educational programmes conceived from a specifically anarchist position. Of course, education is only one of the channels through which anarchists sought to create an alternative social reality to that which, they believed, was characteristic of social relations constituted by the state. As Bookchin notes:

> Sensibility, ethics, ways of building reality, and selfhood have to be changed by educational means, by a politics of reasoned discourse, experimentation and the expectation of repeated failures from which we have to learn, if humanity is to achieve the self-consciousness it needs to finally engage in self-management.
>
> (Bookchin 1990: 189)

The questions to be addressed now are how this perspective might be translated into educational policy and practice, and how might the normative core of anarchist values discussed here be reflected in the content of specific educational programmes. This is the task of the next two chapters.

6 Anarchism goes to school

In the light of the outline of anarchism discussed, the role of education in anarchist thought may seem more confusing than ever. On the one hand, given the anarchist aversion to blueprints and the demand for constant experimentation in the endeavour to improve society, it may seem quite reasonable to argue that doing away with schools and formal education altogether would be a crucial step towards the creation of an anarchist society. Indeed, the anarchists' insistence that individuals be 'active agents creating the possibilities of their own future' (McKenna 2001: 52) seems to demand that any education be broadly libertarian – allowing, as far as possible, freedom for creative experimentation, critical thought and active problem-solving. This view is also, of course, a consequence of the anarchist insistence that the means for achieving social revolution be consistent with its ends.

Yet on the other hand, the earlier discussion of the substantive core of anarchism suggests that any educational practice consistent with these values cannot coherently adopt a libertarian position, in the sense of a *laissez-faire* attitude to children's upbringing. Although the terms 'anarchist education' and 'libertarian education' are often conflated (not least by writers themselves sympathetic to the anarchist tradition, such as John Shotton, or Michael Smith, whose book on the subject is titled *The Libertarians and Education*), it is important to distinguish between the libertarian position and the anarchist position. One of the points I wish to argue in favour of here is that although many anarchists can be described as libertarian, the anarchist educational tradition is distinct from the tradition commonly described as 'libertarian education'.

The term 'libertarian' is used to refer, broadly, to all educational approaches which reject traditional models of teacher authority and hierarchical school structure, and which advocate maximum freedom for the individual child within the educational process – including, in its extreme version, the option to opt out of this process altogether. In the following discussion, I shall use the term 'anarchist education' to refer specifically to a tradition of educational practice and theory which, I shall argue, although it appears to overlap with libertarian ideas in certain respects, is significantly different from the mainstream libertarian tradition. Accordingly, I shall focus on descriptions of schools which were established and run out of an explicitly anarchist commitment, mentioning non-anarchist libertarian educational approaches merely in order to bring out the contrast which I want to make between these two terms.

For example, many accounts of libertarian education, which, as mentioned, include both anarchist and non-anarchist educators in their descriptions, cite Tolstoy's educational experiments in the 1870s as one of the first attempts at libertarian education. Tolstoy is often described as an anarcho-pacifist, or a Christian anarchist, and although his emphasis on individual responsibility and freedom places him at some distance from the social anarchists, he shared their objections to the state, the church, and the institution of private property. However, he was not part of the anarchist movement and, as Michael Smith points out (Smith 1983: 64) his commitment to non-coercive pedagogy stemmed from an educational and moral principle rather than a political one. Tolstoy's chief argument – expressed eloquently in his essay 'Education and Culture' (in Weiner 1967) – was that 'for education to be effective it had to be free' (Smith 1983: 64). In formulating his educational ideas, Tolstoy seemed to be driven more by moral concerns about interference in children's development than by a vision of the kind of society he would like to help create.

It has of course been argued by certain theorists within the libertarian tradition, for example, Stephen Cullen (Cullen 1991), and to a certain extent A.S. Neill (see below) – certainly with regard to moral education – that any form of education is a kind of coercion and as such has no place in a truly free society. The alternative could be something like Ivan Illich's 'learning webs' (see Illich 1971), educational relationships entered into on a contractual basis, or a reconception along the lines suggested by Carl Bereiter's vision, where, although society may not undergo any radical structural changes, all pretence at 'educating' people has been abandoned as morally unacceptable (Bereiter 1974). In such cases, what effectively happens is that society itself becomes the educating force. In Bereiter's case, it is not clear how this is going to happen, as he makes no explicit commitment to particular political principles, whereas in Illich's case, there is more of a clue as to the kind of society he would like to see – one in which 'convivial' institutions replace the coercive institutions of the state – a vision similar to the original social anarchist one but without the egalitarian commitment or the working out of economic principles.

However, as evidenced by the sheer volume of anarchist literature devoted to educational issues, and the efforts invested by anarchist activists in educational projects, the social anarchists, unlike the earlier theorists, seemed to agree that schools, and education in general, are a valuable aspect of the project for social change, rather than proposing to do away with them altogether along with the other machinery of state bureaucracy.

Of course, to a certain extent, this point is a logical conclusion from the anarchist conception of human nature. If, as has been often contended, the anarchists believed that human nature is naturally benevolent, that children have in some sense an innate capacity for altruism and mutual aid – the virtues deemed necessary to sustain a social anarchist society – then, one could argue, it would be enough to do away with the repressive institutions of the state; in the absence of such coercive and hierarchical structures, these positive human qualities would flourish, without any need for further intervention. Any learning necessary for practical purposes could be accomplished by some sort of informal network like that proposed by Illich. Yet given the anarchist belief, discussed in Chapter 2, that human nature involves both an altruistic and a selfish aspect, and that it is environmental factors that determine which of these aspects will dominate at any given time, anarchists could clearly not leave processes of education and socialization to pure chance.

This is not to say that a libertarian approach to education is not often suggested by certain anarchist writers – for example, Emma Goldman who, upon visiting Sebastian Faure's libertarian anarchist school in France at the beginning of the last century, commented,

> If education should really mean anything at all, it must insist upon the free growth and development of the innate forces and tendencies of the child. In this way alone can we hope for the free individual and eventually also for a free community which shall make interference and coercion of human growth impossible.
>
> (Goldman 1906)

Without an understanding of the ideological context of anarchism, and particularly the contextualist anarchist view of human nature, these remarks by Emma Goldman could be construed as calling for a reconceptualization of education; a perspective which would replace the narrow understanding of education as a formal system that goes on in institutions, with a broader view of how society should educate its members. Yet, as discussed earlier, the contextualist view of human nature goes a long way towards explaining the need for a substantive programme of education. And indeed, what Goldman and the many other anarchists involved with educational theories and experiments over the years had in mind was a consciously planned process of education which was to occur in places which, although perhaps very different from the traditional schools of the time, were nevertheless undoubtedly kinds of schools.

Just what, though, did such schools look like? What, in other words, is 'anarchist education', in its practical manifestation? In posing this question, I cannot help recalling a conversation I had some time ago with Colin Ward, the contemporary British anarchist, who commented, perhaps with a touch of irony, 'There is no such thing as "anarchist education." There are just different kinds of educational experiments which anarchists have supported and been involved in'. This comment is important in that it reminds us of one of the essential principles of anarchism, namely, that there is no single theory or doctrine as to the correct form of social organization, including education.

It also indicates the need to answer the question of why it is that anarchists have always been sympathetic to particular kinds of educational practice.

Nevertheless, there is, I believe, a particular anarchist perspective on education and the educational experiments which have been conducted over the years by people aligning themselves with this perspective share, in spite of their differences, important and fundamental features. These features, in turn, need to be understood in the context of anarchism as a political ideology. Thus to answer the question 'what is anarchist education?', while keeping in mind the aforementioned reservation, it is necessary to examine both the educational experiments undertaken over the years by individuals committed to anarchist principles, and the theoretical ideas behind these experiments. The aim of this chapter is to describe some typical educational projects, initiated in various different historical, cultural and political contexts, and with varying degrees of success, which share key features that, as I shall argue later, are unique in the sense that they are logically connected to a set of specifically anarchist beliefs. The question of the logic of this connection, and the possible tensions between the theory and the practice, will be discussed later on.

This chapter is not intended to provide a comprehensive historical account of the development of the movement for anarchist education. This has already been done, in admirable detail, by Paul Avrich in his fascinating study of the Modern School Movement in the United States (Avrich 1980), and by Michael Smith in his study of libertarian educational ideas (Smith 1983), to name two central works in the field. I rely heavily on these works in what follows, with the aim of painting a picture of what a typical anarchist school would look like, as a basis for the ensuing philosophical discussion. In addition, I draw on first-hand accounts by pupils and teachers of life in anarchist schools and communities. As, apart from the aforementioned books, the available documentation on such projects is often sketchy, the educational experiments described here have been selected largely on the basis of the wealth and quality of such first- and second-hand accounts that are readily available to the English reader.

The Escuela Moderna, Barcelona, 1904–1907

One of the first systematic attempts to translate anarchist ideas into educational practice took place in Spain at the beginning of the twentieth century, amidst a climate of severe social unrest, high illiteracy levels, and a public school system completely in the grip of the Catholic Church. The anarchist movement was relatively strong in Spain at the time, and Francisco Ferrer, a long-time political radical, was active in anarchist circles both in France, where he lived in exile for several years, and on his return, in his native Barcelona. While in France, Ferrer had become interested in experiments in libertarian education, particularly those of Paul Robin and Jean Grave, both influential theorists of libertarian education and was familiar with the educational ideas of the utopian socialist Fourier. He became convinced that 'a new society can be the product only of men and women whose whole mental and social training has made them embodiments of new social ideals and conceptions' (Kelly 1916). On 8 September 1901, Ferrer, with the generous financial support of a sympathetic patron, opened The Escuela Moderna in Barcelona. By the end of the first year, the number of pupils had grown from 30 to 70, and by 1905, 126 pupils were enrolled.

In his prospectus, Ferrer declared: 'I will teach them only the simple truth. I will not ram a dogma into their heads. I will not conceal from them one iota of fact. I will teach them not what to think but how to think.' (Avrich 1980: 20).

This attitude was typical of early anarchist educators, who emphasized the 'rational' nature of the education they were proposing – which they contrasted to the dogmatic teaching of the Church, on the one hand, and the nationalistic 'political' education of the capitalist state, on the other. Indeed, Ferrer later established the League for the Rational Education of Children, which became an important forum for the exchange of anarchist and libertarian ideas on education.

The Escuela Moderna was co-educational – a fact which seems to have been perceived by the authorities as more of a threat than any of its other features – and was also quite heterogeneous in terms of the socio-economic backgrounds of its pupils.

Another important aspect of the school was the absence of grades, prizes and punishments. 'Having admitted and practiced', wrote Ferrer,

> the coeducation of boys and girls, of rich and poor – having, that is to say, started from the principle of solidarity and equality – we are not prepared to create a new inequality. Hence in the Modern School there will be no rewards and no punishments; there will be no examinations to puff up some children with the flattering title of 'excellent', to give others the vulgar title of 'good', and make others unhappy with a consciousness of incapacity and failure.
>
> (Ferrer 1913: 55)

Although Ferrer acknowledged that in the case of teaching a trade or specific skills requiring special conditions it may be useful to the teacher to employ tests or exams in order to monitor a pupil's progress, he made it clear that, if not conducive to the pupils' personal development, such devices had no part to play in the kind of education he was advocating. In one of the first bulletins issued by the school, Ferrer noted that, in spite of some initial hesitation, the parents of children at the school gradually came to accept and value this approach, and he went on to point out that 'the rituals and accompanying solemnities of conventional examinations in schools' seemed indeed to serve the sole purpose 'of satisfying the vanity of parents and the selfish interests of many teachers, and in order to put the children to torture before the exam and make them ill afterwards' (ibid.).

There was no rigid timetable at the school, and pupils were allowed to come and go as they wished and to organize their own work schedules.

Although sympathetic to the anti-intellectualism of Rousseau, Ferrer did not scorn 'book-learning' altogether, but a great emphasis was placed on 'learning by doing', and accordingly, much of the curriculum of the school consisted in practical training, visits to museums, factories and laboratories, or field-trips to study physical geography, geology and botanics.

'Let us suppose ourselves', Ferrer writes,

> in a village. A few yards from the threshold of the school, the grass is springing, the flowers are blooming; insects hum against the classroom window-panes; but the pupils are studying natural history out of books!
>
> (Ferrer 1909: 2)

This insistence on the role of practical training and experience in the curriculum also reflected a central anarchist educational idea which Ferrer was keen to put into practice, namely the idea of 'integral education'. This concept essentially involved an understanding of the class structure of capitalist society as being reflected in the distinction between manual labour and intellectual work. It received considerable theoretical treatment at the hands of several social-anarchist theorists, notably Kropotkin and was a crucial element of the anarchist perspective on education. I shall offer a more detailed discussion of this notion and its theoretical underpinnings in Chapter 7.

Ferrer was also adamant about the need for teachers to have complete 'professional independence'. Criticizing the system by which the educator is regarded as a public official, an 'official servant, narrowly enslaved to minute regulations, inexorable programmes' (ibid.) he proclaimed that the principle of free, spontaneous learning should apply not only to the pupil, but to the teacher. 'He who has charge of a group of children, and is responsible for them, should alone be qualified to decide what to do and what not to do' (ibid.).

The avowedly anti-dogmatic principles behind Ferrer's curriculum, and his apparent faith in his ability to create a curriculum which reflected nothing but rational, scientific truth, is revealed in the story of the school library. On the eve of the school's opening, Ferrer scoured the libraries of France and Spain in search of suitable textbooks for his school. To his horror, he reports, he found not a single one. The religious dogma of the Church on the one hand was matched by the 'political' (i.e. patriotic) dogma of the state on the other. He thus opened the school without a single book in the library and sent out a call to leading intellectuals across Europe, commissioning textbooks which would reflect the latest scientific discoveries. To this end, he installed a printing press on the school premises and enlisted a team of translators. The works eventually approved for inclusion in the school library included, to quote Avrich, texts on 'the injustices connected with patriotism, the horrors of war, and the iniquity of conquest' (Avrich 1980: 23). Alongside titles such as *The Compendium of Universal History*, *The Origins of Christianity* and *Poverty: Its Cause and Cure*, the children regularly read a utopian fairy tale by Jean Grave, *The Adventures of Nono*, in which, as Ferrer puts it, 'the happier future is ingeniously and dramatically contrasted with the sordid realities of the present order' (ibid.).

Thus, it would be wrong to assume that Ferrer naively believed that he could provide an education which, as opposed to that of the Church and the state, was politically neutral. As he said in his prospectus, 'It must be the aim of the rationalist school to show the children that there will be tyranny and slavery as long as one man depends on another' (Avrich 1980: 24). Accordingly, the children were encouraged to value brotherhood and cooperation, and to develop a keen sense of social justice, and the curriculum carried a clear anti-capitalist, anti-statist and anti-militarist message. Another example of this commitment is the teaching of Esperanto, which was seen as a way to promote international solidarity.

In short, Ferrer saw his school as an embryo of the future, anarchist society; as proof that, even within the authoritarian society surrounding it, an alternative was possible. He hoped that the school would be nothing less than the vanguard of the social-anarchist revolution. His emphasis on 'rational' and 'scientific' education reflected the Enlightenment ideal of progress which, as discussed earlier, underpinned much of anarchist thought. Yet at the same time, his insistence that the school itself be a microcosm of anarchist society, in the sense of constituting a community based on solidarity and equality, seems to go one step further than the liberal humanist ideal that the way to moral progress lies in gradual intellectual enlightenment. While obviously allowing both children and teachers a great deal more freedom than was common in schools at the time, Ferrer was clearly no libertarian – as the substantive agenda of the school illustrates. This reflects the theoretical point made earlier that the anarchist stance involves more than just doing away with the state by establishing alternative means of social organization; it involves a normative, substantive and ongoing commitment to a set of values and principles. One educational implication of this point is that an implicit or explicit form of moral education underpins all aspects of the anarchist educational process and curriculum.

Under these circumstances, it is no wonder that the Spanish authorities saw the Escuela Moderna, and Ferrer himself, as a threat. Although Ferrer was not directly involved in anarchist activity during the years of the school, and indeed saw himself first and foremost as an educator, his anarchist sympathies were obvious, and the school was constantly under surveillance and was frequently denounced by the clerical authorities as a nest of subversion. In 1906, after years of official harassment, it was closed down. Ferrer himself was arrested in August 1909 on false charges of instigating the mass uprising, anti-war riots and general strike which had plunged Barcelona into violence following Spain's colonial war in Morocco. In spite of attempts by the international liberal community to intervene, Ferrer was found guilty at a mock trial, and condemned to death by firing squad.

Ferrer's death, on 13 October 1909, predictably sparked off a wave of international protest, and is probably, as Avrich notes, the reason why he rather than anyone else became the most famous representative of anarchist education. In the wake of his execution, anarchist activists and enthusiasts for libertarian education around the world were moved to establish educational projects designed to continue and promote Ferrer's ideas. The most extensive and long-lived Ferrer movement arose in the United States, and it is to a study of a typical school of this movement that I now turn.

The Ferrer School, New York and Stelton, 1911–1953

The Ferrer School in New York (or, as it later came to be known, the Modern School) obviously took Ferrer's educational creed as its inspiration, its founding members being convinced that rational, libertarian educational practice was the most likely to advance anarchist ideas. Thus the 1914–1915 prospectus for the school states:

> The Modern School has been established by men and women who believe that a child educated in a natural way, unspoiled by the dogmas and conventionalities of the adult, may be trusted in later life to set his face against injustice and oppression.
>
> (Kelly 1916)

Accordingly, the basic organizational principles of the school were very similar to those of the Barcelona school, namely, coeducation, an emphasis on 'learning by doing', an anti-authoritarian pedagogy, and a heavily anti-capitalistic, anti-statist and anti-religious tone throughout the curriculum. However, the New York group seems to have taken the idea of the school as a vanguard of the socialist–anarchist revolution, and as a microcosm of an alternative society organized on non-hierarchical, cooperative grounds, further than Ferrer did. They believed that in order for the children to develop an adequate understanding of ideas such as justice, equality and cooperation, they must experience them first-hand in the fullest possible way. Thus:

> We hold that children do not and cannot learn the meaning of duties or rights in an economic system composed of masters and slaves. That is why the children of the public schools and the vast majority of children who are pampered and petted by their ignorant or blinded parents know nothing clearly of either rights or duties. Where alone can children, or any others, learn the meaning of rights and duties? In a mode of life which is genuinely cooperative. A life whose products all justly share and whose labour all justly share. This points inevitably to a school which is based upon complete and inclusive cooperation.
>
> (Kelly 1916: 4–5)

Accordingly, a key feature of the New York school was the communal garden, where children learned to plan, plant, care for and gather plants communally.

In addition, all maintenance and domestic work on the school premises was shared cooperatively by the children and staff. In fact, the New York school also served as a kind of community centre, offering a wide range of adult education courses, public lectures and social gatherings, and as a centre for political activity. In 1915, pursuing their ideal of communal life even further, the New York anarchist group purchased a tract of farming land at Stelton, New Jersey, where they set about founding an anarchist colony. The school, which moved there, became a focal point of the colony. Here the community attempted to put their social anarchist ideals into practice, working the land and sharing administration of community matters. A key element of their ideology, which was reflected in the school, was the idea of breaking down the distinction between 'brain work' and 'manual work' — a theme which, as mentioned earlier, was repeatedly taken up by anarchist theorists (see Chapter 7) and which can be seen in Ferrer's insistence on integral education. The justification for this approach was, first and foremost, a political one: as Harry Kelly writes

> The curse of existing capitalist society is its parasitism. It permits idle and useless people to live on the products of its useful members. No society is tolerable in which all are not workers. In the Modern School, all are workers.
>
> (Kelly 1916: 5)

The anarchist ideal of a socialist, communal society also stressed the need for a natural continuity between the world of the school and that of the community. This ideal was more practically feasible once the school moved to Stelton, where many of the teachers and parents involved in the school were also active members of the colony, and the children naturally combined schoolwork with work in the community.

The educators involved in the experiment saw their creation of the community around the school as naturally connected to the libertarian call for a more spontaneous, child-centred pedagogy. Thus, in an argument which anticipates the critique of the institutionalization of education by the capitalist state voiced by the de-schoolers some 50 years on, Elizabeth Ferm, an influential teacher at Stelton, states:

> Herding children in child centers has made it necessary to control and regulate their activities. As the child does not understand the reason for his being gathered in with so many strange children and strange adults, one of the first problems of the teacher is how to adjust him as quickly and as pleasantly as possible into a grade or group where he seems to fit. There is no time to let the child adjust himself slowly and to find his own place.
>
> (Ferm 1949: 11)

However, it would appear that the enthusiasm of anarchist educators like Ferm for child-centred pedagogy stemmed more out of a general sympathy for any calls for radically challenging mainstream educational practice and therefore constituting an alternative to state-controlled schools than out of any carefully worked-out theoretical arguments. Furthermore, at the beginning of the twentieth century, the child-centred, or progressive education movement was heralded as the most 'scientific' approach to education, which partly explains its appeal for anarchist educators. Like the European anarchists, the American anarchists associated with the founding of the Ferrer school (amongst them leading activists such as Emma Goldman, Alexander Berkman and Harry Kelly) saw themselves and the education they were promoting as essentially 'rational' and 'scientific' – in contrast with what they saw as the dogmatic, superstitious beliefs which prevailed in the state system. Thus Kelly stated, in an editorial entitled 'The Meaning of Libertarian Education',

> Our aim in the Ferrer School is to free both the child and the adult from the false conventionalities and superstitions which now hinder the progress of the race. We believe that these superstitions operate chiefly in the fields of industry, religion and sex, so that we especially direct attention to those three subjects. [...] We are not dogmatics in the sense that we teach any one ism or point of view to the exclusion of others. We believe that every human being has the right to make his or her choice of life philosophy.
>
> (Kelly 1913)

Indeed, the anarchists' suspicion of anything clearly systemized and prescriptive, along with their revolutionary social outlook, led the New York group to be highly critical even of some progressive educational theorists, such as Montessori and Pestalozzi. Emphasizing the difference between the anarchist–libertarian approach and that of the Montessori system, a further editorial in the *Modern School* journal states:

> Ferrer, a freethinker and social revolutionist, treats of the school as an essential factor in the struggle for a new society; Montessori, a Roman Catholic and social reformer, regards the school as a means to prepare the child for the present society – admittedly an imperfect society, but one gradually improving [...] Montessori's work indicates that she desires not much more for society than remedial measures for its ills. Several times in her book she writes of the yoke of slavery growing easier from century to century. It is the voice of the conservative shrinking at the thought of the larger scheme, and regarding the prolonged existence of things as they are with complete equanimity. Not so Ferrer. It is not enough for him to lighten the yoke from century to century. He demands its utter removal.
>
> (Kerr 1913)

The author goes on to conclude that in order to develop in children such an objective, enlightened view of society and a commitment to the desired social change, it is essential to remove all 'political' (a term seen as equivalent to 'patriotic') or religious education from the curriculum. The ideal was that 'every pupil shall go forth from it into social life with the ability to be his own master, and guide his life in all things' (Avrich 1980: 75). In theory, then, the curriculum of the Modern School in New York and Stelton was to be less prescriptive than that offered by Ferrer, which, as discussed, contained explicitly anti-statist and anti-capitalist messages. In practice, however, the American Modern School was far from apolitical, both in terms of the formal study programme and in terms of the inter-connectedness between the school and the community, which led to participation by pupils and teachers in workers' rallies, political meetings and so on.

In short, there seems to have been some confusion amongst anarchist educators as to the extent to which a libertarian pedagogy could be combined with a substantive curriculum and school ethos. In spite of their general sympathy for the idea of child-centred education, their reservations about this approach clearly reflect their belief in the necessity of radical social change, and their conviction that such change could only be achieved by people 'whose education has trained them [. . .] to cherish and practice the ideas of liberty, equality, and fraternity' (Kelly 1916: 51). It is a serious failing of the work of anarchist educators that they made little systematic attempt to provide a theoretical account of the relationship between child-centred pedagogical practice and their own anarchist goals and values. Nevertheless, I would suggest that the emphasis, in their writing and practice, on expressions of the basic idea formulated in the aforementioned quote, reinforces the impression that what gave these projects their distinct identity was not their espousal of particular educational practices but their underlying moral and political vision.

So although the educational philosophy of the Ferrer schools in New York and Stelton was, in some sense, child-centred, this was understood in a far looser sense than that developed in the work of Dewey and Montessori. Indeed, the founders of the school claimed (Kelly 1914) that the idea of highly trained teachers implementing the Montessori method with the appropriate apparatus was nothing less than 'a contradiction of the rational idea of education', which they saw as essentially concerned with the spontaneous development of the child:

> A normal child is capricious, whimsical and spasmodic in activity. Unless he is under control he will not persist in the use of didactic toys or any set apparatus for play [. . .] The Montessori method presupposes that children are interested in building correct staircases, in discriminating among shades of a colour. It takes for granted that little folks should learn to be economical in movements; that they should be quiet and orderly; that they should persist, that they should learn to endure.
>
> (Kelly 1914)

Although acknowledging that this inhibition of the child's instincts may often not be conscious on the part of Montessori educators, the author cites the physical and psychological dangers of such practice – which, he argues, hinder emotional growth and independent thought.

In comparison, the Modern School had no rigid structure, curriculum or schedules, but maintained 'what order we feel necessary' (ibid.), relying on the anarchist principle of natural order – that is, an order evolved from below, as opposed to imposed from above. In this, anarchist educators were taking a stand against what they regarded as the essentially authoritarian order of the conventional school – an authoritarianism which is reflected and reinforced throughout the social practices of the capitalist state. This stance also reflects the basic anarchist insight that the ideal mode of social organization is a non-hierachical, decentralized one, in which any system of authority and rules is functional and temporary.

It is worth noting that other anarchist schools established following the execution of Ferrer took a somewhat more systematic approach to issues of pedagogy. Thus Mathew Thomas has shown, in his historical study of anarchist schools in Britain in 1890–1916 (Thomas 2004), that the organizers of the International Modern School established in London in 1906, adopted a Froebelian method of teaching. Believing that Froebel's developmental theory was in keeping with the anarchist view of the spontaneous development of the child, the educators involved in this project thus had no problem in 'teaching according to age and stage', as suggested by Froebel.

The conviction of the educators involved in the Ferrer School, and later at Stelton, that what they were doing was providing an education that was above all rational and scientific, is witnessed by several amusing anecdotes about interaction with the children. On one occasion, for example (described in Ferm 1949), a teacher reports a small child running up to her from the kitchen to say that 'The potatoes are ready!' At which, the child is confronted with a series of interrogations – 'How do you know?', 'Did you test them?', 'What makes you think so?' – all designed to encourage children to appreciate the difference between facts and judgements, to develop their abilities to think in a rational fashion, to rely on observation and empirical verification – in short, to make them 'scientific'.

Although there was no formal timetable at the Modern School, lessons were offered along the lines of fairly traditional academic subjects, and children were free to attend them if and when they wished. The classes on offer are listed in the prospectus as follows:

> English, History, Geography, Physiology, Biology, Astronomy.... Big words, these, but we have no others to use and to employ them here means that normal young people want to know what the stars are, how the earth and the soil and the sea and themselves were made.
>
> (Kelly 1916)

For most of these classes, the children did group work, with very little frontal teaching by the teacher. Yet one teacher described how, in the case of arithmetic, 'the individual system of research' seemed to prevail, as opposed to the other classes, where group work was the norm. Apparently, the pupils, by mutual consent, had hit on an arrangement whereby they began 'doing sums' individually on coming into class in the mornings. 'In an extreme emergency', writes the author,

> or if his faculty of perseverance is not working as well as usual, one calls on the teacher or some other pupil to help him out of a tight place. But the general feeling is that it is much better to 'get stuck', to turn back and see where the difficulty is. Whatever may be said against this lonely struggle in the arithmetic field, it certainly develops powers of initiative and perseverance.
>
> (Ibid.)

In short, the founders and, to a large extent the teachers, of the Ferrer School in New York and later at Stelton, like Ferrer himself, made no pretense at political neutrality in education. They saw what they were doing as an important attempt to challenge what they regarded as the conservative forces at work in all aspects of the state system, and to further the development of a radically different kind of society. Like the Escuela Moderna in Barcelona, the New York school appealed primarily to working-class parents, many of whom were already involved in radical social movements, and who objected to the values being promoted in the public schools. Defending the need for the Modern School in a country like the United States, where there is free public schooling, Stewart Kerr (1913) puts forth the classic anarchist argument against state schooling: 'The ruling classes everywhere [...] use the school, often unconsciously, as a means to keep themselves in power, to maintain things as they are'. The Modern School, in contrast,

> is consciously dynamic, aims to cultivate the critical attitude of mind, the indispensable factor in every step forward the world has ever made [...]. The avowed purpose of the public school is to equip the child for his environment. The order of the environment is not questioned [...]. It is the function of the Modern School to strip the social system of its economic fallacies and expose its sordid selfishness.
>
> (Ibid.)

Thomas's study suggests that anarchist educators elsewhere may have been somewhat more uncomfortable than Kelly and his American colleagues with the idea that the education promoted in their schools could be construed as another form of indoctrination. Thomas suggests that there was some controversy, in the British schools, 'about the politicized nature of the subject matter' (Thomas 2004: 428). Yet Thomas's account merely serves to underline the important differences between the social anarchists, who formed the bulk of those involved in the schools discussed here, and individualist anarchists who, following Stirner, 'rejected the entire concept of the school as an affront to the child's autonomy' (ibid.). What characterized those involved in the anarchist school movement was their 'belief in the transformative potential of alternative schools' (ibid.).

Although longer lived than most experiments in communal living, the Stelton colony, and with it the school, was in decline from the late 1920s onwards and finally disintegrated in 1953. Avrich cites both the impact of the Depression and the rift created in the community between the anarchists and communists during the First World War as the main reasons for its demise.

> Before the war, radicals of different stripes could still argue about their differences, could still have their different groups and theories and yet agree about a common enemy, capitalism, and be friends – could even start colonies together. But after the war and the Russian Revolution, this became more and more difficult.
>
> (Ben Liberman, in Avrich 1980: 327)

Ben Lieberman, a former colonist, pinpoints the final rift at a somewhat later date, citing Stalinism as the decisive reason for the break-up of the community (see Avrich, ibid.).

The Walden Center and School, Berkeley, 1956–

Although the Walden Center and School is still in existence, it does not appear to be explicitly associated with the anarchist movement, and indeed makes no reference to anarchism (or indeed libertarian education) in its prospectus or mission statement. The school's website (http://www.walden-school.net) describes it as 'an arts-based progressive, teacher-run elementary school'. The term 'progressive' here is understood as referring to the fact that classes are mixed-age, there are no grades or standardized testing, and there is an emphasis on the arts and on experiential learning. However, I am including this school in the present discussion as its original founding group all shared anarchist views (see Walden Foundation 1996: 21), and the documentation describing the early years of the school provides a valuable example of an attempt to translate anarchist ideas into educational practice.

The idea of setting up the Walden Center and School grew out of the long association and friendship of a group of committed anarchists, communists and pacifists, most of whom had been active in anti-conscription movements, workers' union struggles and various other social causes. On becoming parents, several of the group, unwilling to send their children to the available state schools, which they regarded as reflecting a cultural conflict 'between human needs and social structures', and attracted by the idea of community life (many of them had already been part of experiments in communal living) developed the idea of founding and running their own school, which was to be not only 'a means of educating children in a freer environment, but also a centre for education and action in the adult community we were a part of' (ibid.: 25). Although not all founding members belonged to the anarchist movement, they all, according to the testimony of several members of the group, 'shared the anarchist–pacifist philosophy that shaped the school' (ibid.: 65).

As political activists throughout the 1940s and 1950s many of the founding group had experienced marked changes in their political thinking, which evolved, according to one testimony, 'from the nineteenth century belief that revolutionary change was possible in our lifetime, to our taking a long view of the role of anarchism in society' (ibid.: 21). Thus their agenda, and their political activities, were somewhat less revolutionary than those of the anarchists involved in the Modern School at the beginning of the twentieth century. Of course, this had to do largely with the changed political context within which they were operating – both at the macro level, and at the level of what was actually going on in state schools at the time. Nevertheless, most of the group still regarded themselves as continuing a line of anarchist thought, and felt, in keeping with this tradition, that 'if revolutionary change wasn't imminent, there must be action we could take that would point to the possibilities inherent in anarchistic relationships' (ibid.). Some of the founding members had in fact, before moving to California, had some contact with teachers and colonists at Stelton.

The process of agreeing, jointly, on the school's programme and structure, was regarded as an experimental, philosophical exercise through which the group tested their educational ideas in the light of their philosophy, and 'strove to build a form, both functional and educational, that most reflected our anarchist/pacifist views' (ibid.: 24).

The form which this initial process took is in itself an example of anarchist principles put into practice: wary of the tendency of ideas to turn into ideology, principles into dogma, and 'carefully wrought attitudes' into slogans, the founders were reluctant to document the countless discussions and debates which preceded and accompanied the initial years of the school, and avoided creating a written programme or prospectus. This suspicion of constitutions, dogmas and blueprints for institutions and practices is, of course, a basic thread common to all anarchists, who believe that to lay down such blueprints would undermine the commitment to human freedom, progress and perfectibility.

Another political principle of anarchism put into practice in these founding sessions, as well as in regular parent–teacher meetings throughout the years, was the rejection of the democratic belief in majority rule – the adherence to which had, according to David Koven, one of the school's founders, destroyed parent–teacher coalitions in other independent schools where the founders of the cooperatives had used it to 'push their Marxist bias' (Walden Foundation 1996: 28). What Koven and his colleagues sought, in contrast, was a form of day-to-day management practice that would 'prevent the creation of a bureaucracy that could dictate life at the school' (Walden Foundation 1996: 27). All decision-making, therefore, took place only after the group had reached consensus. Furthermore, in order to prevent the founding group from becoming 'stodgy and self-satisfied', it was agreed that every new teacher or family was entitled to join in the decision-making process after having been at the school for an initial period of 1 to 2 years. The commitment to consensus meant that no proposed new action or policy to which any member of the school community objected could be carried out until the principled objection had been heard and discussed and a workable compromise had been reached. Of course, the insistence on consensus by no means rules out the possibility of power-struggles and, furthermore, as testified by the founders, running the school this way meant that the process of decision-making was slow and painstaking. However, they felt it was an essential element of their anarchist commitments and seemed convinced that it insured the community, to a considerable degree, against power-struggles over the control of the school and the development of an ambitious, power-seeking minority.

What is of particular interest in this context is that all the founders were adamant that the school was not to be a 'parent–teacher cooperative'. Although the founding parents outlined the basic philosophy of the school, they felt very strongly that on a day-to-day basis, the teachers needed to be in charge, as the ongoing continuity essential to good education could not occur if the teachers were constantly functioning at the whim of the parents. Ultimately, the founders believed, education was the concern of teachers and children, and thus, 'parents could raise hell, but in the end, decisions were made at the teacher–child level' (ibid.: 79), with many decisions made by the children themselves.

As the Fourth Draft of the Philosophy Statement (the only surviving document from the early years of the school) states:

'We do not visualize the teacher as a technician, mass-producing according to someone else's plan, but as a sensitive, creative force at innumerable moments in the learning experience' (ibid.: 10).

Another basic anarchist tenet which was translated into educational practice at Walden is the belief in small communities as the optimal units of social organization. This belief is reflected not only in the organization of the community around the school – which relied heavily on personal contacts, mutual support and friendship as a basis for commitment to this and other projects – but in the pedagogical principle that class size should be limited (15 was eventually agreed upon as the maximum number of children per class) in order to promote an ideal learning environment for children – one in which the teacher could be responsive and sensitive to individual needs and could relate to the children on a personal basis.

In keeping with these anarchist principles of social organization, the school in effect had no central authority, and thus each teacher was autonomous and was responsible for determining procedures, developing curricula and planning programmes – aided in this process, of course, by the ongoing discussions with other members of the staff and the board.

What is surprising, however, in the context of this emphasis on freedom, is that, in contrast to many accounts of experiments in anarchist education (notably those discussed earlier), there is very little mention in the accounts of Walden of the notion of the freedom of the individual child. Of course, there is frequent mention of general principles designed to promote the child's freedom – for example, 'We do not believe in simple indoctrination, even for the sake of the good' (ibid.), and of the vision of a school that would help children to 'think independently, would give them all the tools for creative existence, [. . .] would be secular, would have no heroes, no presidents, no icons' (ibid.: 40). Likewise, several of the founders point to an explicit connection between anarchist principles and pedagogic practice in the notion that 'the needs of children rather than the needs of the state' should be the driving motives behind educational practice. However, there is very little mention of the way these ideas were reflected in the day-to-day life of the school. It is not at all clear, for example, what Walden's position was on the issue of compulsory attendance – abolishment of which is commonly a central principle of anarchist educational initiatives. Denny Wilcher, one of the original founders, testifies that 'no teacher ever forced a child to attend structured classes' (Walden Foundation 1996: 79), but the emphasis in the school's philosophy seems to be more on a commitment to the individual development and emotional and intellectual needs of the child, rather than to the principle of non-coercion *per se*. In fact, the school's apparent reluctance to make non-attendance a central and viable option for children is suggested by the fact that, from the beginning, they attempted to deal with this issue by carving out spaces in the curriculum in which such practice was legitimated. 'On Wednesdays', as Wilcher describes, 'there was no school at all and groups and individuals did whatever interested them' (Walden Foundation 1996: 78), and another founding parent and teacher, Alan MacRae, is credited with having invented 'Hookey Day', held on the first day of Spring, when the entire school, parents included, went to the park and played.

Another point on which Walden seems to differ from the anarchist educational initiatives of the late nineteenth and early twentieth century is in its emphasis on the arts and creativity in general. In contrast to schools such as the Ferrer School in New York or the Modern School at Stelton, where great emphasis was placed on rationality and 'scientific' approaches, the first few years at Walden were characterized by an emphasis on dance, music and plastic arts, and the high points of the school year were always lavish productions of various musical dramas on which the parents, teachers and children collaborated. This emphasis could have been due in part to the fact that many of the founders were themselves professional dancers, musicians or skilled craftspeople, and brought their skills in these fields to the school when they became involved as teachers. But there does also seem to have been an explicit commitment to the role of artistic creativity in creating the kind of educational environment and, indeed, the kind of society envisioned by the founders. The classes at the school took the form of a confederation of groups, each new child being admitted not to the school but to a particular group, and each group made a commitment to engage in a significant amount of music, dance and arts and craft, which, according to Wilcher, 'were seen as basics, not luxuries' (Walden Foundation 1996: 79).

Many of the aforementioned features, particularly the emphasis on the arts, have endured over the years and are clearly an essential element of the school's identity. However, several founding members, reflecting, in the mid 1980s, on the development of the school over the years, expressed the view that the political ethos of the school community had changed considerably. The current parent body seemed, in the words of one of the founding members, to be 'more interested in success' and less open to radical ideas on education and society. This sense can be confirmed by a glance at the comments recently posted about the school on the local web-based parents' network, where enthusiastic testimonies about the school's unique environment typically contain comments such as: 'current studies are showing that this type of environment is excellent for developing upper reasoning math skills' [http://parents.berkeley.edu/recommend/schools/walden.html]. A cynical reader may conclude that, while Walden Center and School still clearly and admirably demonstrates an emphasis on creativity, a commitment to collective decision-making, and an atmosphere of mutual respect between teachers and children, the radical dissenting philosophy on which it was founded has all but been replaced by an acquiescence in the mainstream race for academic achievement and accreditation. Nevertheless, Koven concluded, in 1987 (Walden Foundation 1996: 33), 'When I think of Walden functioning for almost thirty years without a director or central authority, I'm filled with both awe and joy. Here is real affirmation of our anarchist insight.'

In short, Walden, in its early days, seems to have differed from earlier anarchist educational experiments primarily in that it saw itself not so much as a vanguard of the anarchist revolution, or a step towards developing the kind of people capable of bringing about and sustaining the free society of the future, but, above all, as an experiment in human living. The underlying idea seems to be a commitment to anarchism as 'a way of life'. As such, the Walden School would seem to be less clearly a reflection of the political ideology of the social anarchists discussed in the preceding chapters, although it echoes many central anarchist ideas. One way of bringing out these differences between Walden and the experiments set up by the nineteenth-century and early twentieth-century anarchists is in terms of how the school community perceived the relationship between the school and the wider society. In the case of the early social anarchists, it is quite clear that the school was intended to be not only a microcosm of a social alternative to the state but also a vanguard of the social anarchist revolution. The school, in other words, had two revolutionary functions: creating a generation of people capable of laying the basis for the future anarchist society, through a process of moral education and engagement in critical social and political activism and serving as an example to the surrounding society of how such an alternative future was possible. In the case of Walden, in contrast, one gets the impression that the school founders saw their school less as a revolutionary vanguard, and more simply as a social experiment, serving primarily to remind the outside world that alternatives are possible.

Other anarchist schools

As documented in several excellent accounts, there have been explicitly anarchist schools in existence since probably the middle of the nineteenth century. Notably, Paul Robin, Sébastien Faure and Madeline Vernet, all of whom founded innovative libertarian schools in France in the late nineteenth and early twentieth century, were associated, to some extent, with the anarchist movement. (See Shotton 1993 and Smith 1983.) During the same period in Britain, there were several experiments in anarchist education, along more socialist or social-anarchist lines (for an account of these see Shotton 1993 and Thomas 2004). However, anarchist schools are more often than not excluded from historical accounts of radical schooling. In their account of Owenist education, for example, Stewart and McCann make the astonishing claim that the Owenist schools established in Britain in the mid-nineteenth century

> were the only popular educational institutions in the nineteenth century that were specifically designed to produce a change in society by changing the character of the knowledge given to the individuals composing it, and through their influencing the society itself.
>
> (Stewart and McCann 1967: 91)

Summerhill – a non-anarchist experiment

The aforementioned description may suggest that the famous Summerhill School, the longest-lived libertarian educational project, founded in Leiston, Suffolk in 1921 by the late A.S. Neill, is a natural candidate for inclusion in this account. Indeed, from a structural point of view, there are many similarities between day-to-day practice at Summerhill and that at the anarchist schools described here. Summerhill, like anarchist schools, has no rigid timetable or curriculum, teaching is informal, children are free to come and go as they like (provided they remain within the school grounds – a compromise Neill was forced to make in order to comply with the Compulsory Education Law), and Neill always rejected traditional roles of teacher authority. Similarly, Neill's writings, which continue to inform the school's policies and practice, are full of references to the freedom of the individual child and damning descriptions of authoritarian child-rearing practice.

One of the few differences which are immediately apparent on the structural level has to do with the avowedly democratic principles involved in the administration of Summerhill. In contrast to the anarchist suspicion of majority rule as a political system (as evidenced earlier by the example of Walden School), Summerhill has always stressed its democratic character, both at the level of policy and day-to-day running of the school. In the context of Summerhill and similar schools (such as the Israeli Democratic School in Hadera, which is modelled on Summerhill), the notion of democracy seems to have been given a very narrow interpretation, emphasizing above all the principle of majority rule. The school meeting, for example, one of the key features of life at Summerhill, is an assembly where every member of the school community – staff and children alike – have equal voice, and where all decisions are reached by democratic voting.

Apart from this obvious example, however, the differences between Summerhill and similar libertarian or 'free' schools, on the one hand, and anarchist schools on the other, may not be immediately apparent. Yet they are, I believe, crucial. In order to understand their significance, one has to examine the philosophical and ideological commitments which informed the educational principles and practice of these two different approaches. A consideration of the philosophical background of anarchist educational ideas, as discussed in the preceding chapters, shows that these two superficially similar types of school in fact reflect very different positions.

First, and perhaps crucially, Neill conceived of freedom in a primarily individual, psychological sense. His chief intellectual influences were those of the psychoanalytical tradition – especially the work of Wilhelm Reich and, later, Homer Lane. Thus, although critical of existing society, he believed that the way forward to a better world lay in gradual reform at the individual level – a sort of mass therapy, in a sense, by which we would gradually achieve a society of self-aware, uninhibited, emotionally stable and happy individuals. In contrast, the notion of freedom behind the anarchist position is, along with other concepts such as those of freedom and cooperation, not, as Smith puts it, 'an abstract, context-free concept', but one which carries 'concrete political connotations' (Smith 1983: 17). The anarchist understanding of freedom in the context of education involves, as discussed in Chapter 4, not only a clear sense of, as Smith notes, 'what pupils are to be freed from' (ibid.: 87), but also a carefully thought-out positive ideal.

In contrast, in *A Dominie Dismissed*, one of Neill's early books, which is a semi-autobiographical story based on his years as a young teacher in rural Scotland, he describes his dissatisfaction with the current state of society: 'Obviously present day civilization is all wrong. "But", a dominie might cry, "can you definitely blame elementary education for that?" I answer "Yes, yes, Yes!" ' (Neill, quoted in Hemmings 1972: 24). Thus Neill, unlike the anarchists, did not seem to believe that broad, structural social change was the main goal of social reform. Rather, he envisaged a process of social transformation whereby educational practice, reformed along the lines he suggested, could remedy the ills of society. Interestingly, Neill echoed many anarchist ideas in his emphasis on the need to remove authority as a basis for relations in the family, the school and the workplace. He was greatly impressed by the work of Homer Lane at the Little Commonwealth, the experimental self-governing community for young delinquents. Self-government, Neill argued, not only serves to remove the negative effects of authority, but also 'breeds altruism', as witnessed by the experiments of Homer Lane and others (Hemmings 1972: 30).

Yet Neill was adamant on his non-political – one may even argue, value-relative – position as an educator. 'Life is so difficult to understand', he remarked in an interview for the *The New Era* (quoted in Hemmings 1972: 35), 'that I personally cannot claim to settle the relative educational values of anyone.' As Hemmings comments, Neill seemed genuinely to believe that 'children must determine their own values, in culture as in morality' (ibid.). This is a far cry from the committed political stance of anarchist educators who, though they may have believed in the educational value of allowing free, critical dialogue and encouraging creative independent thinking on the part of pupils, had no qualms about stating their own ideological convictions, and indeed designed a curriculum and a school climate which would reflect the values implicit in these convictions. For 'neutrality in the school', the anarchist founders of the Modern School declared, 'can be nothing but hypocrisy', and they went on to state:

> We should not, in the school, hide the fact that we would awaken in the children a desire for a society of men truly free and truly equal [...], a society without violence, without hierarchies, and without privilege of any sort.
>
> (Ferrer 1909: 6)

Neill, although he began his professional life as a teacher, developed a growing fascination with Freudian psychology early on in his career, and in fact described himself on several occasions as a psychologist rather than an educationalist – his preface to *The Problem Child* (Neill 1926) begins with the words: 'Since I left education and took up child psychology...' and, as early as 1922, in *A Dominie Abroad*, he states 'It has come to me as something of a sudden shock that I am no longer interested in teaching. Teaching English bores me stiff. All my interest is in psychology' (Hemmings 1972: 48).

As Hemmings notes, Neill's agreement with Homer Lane's idea of 'original virtue' – reflected in his insistence that all moral instruction perverts the innate goodness of the child – entails certain philosophical difficulties when placed alongside his apparent moral relativism. Neill's position on this issue is also strikingly at odds with the anarchists' rejection of the romantic, Rousseauian view of a pre-social, naturally benign human nature, and with their insistence that human nature is actually twofold and contextualist.

A more explicit statement of Neill's views on society and the individual can be found in his comment, in *The Problem Child*, that 'When the individual and the social interests clash, the individual interests should be allowed to take precedence' (Neill 1926: 216). This suggests that Neill did not share the anarchist view of humans as essentially social by nature and of the impossibility of talking about individual self-fulfilment in isolation from the social context.

Hemmings goes as far as to suggest, based on Neill's comments about the primacy of individual interests and the need for the child to create his own culture and values, that

> Such insistence on individual freedom led Neill to avoid serious consideration of the social consequences of his education: he was prepared to let these evolve their own way. On the individual level, he was saying that if the emotions were right the intellect would look after itself, and as regards social structure he seemed to be assuming that, given emotionally healthy individuals, their culture could safely be left to develop.
> (Hemmings 1972: 109)

Smith, too, notes that at Summerhill, there is 'no systematic attempt to introduce the discussion of political values [...] and no real attempt to promote cooperative values' (Smith 1983: 100).

This view is in fact backed up by my own impressions of visits to Summerhill today. One has the impression of a lively group of self-confident, happy children, who may, as one imagines, very well grow up to be happy, but completely self-centred individuals. As witnessed by the account by a new teacher of the opposition he encountered from the school staff to his proposal to develop a P.S.E. project involving children from the local town, there is little attempt to engage with broader social issues or to confront present socio-political reality. Indeed, there is very much a sense (again, this is supported by comments of parents at the school) of the school having created a little island, in which Summerhill, and the superior kind of education which it represents, is regarded as being against the rest of the world, with its misguided ideas. Whereas the anarchists associated with the schools described earlier were always deeply involved in the social and political environment in which they lived, and seemed to feel themselves to be in some sense a part of something greater, in contrast, as Hemmings notes (Hemmings 1972: 174), for the children and teachers at Summerhill, the school itself represents the 'real, present society – the conflicts and demands of the "outside" society being somewhat removed from experience'.

This contrast is reflected, too, in the way in which Summerhill recently conducted its battle against the threat of closure from the current government, following a damning OFSTED inspection. Instead of addressing the broader social implications of the threat by a centralist government to an alternative school and broadening support for their campaign by engaging with other groups (such as struggling comprehensive schools in deprived areas, frustrated teachers and parents) who felt their autonomy and rights to make educational choices similarly threatened – the school community chose to focus their campaign on the particular validity of Neill's educational philosophy and their right to defend this philosophy against that of the mainstream educational establishment. Anarchist educators, although they did indeed aim to create a community that represented a particular way of social organization and a way of life different from that typical of the surrounding society, nevertheless saw themselves as constantly engaging in the outside world – as, indeed, involved in an ongoing process of interaction with it in their efforts to bring about the social change they saw as so essential. As Hemmings suggests, what Neill was really after was an appreciation of freedom for its own sake (Hemmings 1972: 73) – a far cry from the social anarchists, who viewed freedom, in the sense described here, as an inherent aspect of creating a society based on mutual aid, socio-economic equality and cooperation.

Anarchist schools versus libertarian education

In short, although many writers, Smith (1983), Shotton (1993) and Spring (1975) among them, include Summerhill and similar schools under the broad heading of 'libertarian education', I believe there is a significant difference between the philosophical and political outlook behind these experiments in alternative education and that of the anarchist schools discussed earlier. It would appear that the anarchist educational experiments are unique in the world of 'progressive', 'libertarian' or 'free' education not in terms of their pedagogical practice but in terms of the substantive ideas and motivations behind them. These ideas can only be grasped in the context of the anarchist commitment to undermining the state by creating alternative forms of social organization and relationships.

As discussed earlier, the anarchist view of human nature as not predominantly or innately 'good' or 'evil', but as determined largely by social context, goes a long way towards explaining the central role that anarchist thinkers over the ages have assigned to educational experiments, and particularly to the moral content and form of these experiments. In contrast, it is in fact the libertarian position associated with educational experiments such as Summerhill which makes the type of optimistic or naïve assumptions about human nature often wrongly attributed to anarchism. John Darling notes this point in his discussion of 'growth theorists' (Darling 1982), where he quotes Neill as assuming that children are 'naturally good' and will turn out to be 'good human beings if [they are] not crippled and thwarted in [their] natural development by interference' (Neill, quoted in Darling 1982: 68).

The picture of typical anarchist schools outlined earlier, then, serves two purposes: first, it makes it abundantly clear that anarchists did not subscribe to the view that one can do away with education, or even with schools, altogether, but seemed to agree that schools, and education in general, are a valuable aspect of the project for social change, rather than simply another objectionable aspect of the machinery of state bureaucracy.

Second, it distinguishes the anarchist view from the pure libertarian view, that there is something morally objectionable in the very attempt by educators to pass on any substantial beliefs or moral principles to children. Although anarchist educators have often been sympathetic to libertarian educational experiments such as Summerhill, this is, I suggest, not because of an underlying commitment to the same set of values and principles, but rather because, as Colin Ward points out,

> The handful of people who have sought to put their ideas of 'free' education into practice have always been so beleagured by the amused hostility of the institutionalised education system on the one hand and by the popular press in the other [...] that they have tended to close ranks and minimise their differences.
>
> (Ward 1990: 15)

Although, as Ehrlich puts it, 'In an anarchist society, the social function of schools and the potential of education would be quite different' (Ehrlich 1996: 15), I think the point made by Morland about Bakunin's thought, namely, that 'some form of schooling will exist after the abolition of state mechanisms' (Morland 1997: 113), generally holds true for the social anarchists.

How such schools would be run, and by whom, is, in keeping with the anarchists' commitment to free experimentation and their aversion to blueprints, to be left to the discretion of individual communes. The following passage from Bakunin provides further illustration of this idea, along with support for the aforementioned point, that the social anarchists, unlike many libertarian educators or individualist anarchists, regarded education as an important social good and were reluctant to leave it in the hands of parents.

> It is society not the parents who will be responsible for the upkeep of the child. This principle once established we believe that we should abstain from specifying the exact manner in which this principle should be applied; to do otherwise would risk trying to achieve a Utopia. Therefore the application must be left to free experimentation and we must await the lessons of practical experience. We say only that *vis à vis* the child, society is represented by the commune, and that each commune will have to determine what would be best for the upbringing of the child; here they would have life in common; there they would leave children in care of the mother, at least up to a certain age, etc.
>
> (Bakunin, in Dolgoff 1973: 372)

However, this passage by Bakunin clearly refers to education in the post-state reality, that is, once the social-anarchist society has been established. Although, as discussed earlier, the anarchist view of human nature explains the need for an ongoing process of moral education alongside the educative function of social institutions run on anarchist principles, many anarchists were theoretically vague on the question of the role of education in bringing about the transition to the anarchist society.

Most anarchist writers on education in fact completely fail to distinguish between the stage of life within the state and the theoretical stage of life beyond the state. Such a failure is responsible for a great deal of confusion and, indeed, largely explains the enthusiasm of many anarchist sympathizers for educational experiments such as Summerhill which, while arguably in keeping with Bakunin's vague remarks about the forms of education acceptable in the future anarchist society, do not, as discussed, provide the substantive moral core necessary to further and sustain such a society. However, in another sense, this very failure to distinguish between these two theoretical stages in itself reflects an important aspect of the anarchist perspective on education and one in which, I suggest, it differs from the mainstream liberal, as well as the Marxist, view. This point will be taken up again in the following chapters.

Means and ends in education

The picture of education that emerges from this discussion then is a complex, dialectical one, in which education for social virtues is both necessary to sustain stateless, cooperative communities, and is itself reinforced by the day-to-day experience of life in such communities. Yet how, one may still insist, are we to get from *a* to *b*? Given that we are faced, today, with the all-pervasive and, to all intents and purposes, permanent reality of the liberal state and its institutions, how are educators with anarchist sympathies expected to use education as one amongst the many means to further their goals?

This question has both a theoretical and a practical aspect. On the theoretical level, it has to do with how we conceptualize the relationship between means and ends.

The means–ends distinction has received considerable attention in the tradition of liberal-analytic philosophy of education. Richard Peters famously argued, in 'Must an Educator Have an Aim?' (Peters 1959), that the inherently normative aspect of the concept 'education' should not mislead us into thinking of education in terms of a model 'like building a bridge or going on a journey' (Peters 1959: 123), where all experiences and processes leading up to the stated end are regarded as means to achieving it. So although talk of education inevitably involves judgements of value, the simple means–ends model, according to Peters, can give us 'the wrong picture of the way in which values must enter education' (ibid.).

Yet what Peters is anxious to avoid here is a notion of aims which implies a simple means–ends model and thus an apparent willingness to employ any means necessary in order to achieve the stated end. He gives as an example of what he calls a 'very general aim', the political aim of equality, arguing that the type of people who regard this as an important aim, lured by the picture of a society without inequalities, often advocate all sorts of drastic structural measures in order to achieve it. The notion of equality, when employed as a 'principle of procedure', on the other hand, would, according to Peters, yield far more moderate, liberal measures – for example, the insistence that 'whatever schemes were put forward must not be introduced in a way which would infringe his procedural principle' (Peters 1959: 127). The second type of reformer would, as Peters notes, not have any 'concrete picture to lure him on his journey' (ibid.).

However, I would criticize Peters on this point, for 'aims' of the kind he has in mind are often important in providing what Noam Chomsky has called an 'animating vision' (Chomsky 1996: 70) for human activity, particularly education. It is the way one thinks of such an aim, and the imaginative use one makes of it, rather than its general nature, that determines whether or not it can become a constructive factor in one's educational endeavours, or a restrictive, potentially dangerous one. Positive, substantive 'pictures' – of a world without poverty, of a society without distinctions of class and wealth – are often valuable in inspiring people to act positively to improve their lives and those of others. The fact that there is always a risk of aims being interpreted rigidly is not an argument against having 'concrete aims' as such but against trying to impose them without any critical evaluation or sensitivity to existing conditions. As John Dewey notes, it is when aims are 'regarded as literally ends to action rather than as directive stimuli to present choice' that they become 'frozen and isolated' (Dewey 1965: 73).

Crucially, for Dewey, the means cannot be determined in advance, and they are in constant interplay with the aim which, far from being a fixed point in the distance, is constantly a part of present activity; not 'an end or terminus of action' but something which directs one's thoughts and deliberations, and stimulates action; 'Ends are foreseen consequences which arise in the course of activity and which are employed to give activity added meaning and to direct its further course.' (Dewey 1964: 72) Furthermore, the original 'aim' is constantly being revised and new aims are 'forever coming into existence as new activities occasion new consequences' (Dewey 1964: 76).

This Deweyan idea goes some way towards capturing what I believe is the anarchist perspective on the relationship between education and social change. Crucial to this perspective is the insight that while aims and goals play an important role in the educational process, they do so not in the sense of ends and means. Thus criticisms such as Erin McKenna's, that 'the anarchist vision lacks a developed method of change' (McKenna 2001: 65) seem to me to fall into the trap of assuming a simplistic ends–means model. This model, whereby educational processes are regarded merely as a means to achieving social or political ends, is an inadequate tool for understanding the anarchist position.

I said, earlier, that the question of how to get from *a* to *b* has both a theoretical and a practical aspect. I hope these remarks on the conceptualization of ends and means go some way towards addressing the theoretical aspect. I shall take up these themes again in the ensuing discussion. As far as the practical aspect goes, it may be helpful to examine this question by looking, in the next chapter, at a specific issue of educational policy. Contrasting the liberal treatment of a particular policy issue with the anarchist treatment of it will, I hope, illustrate these theoretical points about the way in which anarchist goals and visions can be reflected in educational processes and about the general differences in perspective between anarchism and liberalism.

7 Education for an anarchist society

Vocational training and political visions

As the preceding discussion suggests, many anarchist ideas and experiments in education stemmed from the belief, informed by the anarchist view of human nature, that a key aspect of the revolutionary process involved nurturing and developing those moral qualities deemed necessary to create and sustain a social-anarchist society. In other words, the emphasis in anarchist educational programmes was not so much on attempting to bring about a pre-conceived alternative model of social organization but on laying the ground for the natural evolution of such a model by means of fostering the attitudes that underpin it, alongside the experiment of creating a microcosm of anarchist society. This perspective underpins the experiments in anarchist education described in Chapter 6, but it is often unarticulated, so it is only by unpacking the philosophical and ideological insights of anarchism as a theory that one can appreciate the uniqueness of such experiments in the world of libertarian education.

As suggested earlier, the means–ends model is insufficient to capture the relationship between education and social change within anarchist thought. Nevertheless, the picture painted in the preceding chapter of some typical anarchist schools, alongside the suggestion for a more fully developed account of moral education, answers, to some extent, the practical question of 'What should an anarchist educator do in order to bring the possibility of an anarchist society a little closer?' The present chapter attempts to answer this question from a different, but related, angle, namely: 'What should the anarchist policy-maker or educational theorist do – in keeping with anarchist theory – in order to bring the possibility of an anarchist society a little closer?'

By focusing on a particular educational question with important policy implications, I hope to draw out what I have described as the anarchist perspective a little more clearly, and to contrast it with other perspectives – notably, the Marxist and the liberal ones. With this aim in mind, I shall discuss the issue of vocational education, which is especially pertinent due to the important anarchist idea of integral education. As the following discussion will reveal, the question of the role of vocational training within the school curriculum, like other educational questions, can, from an anarchist point of view, only be understood within a broad political context. Therefore, this discussion will lead into a further development of the idea of the moral and political content of anarchist education, and will tie this in with the general theme of the anarchist perspective on the relationship between education and social change. Accordingly, this chapter consists of two interrelated sections. In the section on Vocational Education: Theory and Practice, I discuss the way the notion of vocational education is understood both within the anarchist tradition and in the work of two contemporary philosophers of education, Christopher Winch and Richard Pring, who have developed rigorous philosophical accounts of this notion in the context of the liberal educational tradition. In the section on The Moral and Political Content of Education, I examine the moral and political content which, I argue, plays a crucial role in anarchist education and which, accordingly, underlines the distinct perspective offered by the anarchist position.

Vocational education: theory and practice

Integral education

The anarchist notion of integral education – that is, an education which combined intellectual and manual training – was an important feature of all anarchist schools, notably the Escuela Moderna in Barcelona (see Chapter 6), and Paul Robin's educational experiments in France (see Smith 1983: 18–61). But the chief theoretical exponent of this idea was Kropotkin who, in 'Brain Work and Manual Work' (Kropotkin 1890) and in *Fields, Factories and Workshops Tomorrow* (Kropotkin 1974), set forth the ideal of a society in which, instead of the current 'pernicious distinction' between 'brain work' and ' manual work', reflecting divisions between a 'labouring' and an ' educated' class, all girls and boys, 'without distinction of birth', should receive a 'complete education'. Kropotkin's theory was informed by the assumption, shared by Marxist theory, that labour – as a central aspect of human life and an element in personal well-being – is to be distinguished from work – which, in capitalist society, becomes merely a commodity, to be sold for a wage. Yet, perhaps more importantly, Kropotkin's views were guided by the belief in social equality as a valuable and attainable goal and the ideal of a society based on mutual cooperation and fraternity.

From this perspective, Kropotkin's analysis of capitalist industrialized states and their inherent inequalities convinced him that it is the capitalist system itself which divorces manual work from mental work and thus creates the false dichotomy between the two and the associated inequalities in social status. The only way to break down these divisions was to provide an education in which, in the words of Proudhon, 'the industrial worker, the man of action and the intellectual will all be rolled into one' (Edwards 1969: 80). In fact, by the late nineteenth century, this idea had become an established tenet of revolutionary socialist educational thinking. This is reflected in the fact that one of the first acts of the Paris Commune was to establish an

Educational Commission committed to providing all the children of the community with integral education. The idea, as described by Edwards in his account of the Commune, 'expressed the desire both to learn a useful trade and at the same time escape from the specialization caused by division of labour and the consequent separation into educated and uneducated classes' (Edwards 1971, quoted in Smith 1983: 273).

Thus the notion of integral education involves more than just a breaking down, at the practical level, of the traditional liberal-vocational distinctions; it does not propose, that is, merely to ensure that all children leave school with a useful trade and appropriate theoretical knowledge so that they may become fully participating members in the productive economy. The theoretical assumptions behind this notion are, first and foremost, political. Integral education programmes along these lines were seen as an essential element of educational experiments such as those of Paul Robin, in France, where the school was intended to create an environment embodying a commitment to social equality and the belief that communities run on the principles of co-education, freedom from coercion, respect for the individual child and self-government could form the vanguard for the socialist revolution. Thus, at Paul Robin's school for orphans, Cempuis, intellectual education was seen

> as essentially complementary to manual and physical training. Questions, problems, needs, arose out of the day-to-day practice of the workshops, but not in a mechanical, over-programmed way [...] If manual training was carried out in the right way, the child would want to know more of the principles behind it.
>
> (Smith 1983: 34)

The political motivation behind this approach, then, was explicit and was an intrinsic part of the project of laying the foundations for the social-anarchist revolution. Similar to the theoretical defence of polytechnical education systems established in the Soviet Union immediately after the revolution, and in Communist China, one of the main reasons for believing in the value of an education which involved real encounters with the world of work was that distancing children from this world in an academic environment would cut them off from the experience which lay at the basis of social and political consciousness. Both Marx and Mao explicitly defended the view that 'combining work with study would keep the young in touch with those moral and political truths which were part of the consciousness of the working class' (Smith 1983: 52). Although Kropotkin was less focused on the struggle of the working class, and emphasized instead the needs of a complex industrial society and the value of cooperative social organization, this theme can nevertheless be found in much anarchist writing on the content of the school curriculum, as illustrated, for example, in the educational writings of Francisco Ferrer (see Chapter 6).

The early social anarchist thinkers were only too aware of the realities of the growing industrialization they were witnessing and of the fact that they were educating workers. They held, with Proudhon, that 'the work a man did was something to be proud of, it was what gave interest, value and dignity to his life' (Smith 1983: 25). Thus,

> An education that was divorced from the world of work, that is, an education that was entirely bookish or grammar-schoolish in conception, was valueless from the point of view of ordinary working-class children. Of course, an education that went too far in the other direction, which brought up children merely to be fodder for factories, was equally unacceptable. What was required was an education which would equip a child for the work-place but would also give him a degree of independence in the labour market.
>
> (Ibid.)

Furthermore, the anarchist concept of integral education, apart from reflecting the anarchist social ideal, also involved an important notion of personal well-being. The social-anarchist challenge to the typical division of labour in society would, it was hoped, help to avoid the sense of monotony involved in working in one occupation throughout life. This was regarded as reflecting what the anarchists called the 'fundamental organizational principle of diversification' (ibid.: 19), which itself was seen as a consequence of the essential human need for diversity.

But, crucially, anarchist educational programmes also involved a commitment to political and moral education, in the sense of challenging the dominant values of the capitalist system – for example, the wage system, the competitive market-place, the control of the means of production, and so on – as well as fostering the social virtues. Thus, while challenging the existing system and trying to minimize its damaging effects on future workers, social anarchist educators never lost sight of the radical new reality that they wanted to create – and which, they believed, was fully within the scope of human capabilities and aspirations. It is in this sense that they represent a shift in perspective from mainstream thinking on these issues.

The social anarchist perspective on vocational education can be interestingly contrasted with both the Marxist and the liberal one. It is of course because Marxists focus on the class dimension as basic to all notions of social struggle and resistance that they see the necessity of educating a proletarian revolutionary vanguard. They are traditionally, then, concerned with the education of workers. Specifically, the role of education from a Marxist perspective is, above all, to bring class political consciousness to the worker (a role which, according to Lenin, could only be done from the outside, by an enlightened educator) (see Bantock 1984: 242).

Bantock suggests that the Marxist enthusiasm for comprehensive education (i.e. an education which combined academic and vocational training) was a result first and foremost of the Marxists' environmentalist position – that is, the fact that it is environmental influences – amongst them education – and not natural capacities which influence human potential. They therefore rejected as bourgeois ideas such as intelligence-testing and streaming. The Marxist attitude to vocational education is also informed by the critique of labour as a commodity in the capitalist system and the conviction that the labour process should be 'a purposive activity carried on for the production of use-values, for the fitting of natural substances to human wants' (ibid.: 229).

While anarchists share with Marxists many assumptions regarding the nature of labour in capitalist society, the anarchist perspective on social change and the role of the state leads to a very different conception of vocational education, as the following discussion will show. Similarly, this distinct anarchist perspective can be illustrated by a contrast with common perceptions of vocational education within the liberal tradition.

Fraternity as a component of integral education

As mentioned earlier, certain commentators have suggested that it is in fact fraternity, rather than freedom or equality, which should be regarded as the chief goal of social anarchism. However, as the preceding discussion suggests, I believe that such philosophical exercises in establishing the theoretical priority of any one goal or value within anarchist thought are misconceived. Of course, one could make a general point about the incommensurability of values within political theories, as Isaiah Berlin has discussed with reference to liberalism. However, in the case of anarchism, this general philosophical point is particularly salient as it is, I believe, partly a reflection of the anti-hierarchical stance of anarchist thinkers. Thus the anarchist antipathy to structural and permanent hierarchies in social and political organization could be read as analogous to a general suspicion of hierarchical thinking when it comes to concepts and values.

The aforementioned remarks notwithstanding, it is certainly true that, as discussed in Chapter 6, fraternity can be regarded as an important educational goal for anarchists.

The educational experiments described in Chapter 6 illustrate how the moral qualities involved in the attitude of fraternity, which are an essential requisite for the creation and maintenance of social anarchist communities, were promoted largely through what we would refer to as 'school climate' – in other words, through the fact that the school itself was run as a microcosm of a social-anarchist community in the making. Geoffrey Fidler, on the basis of research into the work of the late nineteenth- and early twentieth-century French anarchist-libertarian educators, has argued for a conceptual connection between fraternity and the anarchist idea of integral education.

The notion of integral education, as described earlier, developed primarily out of the anarchist aim of breaking down the class divisions of capitalist society by doing away with the distinction between intellectual and manual labour. But, Fidler argues, in his analysis of early nineteenth-century French experiments in anarchist education,

> At the heart of libertarian as 'complete' education lay the urge to realize an equal, voluntary and 'right' espousal of the mutual arrangements of the fraternal community. This was construed as 'natural' and 'spontaneous' in the particular sense of self-realization succinctly expressed by *Les Temps Nouveaux* [the journal of Libertarian education, edited by Sebastian Faure].
>
> (Fidler 1989: 46)

What Fidler seems to be suggesting here is that the anarchists' critique of capitalist society hinged primarily on their objection to the socio-economic inequalities created by the division of labour in such a society. In positing an ideal society, therefore, they regarded it as crucial that no such division should obtain, out of both a commitment to social equality, and a notion of individual well-being as conceptually and psychologically connected to the well-being of the community (see the discussion on Bakunin and freedom, in Chapter 4). Yet such a society could not be created or maintained without promoting and nurturing the human propensity (already present, but often suppressed by capitalist institutions and values) for benevolence, mutual aid and fraternity.

Fidler, in fact, in a passage reminiscent of Ritter's discussion of 'reciprocal awareness' as the moral underpinning of social anarchist society, talks of anarchist education as being, at heart, an endeavour to 'awaken the social instinct'. This was to be achieved, as illustrated by the educational projects discussed in Chapter 6, largely through the climate of the school and the moral example of teachers who were expected to exhibit what Kropotkin regarded as the ultimate moral principle of anarchism, namely, 'treating others as one wishes to be treated oneself' (Fidler 1989: 37).

Fidler argues that this anarchist perspective, best reflected in the work of Kropotkin and Reclus, makes a distinctive addition to the world of libertarian education, in that the notion of integral education was regarded, above all, in an essentially moral light, as 'a means of achieving the conscious or ethical form of fraternity' (Fidler 1989: 35). The social anarchists involved in such educational experiments, according to Fidler, 'enunciate a practical utopianism by affirming their commitment to apparently unrealistic moral principles as a vehicle for the realistic purposes of persuasion, education and guidance in present conduct' (ibid.).

The anarchist emphasis on the moral qualities necessary to sustain a society characterized by a breakdown of the manual-intellectual distinctions and their resulting inequalities, then, is part of their radical vision of the possibility of a stateless society. As such, it seems more linked to a specific political vision than the general idea of polytechnic education. However, many theorists within the liberal tradition have also dealt with the conceptual problems involved in the traditional liberal/vocational distinction, and it is important to understand how the anarchist treatment of this distinction differs from the liberal one.

Reconceptualizing the liberal-vocational distinction

In recent years, some philosophers of education have raised philosophical challenges to the apparent dichotomy between liberal and vocational education. Notably, Richard Pring has argued for a broadening and reformulating of the liberal ideal so as to embrace the idea of vocational relevance, along with 'practical intelligence, personal development [and] social and community relevance' (Pring 1995: 195). Similarly, Christopher Winch has developed a detailed and rich conception of vocational education, embracing concerns about 'moral and spiritual well-being' alongside notions of economic and political goods (Winch 2000).[1] Pring's motivation for this reconceptualization seems to be primarily the recent attacks that the traditional liberal view has come under – notably the claim that it excludes many people from the 'liberal conversation' – and the threat to liberal educational values from those who, in response to such attacks, reduce educational goals to the language of 'efficiency' or to narrow economic ends. In contrast, Winch's chief motivation seems to be a sense that the issue of vocational education has not been given the serious philosophical treatment it deserves – presumably partly because of the dominance of the traditional liberal conception.

Richard Pring is rightly critical of the tendency to talk of liberal education as if it were, conceptually, diametrically opposed to vocational education. Yet his chief criticism is the point that this implies that

> the vocational, properly taught, cannot itself be liberating – a way into those forms of knowledge through which a person is freed from ignorance, and opened to new imaginings, new possibilities: the craftsman who finds aesthetic delight in the object of his craft, the technician who sees the science behind the artefact, the reflective teacher making theoretical sense of practice.
>
> (Pring 1995: 189)

Pring's criticism, in other words, is not an external critique from a socio-political perspective (a perspective which, as the foregoing discussion shows, characterizes all anarchist thought on education) but comes from within the educational sphere itself. He argues that vocational education, just like the traditional conception of liberal education, can be intrinsically valuable and connected to a sense of personal well-being and therefore should not be so rigidly conceptually separated.

The conception of freedom which Pring appeals to here is the very conception which lies at the core of the classic liberal account of education from Plato onwards, namely the idea of education as liberating in the sense of freeing the mind. This impression is strengthened by the role Pring assigns to the work of Oakeshott in his discussion of the model of education which forms the background of his analysis. In Oakeshott's idea of education as conversation, freedom is conceived as a freeing of the mind from everyday, concrete concerns; liberal education, on this account, involves an 'invitation to disentangle oneself from the here and now of current happenings and engagements, to detach oneself from the urgencies of the local and the contemporary...' (Oakeshott, quoted in Pring 1995: 186). As Pring notes, this particular conception of liberal education, in focusing upon the world of ideas, 'ignores the world of practice – the world of industry, of commerce, of earning a living...' (ibid.). Yet in arguing that, in our reconceptualizing of the liberal ideal, it is this 'art of reflection' that we must preserve, Pring, it seems, is still subscribing to a basically liberal notion of what it means to be free.

In anarchist thought, in contrast, the concern with the concrete aspects of social justice, distribution of goods, and the material well-being of the community, is always at the forefront of educational thought and practice. Freedom is understood as, first and foremost, effective freedom from all forms of oppression. Thus the emphasis, for the anarchists, in breaking down the liberal-vocational distinction, is not on encouraging critical, detached reflection in the sphere of vocational training in order to create more reflective, more intellectually developed craftsmen, but on paving the way for the concrete freedom of the worker from the restrictions of the capitalist state by, amongst other things, abolishing the division into manual and non-manual labourers.

Of course, at the time at which Kropotkin was writing, the social divisions into 'brain workers' and 'manual workers' of which he speaks were far more apparent and clear-cut than they are today. Early socialist thinkers could not have predicted the socio-economic developments of late capitalism, in which the traditional category of 'workers' is no longer such a clearly demarcated social class. Yet the important point to understand in this context concerns precisely this relationship between educational goals and existing economic and social reality. For Pring, Winch, and many other writers in this field, the structure of the economy, the labour market, and the social and political institutions in which such educational debates take place are obviously acknowledged to be subject to critical appraisal on the part of active citizenship, but it is not the aspiration to radically reform them which forms the basis for educational philosophy and theory. This may appear to be a subtle difference, and, indeed, it is important not to understate the presence, within liberal theory, of a tradition of critical enquiry and reform, and of the idea of citizens as actively shaping society. But, especially within the context of liberal philosophy of education which, over the years, has increasingly become concerned with education in the liberal state, this assumption of the liberal state's inevitability as a basic framework sets thinkers in this tradition apart from the radical social anarchists, in spite of their agreement on certain underlying values. Even theorists like Winch and Pring, whose analyses present a radical challenge to the traditional conceptual parameters of liberal education, still operate within these basic assumptions regarding the inevitability of the liberal state.

As argued earlier, although the aspiration to radically restructure social and political organization lies at the heart of anarchist thought, the chief concern of anarchist educators is not to directly promote a specific model of the good society but to create an environment which will foster and encourage the development of the human propensities and virtues necessary to create and sustain new forms of social organization without the state. Thus the school, for anarchist educators, is seen primarily as a microcosm of one of the many possible forms of anarchist society; an experiment in non-hierarchical, communal forms of human interaction where, crucially, alongside a rigorous critique of existing capitalist society, the interpersonal relationships which constitute educational interaction are based on the normative role assigned to the human qualities of benevolence, mutual aid and social cooperation.

Pring and other writers in the liberal tradition note the importance of fostering critical attitudes in pupils, but because of the liberal state perspective which informs their work, their discussion seems to lack the normative vision which guides anarchist educators. Indeed, whether out of an explicit commitment to autonomy or an endorsement of some version of liberal neutrality, liberal educators are often reluctant to speak in anything other than general terms of providing pupils with the tools needed to make critical judgements and life-choices. In arguing, for example, for a breakdown of the distinction between education and training, Pring makes the point that one and the same activity could be both 'educational' and 'training' (ibid.). But, again, the political, moral aspect is entirely absent from this discussion. One can, as Pring says, change vocational approaches to education so as to aim to educate 'broadly liberal, critical' people through the activity of training them; but this in itself does not challenge the way we conceptualise society; the basic socio-economic distinctions would still hold, even if one aspires to have educated workers.

All this is not to suggest that theorists like Pring and Winch overlook the political and economic context of educational policy. Indeed one important contribution of such critiques of the traditional ideal of liberal education is the claim that it does not fully take into account the importance of addressing, at the level of educational goals, the needs of society and the economy. As Pring puts it, 'there is a political and economic context to education that we need to take seriously' (Pring 1995: 22).

Much of Winch's work has been devoted to developing a detailed account of this point, drawing on the notion of social capital. Starting from the assumption that all education aims at personal development and fulfilment, Winch develops the idea of 'liberal vocationalism', which embraces civic and vocational education, entailing a concept of vocational education which is at once far richer and broader than the instrumentalist conception and also, in drawing on social capital theory, implies a far wider definition of productive labour than the influential one developed by Adam Smith and later by Marx.

In thereby insisting that vocational education should by no means be conceptually confined to 'preparation for producing commodities, or even necessarily for paid employment', but that it involves such aspects as civic responsibility, cognitive skills, social practices and spiritual development, Winch's analysis may, at first glance, seem to be completely in tune with the anarchist aspiration to breakdown the narrow delineation of vocational, as opposed to academic, education.

However, in social anarchist theory, the political and economic context is defined by a normative set of values, the concrete implications of which demand a radical restructuring of our social arrangements and institutions.

Writers within the liberal tradition commonly refer to the 'liberal traditions of education' (Pring 1995: 9) as opposed to the 'utilitarian ones of training' (ibid.). The point of both Winch's and Pring's analyses is to break down these distinctions so as to provide a broader conception of what it means, within a liberal conception of the good society, to be educated. Yet the conflict to be resolved, for the anarchist, is not that between 'Those who see the aim of education to be intellectual excellence (accessible to the few) and those who see its aim to be social utility (and thus accessible to the many)' (Pring 1995: 114) – a conflict which Pring regards as 'the most important and most difficult to resolve' (ibid.) – but that between our vision of what kind of society we want, and what kind of society we have. Education, on this view, is an inherently normative process, and, crucially, a form of human interaction and relationship. Yet as such, it is not merely a means for achieving our political ideals, but part of the process for discovering, articulating and constantly experimenting with these ideals, in the course of which those particular human qualities assigned a normative role in our concept of the good society, need to be continually reinforced, articulated and translated into educational practice.

Thus, while most social anarchists would probably agree with Winch that 'it is important to maintain a very broad vision of "preparation for work" ' (Winch 2000: 163), they would go further than his conceptual point that 'a society that sees the development of individuals, of economic strength and of civil institutions as closely connected, would find it natural to attempt to achieve a balance in combining liberal, vocational and civic education' (ibid.: 191). For social anarchists are not concerned merely with insisting that any discussion of education in society must take these issues into account, but are motivated by the belief that there is something radically wrong with current society, and that reconceptualizing education and engaging in specific, normative educational practices, is one way to go about changing it.

It would be misleading to characterize either the traditional liberal view or the kind of liberal vocationalism promoted by Winch as views lacking in aspirations for improvement or for social reform. It does however seem true to say that both these views – as evident in the work of the authors cited here – assume that the way forward lies in a broadening and deepening of the democratic aspects of our social institutions, out of a belief that this will both contribute to personal well-being and strengthen the moral fabric of society. The unwritten assumption behind much of this work is that the basic structure of the liberal state is not itself subject to debate. Thus Winch, while clearly committed to democracy and to further democratization of social institutions, carefully avoids making any normative pronouncements as to the preferred mode of social organization. Indeed he attests to this position early on in the book, defining the brand of liberalism to which he subscribes as 'the contingent and non-foundational kind described by Gray as "agnostic" or "contested"' (Winch 2000: 2).

Likewise, liberal theorists of vocational education cannot be accused of insensitivity to the moral and political aspects of the kind of educational values being promoted. Pring, for example, mentions the moral aspect of the social utility conception. However he discusses this in the narrow sense of the promotion of virtues (such as enterprise) seen to be essential for helping learners function more positively (i.e. morally) in the world of work and business.

Similarly, in arguing for a broadening and elaboration of the often vague concepts of personal development and flourishing employed in educational policy documents, Pring outlines a philosophical concept of what it means to be a person. In discussing the moral aspects of this concept, he refers to two senses in which it is a moral one: 'It implies the capacity to take responsibility for one's own actions and one's own life. On the other hand, it indicates the desirability of being so treated – of being given the opportunity for taking on that responsibility and of respecting it in others' (Pring 1995: 126–127). This seems, in contrast to the anarchist perspective, to imply a rather passive idea of what being moral is; it leaves out completely the idea of the subject as creator of social reality, or as engaged in the ongoing project of making the world a better place. It is true that Pring, in the course of his discussion, does emphasize the notion of the person as a 'social animal' (ibid.: 132) and refers to the Greek tradition that true human life requires participation in the political life of the state (ibid.: 133). However, one cannot get away from the sense that 'social and political life' in this perspective, is not viewed primarily, as it is for the anarchists, as something essentially malleable and subject to constant, and often radical, experimentation.

Winch, too, notes the importance of moral education. But this, again, is in terms of virtues required by workers as people interacting with others – the workplace, in other words, is seen as

> an essential location for the validation of life-choices, for the acquisition of technical skills in conditions where they are to be applied seriously, in forming young people into the values, disciplines and virtues that are prized in a particular occupational context and in making them aware of the social ramifications of their chosen occupation.
>
> (Winch 2000: 79)

It is in this context that Winch argues for the role of schools in preparing people for such choice-making, and for the continuation of this moral aspect of education in the world of the workplace. Again, this world, it is implied, is simply 'out there'. In other words, it is not at the meta-level that moral and political questions seem to enter such debates on educational aims but at the level of implementation of educational programmes within an already accepted social structure.

So both Winch and Pring, although rejecting the narrow conception of vocational education as 'preparation for the world of work', still seem to remain pretty much within the tradition that regards 'the world' – however richly theorized – as something which is simply out there, to be prepared for and adapted to by the education system and its graduates, rather than to be created or changed.[2]

Education and the socio-economic structure: cause or effect?

In general, although most philosophers in the liberal tradition now acknowledge the relationship between educational ideas and political and economic issues, this relationship is often implied to be one-way: education should fit in with economic and political trends, rather than, as has been traditionally argued by radical dissenters, opposing them and standing for something different.

The danger, for Pring, is that education may, by clinging to the traditional liberal ideals, become 'disconnected from the social and economic world which it should enlighten' (Pring 1995: 123). This is, indeed, a welcome criticism and an important reassessment of the traditional liberal ideal. However, it reveals the central contrast between this and the far more radical anarchist vision which, rather than merely 'enlightening' the social and economic world, seeks to radically change it. So while Winch's general conclusion seems to be in favour of the idea that 'educational, moral and economic ideals are linked, both conceptually and causally' (Winch 2000: 134), the interesting question here is which way the causality goes. For the social anarchists, 'politics, and for that matter economics, is subservient to morality' (Adan 1992: 175). Although one suspects that both Winch and Pring would sympathize with this remark, it is hard to find explicit support for it within their writings on vocational education.

Another interesting illustration of this difference in perspective comes from John White's recent book, *Education and the End of Work* (White 1997). In criticizing dominant theoretical analyses of the role and nature of work in society, White, while questioning Marxist-influenced views on the centrality of labour to human life, nevertheless acknowledges, in a way which may seem in tune with the anarchist account discussed earlier, that 'any reasonable account of education should make work-related aims central' (ibid.: 16). He goes on to address the question of how parents, teachers and policy makers should conceive the relationship between education and work. This question, he says, cannot be answered in the abstract. 'If we could see into the future how things will be in 2050 or 2100, we would be better placed. But the future of work is radically uncertain' (ibid.: 69). White then goes on to discuss two possible scenarios: one involving the 'continuance of the status quo' with regard to the dominance of what he refers to as heteronomous work in societies like Britain; the other involving a 'transformation into a society in which heteronomous work is less dominant'. Interestingly, White himself acknowledges the implications of this approach whereby education may be seen to have a primarily reactive function, and makes the important point – a point in keeping with the anarchist perspective – that 'education can help to create social futures as well as reflect them' (ibid.: 78). However, in spite of these important broad points, the focus of White's analysis is a far narrower one, namely, the role of work in individuals' lives. Thus, to the extent to which social questions such as equality play a part in his work, they do so in the context of notions like 'universal equality of respect', intended to further the aim of helping everyone to attain the means for a life of autonomous well-being. Although White acknowledges that this liberal ideal will in all likelihood entail a policy of educational investment in the less well-off, any social restructuring involved is secondary to the educational goal of fostering children's ability to become autonomous adults. White's preference for a society in which industriousness is no longer regarded as a central moral value, and in which there is a reduction in heteronomous work and a more pluralistic social and cultural perception of work, is ultimately a result of this ideal rather than, as in the anarchist case, the reflection of a vision of a particular kind of society.

The social-anarchist revolution: within the state and beyond the state

These issues may be further clarified with reference to the distinction (a distinction that, as mentioned, anarchist theorists commonly fail to make) between the pre-revolutionary and the post-revolutionary stage, or, more accurately, between life within the state and life beyond the state. This is not a purely temporal distinction for, in the anarchist view, the social revolution is an ongoing endeavour. Therefore one cannot talk of a clear distinction between pre-revolutionary and post-revolutionary reality. I suggest, however, that it is helpful to distinguish between life in a stateless, social-anarchist society and life within the state.

Thus for example it is, of course, quite possible that once the social-anarchist revolution is successful and society is organized in such a way that basic needs are met and communal arrangements, ideally, have secured relatively stable economic relations, it may make sense to talk of the kind of 'liberal-vocationalism' that Winch is sympathetic to – in other words, an education which, in addition to providing a sound intellectual and moral basis, 'encourage[s] young people to make occupational choices from amongst those that society considers worthwhile' (Winch 2000: 31). However, within the nation state, where, according to the anarchist critique, inequalities are entrenched and reflected in, amongst other things, the division of labour and the market economy, such 'choices' cannot be made freely for they are dictated by the economic needs of the state which, by definition, is inimical to human freedom and flourishing.

Furthermore, even if the state is successfully dismantled, given the anarchist commitment to perfectibility and to constant experimentation, and bearing in mind the contextualist conception of human nature, it is important for the community to continue to provide an education which maintains a critical attitude towards existing practices and institutions and fosters attitudes of fraternity and mutual aid.

The aforementioned points about the anarchist perspective on education may suggest that the anarchists were unduly concerned with questions about the social good, overlooking the question of personal fulfilment and well-being. Indeed, Richard Pring makes the point that the apparent conflict between liberal education and social utility 'reflects a deeper divide between the pursuit of individual good and the pursuit of social welfare' (Pring 1995: 121). But this again presupposes a particular way of looking at the individual. In anarchist ethics, as discussed earlier, individual freedom and well-being are created and sustained in the context of social interaction; one cannot consistently talk of the individual good without taking the social context into account. In the anarchist view of morality, indeed, the individual and the moral good are conceptually and logically bound (see Adan 1992: 49–60). Many anarchist theorists, most notably Bakunin, were concerned to develop a conceptual defence of 'the intrinsic identity between the individual and the common good' (Adan 1992: 56). Their conception of the community as the basic social unit was of

> a whole of wholes, whose function is making possible the fullest realization of common good; i.e. the creation of conditions for personal actualization to an unlimited degree [...]. The individual is a whole in itself and the good it attains is also an objective good, not merely subjective and thus, in a way, the actualization of society at large.
>
> (Ibid.)

On the policy level of devising specific educational programmes which would help children enter the world of work, Winch's analysis makes several important points, some of which have interesting connections to the anarchist view. But again, from an anarchist point of view, these points are mostly relevant to education beyond the state. For example, in his discussion of the issue of transparency of markets, Winch points out that all vocational education depends to some extent, for it to have been considered a success, on speculation as to the availability of certain jobs in the labour market. But, as he explains,

> at the level of skills acquisition, the labour market is often a futures market, trading in commodities whose value will only become clear at some point in the future [...] One is, in effect, betting that a current investment will be worthwhile in two or three years' time.
>
> (Winch 2000: 128)

The implicit picture of economic life behind these remarks is of the economic sphere as something which is, as John White puts it (White 1997: 78), 'reflected by' rather than 'created by' education. Anarchist educators like those discussed in Chapter 6, fuelled by the desire to replace the capitalist state system with what they regarded as a morally superior social model, assume a very different picture. An outspoken and, perhaps, rather extreme expression of this view comes from Harry Kelly, in his outline of the purpose of the Modern School in New York at the beginning of the twentieth century (see Chapter 6). The anarchist educational movement involves, Kelly argues, 'the idea of making all industry cooperative,' from which it follows that 'it is inconceivable that education in its future evolution will not sometime take complete control and possession of the world's industry' (Kelly 1916: 53). Sinister as this may sound, I believe the main point of Kelly's remarks is not the proposal of any revolutionary tactics for seizing control of the capitalist state infrastructure, but rather the insight that socio-economic structures, moral values and educational ideals are all bound up in the normative project of constructing educational policy and processes. In this, Kelly was echoing Kropotkin's belief that the social anarchist socio-economic model is

> of absolute necessity for society, not only to solve economic difficulties, but also to maintain and develop social customs that bring men in contact with one another; [it] must be looked to for establishing such relations between men that the interest of each should be the interest of all; and this alone can unite men instead of dividing them.
>
> (Kropotkin 1897: 16)

Accordingly, while anarchist educational projects run within the reality of the (capitalist) state sought to embody, in their structure and day-to-day management, the principles and practice of communal living, their long-term programmes for vocational education also embodied the hope that the 'outside world' for which they were preparing their children would be – largely as a result of this moral groundwork – a very different one from that of the present.

Education and the market

Winch notes that in neo-classical economic theory, the assumption is that markets are 'transparent', in the sense that all participants in the market place have access to information about price, quality, supply and demand. But, as he remarks (Winch 2000: 128), 'this is patently false', and

> it is now much more widely admitted, particularly through the influence of the 'Austrian' school of economics, that markets are not completely transparent, that they filter information and depend on local and tacit knowledge of buyers and sellers for their successful operation.

In the case of labour markets, even though professionals may be available to advise novices – for example, pupils undergoing vocational education programmes – 'it is still highly likely that there will be insufficient information to make an informed decision when the availability of jobs depends on larger macro-economic factors that most people will not be in a good position to understand' (ibid.: 129).

In an anarchist society, the market would be run along cooperative lines – a point which, anarchist theorists were keen to stress, was not hostile to competition. Indeed, as the anarchist economist Stephen P. Andrews has argued, 'competition itself is not socially negative. [...] Correctly employed, economical competition leads to the growth of a perfectly balanced system of social cooperation' (in Adan 1992: 190). The term 'correctly employed' here presumably refers to a climate of individuals cooperating in freedom on the basis of a sound moral education. But aside from this point, Winch's point about market transparency may be relevant in the reality of anarchist society beyond the state, and in fact suggests that small-scale economies, such as that of the anarchist commune, would be more conducive to such transparency than the markets of the capitalist state, due not only to the simple question of size but also to the anarchist commitment to participatory self-government and bottom-up forms of social organization.

So although Winch is in agreement with elements of the anarchist critique in stating that young people are

> potentially at the mercy of a market which may not have a particular call for their skills and knowledge at a stage in life when, by definition, and according to a well-established account of how markets work, they are in a poor position to make rational decisions on the labour and training market.
>
> (Winch 2000: 130)

His solution to this problem is to find ways of linking demand and supply of labour so that vocational education can successfully provide students with jobs in the market. He does not see these problems as inherent features of market capitalism which can only be remedied by radical political and social change.

Similarly, Winch argues convincingly that

> for vocational education, it is important to maintain a very broad vision of 'preparation for work' which not only encompasses the different forms of paid employment, but also domestic and voluntary labour. It also

follows, from the reluctance that I have argued one should have towards unduly elevating the value of some occupations and denigrating others according to personal taste and preference, that a society that wishes to continue to develop various currents not just of skill, but of value and outlook on life, needs to take a generous attitude to the provision of vocational education, so as to allow for the proper development of a wide variety of occupations.

(Ibid.: 163)

But the denigration and preferences which Winch refers to may in fact be, as the anarchists would argue, largely a result of the inherent structural features of our society. If this is the case then, again, only a radical reconceptualization of our social institutions could adequately address these issues.

We have seen, then, how the anarchist conception of integral education breaks down the traditional distinctions between the liberal and the vocational ideal not just from a conceptual point of view, nor from the point of view of creating a broader educational goal for modern liberal states, but as part of the radical challenge to the existing political order.

When working within the constraints of life within the state, the task for the anarchist educator is to lay the grounds for the transition to an anarchist, self-governing, equitable community. One can begin this process, as argued by Kropotkin, Ward and others, on the smallest possible scale, by challenging dominant values and encouraging the human propensity for mutual aid, cooperation and self-governance. Indeed, as discussed in previous chapters, the anarchist revolution is conceptualized by most of the social anarchists not as a violent dismantling of the present system in order to replace it with a radically new one, nor, as in the case of Marxism, as a remoulding of human tendencies and attitudes, but as a process of creating a new society from the seeds of aspirations, tendencies and trends already present in human action. As Kropotkin emphasizes, the foundations of anarchist society are, above all, moral, and thus one cannot escape the conclusion that the emphasis of the educational process must be on fostering those moral attitudes which can further and sustain a viable anarchist society. Of course, part of this process involves adopting a critical attitude towards current institutional and political practices and arrangements, with an emphasis on the manifestations of oppression and social injustice. But this critical stance has to be encouraged in a climate which itself reflects the values of solidarity and equality.

Another essential ingredient in this educational process is the absence of fixed blueprints for future organization; in other words, although pupils should be encouraged to reflect on broad social and political issues, and to question current institutional arrangements, they must not, in the anarchist view, be manipulated into advocating a specific form of social organization, but should be encouraged to see themselves, first and foremost, as potential social innovators and creators. Of course, the question of whether the anarchist educational projects discussed here in fact succeeded in avoiding such manipulation is open to debate. The crucial point of such educational endeavours, nevertheless, is to encourage pupils to grasp the central anarchist idea that society and political life are malleable and potentially subject to constant improvement, rather than a fixed backdrop to passive consumers or bystanders. It is in this context that the idea of integral education plays such an important role. Thus, although for the social anarchists, the aim of creating a different form of social organization remains at the level of an aspiration, with no fixed delineations, the moral qualities necessary to sustain such a society are clearly determinate – based on solidarity and mutual aid.

Scarcity and the circumstances of justice

The aforementioned discussion has interesting conceptual connections with the discussion of the Rawlsian notion of the circumstances of justice. For the circumstances of justice which form the starting point for Rawlsian liberalism not only assume the absence of fraternal interpersonal ties as a basis for human action (see Chapter 5) and thus for decisions taken under the veil of ignorance but also make assumptions regarding the level of scarcity of resources. Kropotkin, in contrast – the principle theorist of anarchist economics – developed a notion of a global economy based on the assumption that sufficient resources are available, on a global scale, to satisfy all basic needs, thus rejecting the basic assumption of fundamental scarcity that underpins both classical political economy and the type of neoclassical economic theories which Winch cites. Kropotkin, as Knowles (2000) discusses, was scathing in his criticism of the way in which Malthusian ideas had permeated economic theory. 'Few books', he remarked, 'have exercised so pernicious an influence upon the general development of economic thought' (ibid.: 30), describing this influence as follows:

> This postulate stands, undiscussed, in the background of whatever political economy, classical or socialist, has to say about exchange-value, wages, sale of labour force, rent, exchange, and consumption. Political economy never rises above the hypothesis of a limited and insufficient supply of the necessaries of life; it takes it for granted. And all theories connected with political economy retain the same erroneous principle. Nearly all socialists, too, admit the postulate.
>
> (Ibid.: 30)

In contrast, Knowles argues, 'The driving force of Kropotkin's political economy arose from his perceived need to satisfy the needs of all; to achieve the "greatest good for all," to provide a measure of "wealth and ease" for all' (ibid.).

Similarly, in arguing that well-being could be guaranteed partly by ensuring that all members of society worked no more than 5 hours a day, Kropotkin claimed to be presenting an important challenge to mainstream economic thought (which he referred to as 'the metaphysics called political economy'), and which had ignored such aspects of economy in the life of the worker: 'few economists, as yet, have recognized that this is the proper domain of economics' (ibid.).

In short, the earlier discussion supports the insight that, for the social anarchists, economic principles and the world of labour were, in an important sense, subservient to moral principles, and that it is the moral picture of an ideal social structure which underlies the anarchist view of education as crucially intertwined with socio-economic reality.

The moral and political content of education

Removing state control of schools

The actual policy steps required to translate this radical political reconceptualization into educational practice bring us back, naturally, to the central anarchist objection to the state. Part of the necessary process of emancipating the workers, for the social anarchists, involved removing education from the control of the state. Proudhon, Godwin and other early anarchist theorists regarded education as a key factor in creating intellectual and moral emancipation, much along the lines of the traditional liberal ideal. Yet in schools controlled by the state, this was virtually impossible, in their view. The first step, then, had to be to remove state control from education. This move, in and of itself, of course would not be enough unless the education offered was substantively different, in moral terms, from the traditional one; that is, unless, as discussed earlier, it challenged competitive, authoritarian instincts and encouraged instead values of mutual aid, cooperativeness and self-management.

Proudhon, one of the first anarchist theorists to develop the concept of integral education, envisaged the school becoming something like a workshop. Crucially, he insisted that the education system must, like other aspects of society, become decentralized, so that the responsibility for the setting up and managing of schools would rest with parents and communities and would be closely tied to local workers' associations (see Smith 1983: 26). In this, Proudhon articulated, perhaps more than any other anarchist theorist, the idea of the necessary intimacy between school and work. He held something similar to the Marxist conception of labour as central to human well-being, and insisted that education should be polytechnical – enabling the students to master a range of skills, including the theoretical knowledge they involved, and only later to specialize. But Proudhon's ideal seems to stem largely from a romantic picture of pre-industrial society. To translate this conception of the school as workshop into our own society would be highly problematic. The 'ties with the world of work' which Proudhon envisaged would be more likely to be ties with huge corporations and financial companies, involving market-capitalist values, than the associations with small artisans' and workers' guilds which formed part of Proudhon's rather naïve romantic vision.

This problem simply illustrates, once again, the point that although decentralization and the consequent undermining of state power are key goals of anarchist programmes, they cannot be achieved without laying the moral and political groundwork – without, that is, fostering values capable of sustaining a truly stateless, decentralized society. For a more detailed discussion of this point, with reference to current proposals for removing education from state control, see Chapter 8.

To sum up the argument so far, and to connect these points back to the discussion of perspective with which I began this chapter; approaching educational (as well as economic) thought from a vision of what the ideal society would look like, and making questions about how feasible this vision is, why it is desirable, how different it is from our present one, and what the transition would involve part of the educational-philosophical debate itself, puts this debate in a very different light. From the point of view of a commitment to anarchist principles, it may well be that the main conclusions of this discussion are that far more emphasis needs to be placed on fostering particular values, aiming to create an educational environment which reflects these values – solidarity, mutual aid, sensitivity to injustice and so on. But even if one disagrees with these specific normative conclusions, one can still appreciate the general point that reconceptualizing the relationship between philosophy of education and political thought so that the two interact in a way which assumes questions about the future form of society to be very much still open to debate, and which approaches children, teachers and parents as people engaged in its creation, can add a valuable perspective to such debates. At the very least, they may help us to rearticulate, re-examine and imbue with greater relevance, some of the very values – such as freedom, critical thinking and justice – which we so often assume lie at the core of liberal thought.

Education for social change

The aforementioned discussion of vocational education has, I hope, helped to draw out the way in which anarchist educational programmes and policy reflect the conviction that there is a substantive, positive core of moral values which is the crucial ingredient in any educational process aimed at transforming society in keeping with the vision of a stateless society. Particularly, anarchist educators were concerned in identifying and nurturing the social virtues which, so they believed, reinforced both the feasibility and the desirability of their ideal.

This analysis illustrates how the political dimension of anarchist thought is reflected at all levels of the educational process – not in terms of imposing a blueprint or training a revolutionary vanguard, but in terms of raising awareness of the radical possibilities for political change and the vision of a society radically different from our own – in which we are concerned not merely to educate workers, but to believe that the distinctions between workers and non-workers will disappear.

The utopian aspect of anarchism is already implied by these comments, and I wish to elaborate on how it is reflected in the curriculum by means of a discussion of political education. This discussion is connected to the idea of vocational education in several important respects.

Roy Edgley (1980) presents the tension between liberal aspirations to break down class-based social inequalities and social-political reality rather depressingly, suggesting that students are 'prepared for manual work, at least in part, by being failed in the predominantly mentalistic process of the schools' (ibid.: 9). Edgley draws on D.H. Lawrence's description of the 'malcontent collier' who, due to the 'myth of equal opportunity' which permeates the liberal education system, cannot be but a failure in his own eyes. If, Edgley argues, education is to take seriously the goal of preparing students for the world of work,

> it must ensure that there is at least a rough and at least a relative match in skills between its student output and the skill levels of the job positions of the occupational structure. That means that education must reproduce, at the skill levels of its students, the gross inequalities, in particular the class inequalities, of that occupational structure. Given such a task, education's commitment to social justice and equality, an essential part of its liberal idealism, is then understood in terms of equality of opportunity. Higher and middle-class job positions and their associated educational qualifications are seen as scarce goods to be distributed as prizes in the time-honoured bourgeois way, by competition, and although the competitors must finish unequal, education meets its moral ideal by ensuring that they start equal and compete fairly.
>
> (Ibid.: 8)

It is, Edgley argues, extremely unlikely that education can eliminate inequalities to such a degree, and thus equality of opportunity represents, in the liberal educational tradition, 'an unhappy compromise between education's liberal ideals and the reality of a class-structured division of labour' (ibid.: 9).

The anarchist response to this depressing scenario is to postulate an ideal reality in which the class-structured division of labour – which, anarchists argue, is a result of the modern capitalist state – simply does not exist, to argue that such an alternative social reality *could* exist and to construct an account of the types of human propensities needed to support such a reality. Education then needs to focus on fostering such propensities and on providing both liberal and vocational training so as to prepare children to be the creators of such a social reality. Yet this approach on its own may seem naïve and, clearly, has to be supplemented by some form of political education, so that students understand the critique of existing society, and have the analytic tools necessary to forge new forms of social organization. A similar realization characterizes some more critical liberal positions and, indeed, one possible way out of Edgley's depressing conclusion is the type of radical political education formulated by Patricia White.

Edgley argues, drawing largely on Patricia White's work, for a radical role for political education. As White theorizes this idea, political education should have as its goal education for action and not 'simply the production of spectatorial armchair politicians' (quoted in Edgley 1980: 13). Specifically, political education should emphasize democractic processes, whereby through experience pupils would be encouraged to democratically transform social institutions into less authoritarian and more democratic structures.

Although Edgley, largely due to his acceptance of some version of Marxist reproduction theory, believes White is overly optimistic with regard to the power of political education to democratize social institutions and practices, he acknowledges the potential of this type of educational approach. And while White's analysis is focused on the democratization of society, the anarchist conception goes further in arguing for a complete transformation of social organization, in which, alongside the role played by school climate, school structure and other informal ways in which social-anarchist values are reflected in educational practice, there is clearly an important role to be played by systematic political education. Such an education, in addition to fostering a critical attitude and an appreciation of democratic principles (both aspects which White would endorse), would take the further step of encouraging students to reflect on the possible construction of radically different social futures.

The descriptions of anarchist schools in Chapter 6 suggest that anarchist educators often indeed assigned something like political education a key role in their curricula. For example, in Ferrer's school, the vocational training which students underwent was accompanied by analyses of the class system and an attempt to critically understand the workings of the capitalist market place. But if political education as a distinct curricular subject is to have any uniquely anarchist significance, it must reflect the utopian element of anarchist thought. The liberal perspective focuses on the notion of autonomy, and from here in calling for greater democratization of the workplace, the school and other social institutions. The anarchist perspective, in contrast, involves not only the 'leap of faith' that a stateless society is possible, and can be sustained along communal, non-hierarchical principles, on the basis of already present human capabilities and propensities but also, crucially for education, the utopian hope that the very imaginative exercise of encouraging people to conceptualize the exact form of this society, and to constantly engage with and experiment with its principles and manifestations, is itself a central part of the revolutionary process. It is here – in this practice of imagining a world radically different from our own, and in daring to believe in its possibility – that the role of political education takes a central place.

Although there is no systematic treatment of such a programme for political education in the historical accounts of anarchist educational projects discussed here, nor in the theoretical works on education by leading anarchist theorists, political education, in some form or another, clearly permeates all aspects of anarchist educational endeavour. Whether in the course of visiting factories at Ferrer's school, or of planting their own vegetable garden and managing the produce at the Stelton school, pupils were encouraged to develop a critical awareness of the problems and complexities of the existing state system and to speculate on alternative modes of socio-economic organization. It is interesting, though, to consider a more specific attempt to translate the utopian, imaginative element of anarchist thought into concrete pedagogical practice. An example of such an attempt is offered by a small pamphlet published by an independent anarchist publishing house, entitled *Design Your Own Utopia* (Bufe and Neotopia 2002). Although there is little if any reference in the writings of anarchist theorists as to how specific educational methods and programmes could be employed to implement anarchist ideas in an educational context, I believe this proposal could serve as a model for political education both within and beyond the nation state.

The programme suggested in this pamphlet offers a model for a classroom discussion in the context of political education, based around a question-posing pattern, whereby each question answered (by the group, or individually) leads, by way of a consideration of various options and implications, to further questions. Posing and answering the questions along the way demands a rigorous and honest treatment of normative commitments and values and a thought experiment whereby one is forced to confront the possible practical implications of one's values.

The pattern is to start not from the current institutions of the liberal state, but from an open-ended discussion, in the course of which values are articulated and principles considered, along with a critical examination of the implications of and justification for the principles under discussion. Of course, such an educational approach requires a certain degree of sophistication and would probably be more suited to older children who have already got some grasp of basic social and political concepts. It could, however, be creatively incorporated into a political education programme involving familiarization with political concepts alongside imaginative utopian thought.

The programme starts with the question of scope: students are asked, as a first step, to consider whether their utopia would be a global utopia, a nation state, a village, a city, a bio-region or some other type of international community (ibid.: 3) before going on to ask questions about the goals of their utopia. This question in itself already opens up the discussion to accommodate theoretical ideas far broader than those usually covered in political education or citizenship courses. The recent QCA recommendations on teaching citizenship in schools, for example, the nearest thing in the British curriculum to political education, centre around the idea of fostering the knowledge, understanding and skills needed for 'the development of pupils into active citizens' (QCA 1998: 2). Although it is hard to find fault with this idea as a general educational aim, the perspective from which it is formulated is clearly one of understanding and reinforcing the current political system rather than radically questioning it. This is not to suggest that the programme is narrowly focused on the state – for it specifically recommends 'an awareness of world affairs and global issues' (ibid.: 22) alongside an 'understanding of democratic practices and institutions' (ibid.). However, the playful element of utopian thought experiments suggested by the anarchist perspective could, I believe, enrich this process of 'understanding' and 'developing skills and knowledge'.

In the anarchist utopian experiment, students are asked to speculate on the feasibility of political structures other than the state and their relationship to each other, not as an informative exercise but as an imaginative one. Of course, the QCA document, as well as several writers on citizenship education (see, e.g. Fogelman 1991) emphasize the need for an active, participatory role on the part of future citizens and attach considerable importance to 'student empowerment' (Lynch and Smalley 1991: 171). However, utopian thought experiments add a valuable dimension to the idea of empowering students through 'experiments in active democracy' (ibid.), in that simply considering the types of questions proposed here can 'help us to understand that the present social, political and economic systems are human inventions, and that we, collectively, have the power to change them' (Bufe and Neotopia 2002: 1).

The anarchist programme outlined in the pamphlet goes on to ask 'What would be the fundamental values of your utopia?' and, interestingly, 'Would individuals choose their own goals and values or would their goals and values be those of your utopian ideology?' – a question which paves the way for a discussion of the liberal ideal, the ideas of community and individual freedom, and other connected issues.

Further on in the course of the exercise, students are presented with questions about the specific content of their utopia, and encouraged to think through their implications. For example, 'What would the rights and duties of members of the utopia be?'; 'Would the number of children per parent be limited?', 'What would your decision-making process be?', 'How would production and distribution be organized?' and ' Would the roles of men and women vary?'

I believe that such an educational approach could constitute an attractive, stimulating alternative – or at least a supplement – to conventional teaching of political and moral issues that, as many writers on utopia have noted (see Chapter 8), encourages creative and critical thinking about our social and political reality. A political education programme along these lines would clearly have to be thought out in further detail and with a great deal of caution. As mentioned, social anarchist theorists themselves failed to provide any such systematic account. However, I believe this kind of approach encapsulates an important aspect of the anarchist educational stance and is valuable in its own right even within a state education system.

Moral education – the missing link

In conclusion, the anarchist idea of integral education may, on the surface, seem very much like notions such as Winch's 'liberal vocationalism', which both challenges the common liberal/vocational distinction and broadens our understanding of productive work and its connection to individual well-being. However, I have argued that what makes the anarchist perspective distinct from the liberal one is first its radical political vision – a vision which hinges on a faith in the possibility of a society organized in stateless, self-governing, equitable communities – and, connectedly, the understanding that while the precise form of such communities is indeterminate, the moral values which underpin them have both descriptive and normative validity and need to be reinforced by the educational process.

It has to be said, at this stage, that this argument for the centrality of some kind of moral education is largely a reconstruction of often indirect and unsystematic writings from a variety of anarchist sources. Although the salience of notions like solidarity, fraternity and mutual aid pervades all social-anarchist work on education, it is hard to find any systematic account of how these notions are to be built into a coherent programme for moral education. Indeed, references to pedagogy and to concrete educational programmes are few and far between in anarchist literature, largely due to the belief that such programmes would and should be determined by individual teachers and students according to the specific needs of the community. The following account by Bakunin (in Dolgoff 1973: 373–375) is one of the few attempts to lay down such a programme, based on what Bakunin regarded as three essential stages in education:[3]

Stage 1   (5–12 years): At this stage, the emphasis should be on the development of the physical faculties, in the course of which 'the culture of the mind' will be developed 'spontaneously'. There will be no formal instruction as such, only 'personal observation, practical experience, conversations between children, or with persons charged with teaching'.

Stage 2   (age 12–16): Here the child will be introduced to 'the various divisions of human knowledge', and will also undergo practical training in a craft or trade. This stage involves more methodological and systematic teaching, along with communal reading and discussion, one effect of which would be to reduce the weight attached to the individual teacher. This stage in essence is the beginning of the child's apprenticeship in a profession, and Bakunin specifies that, from the early stages, visits to factories and so on must form a part of the curriculum, leading to the child's eventual choice of a trade for specialization, alongside theoretical studies.

Bakunin's second stage is remarkably similar to Winch's idea of liberal vocationalism, with his talk of the 'branches of knowledge' clearly referring to something very like the liberal idea of initiation into the disciplines.

However, as stated, this educational programme has to be understood in the context of a political vision far more radical in its scope than the liberal one, and a faith – perhaps, as Ritter suggests, a 'leap of faith' – that this vision can be brought a little closer by the very organization and day-to-day running of the educational process in such a manner as to embody the moral values underpinning this vision. Precisely how these values are to be built into the educational process, beyond the informal means of pupil–teacher relationships, decentralized school management, non-coercive classroom practices and constant experimentation (all of which are evident in the anarchist schools discussed in Chapter 6) is, as mentioned, unclear from the literature. Given the anarchist understanding of human nature and the consequent acknowledgement that some form of moral education will be necessary, even in the post-revolutionary society, to ensure the flourishing of the social virtues, I believe that the lack of clarity on this subject is, perhaps, the central weakness of the anarchist position on education. Constructing a systematic account of moral education is, thus, a key task for the anarchist educator. The anarchist idea of the school as a microcosm of the ideal society, and the emphasis on direct encounters and on 'learning by doing', alongside the clear acknowledgement of the educational role of social institutions and practices, suggest that such an account could be broadly Aristotelian in its conception. Unfortunately, however, the task of constructing such an account is beyond the scope of this book.

8   What's so funny about anarchism?

The task of the anarchist philosopher is not to prove the imminence of a Golden Age,
but to justify the value of believing in its possibility.

(Read 1974: 14)

The social-anarchist perspective on education, as I have argued, is underpinned by a specific, substantive vision of the good. While the anarchist belief in the possibility of society without the state implies a radical challenge to the dominant liberal view, the vision of what this society may look like is based on values that, as discussed in the earlier chapters, are not at odds with liberal values. In fact, one could argue, as Noam Chomsky has done, that the social-anarchist tradition is the 'true inheritor of the classic liberal tradition of the Enlightenment' (in Guerin 1970: xii). Furthermore, this tradition perhaps rearticulates the utopian element of classical liberal thought.

Zygmunt Bauman, for example, describes the liberal project as 'one of the most potent modern utopias' in its promotion of a model of the good society, and argues that, at the time of its inception, it may have signified a 'great leap forward' (Bauman 1999: 4).

The aforementioned remarks notwithstanding, there does nevertheless seem to be a tension between the agenda of anarchist education, as reflected in the programmes and curricula developed by educators working within the anarchist tradition (see Chapter 6) and that of what is generally referred to as liberal education. Specifically, and peculiarly, anarchism as an educational stance seems almost both too normative and too open-ended to be palatable to the liberal educator. The explicitly anti-statist, anti-capitalist and egalitarian views espoused by anarchist educators, and built into their curricula (see Chapter 6), smack too much of dogma, perhaps, to those with liberal sensibilities. Yet at the same time, the insistence on the indeterminacy of the future society, the demand for constant, free experimentation and the faith in the power of communities to establish their own educational practices are risky ideas to many liberals who, like Eamonn Callan (1997) and Meira Levinson (1999), see a formal state education system not just as an important social good but also as an essential guarantor of liberal freedoms, social justice and political stability.

Yet, as the preceding discussion shows, the underlying values of the anarchist position are not at odds with those of the liberal one. Although they may assign them different normative and methodological status, few liberals would be inclined to reject such values as freedom, equality, fraternity or solidarity.

Liberal neutrality, education and the liberal state

Why, then, does the notion of 'anarchist education' seem, at best, laughable and, at worst, threatening, from a liberal point of view? I would argue that the reason this is so is because 'liberal education' has, in recent years, become synonymous with education in a liberal state. Many writers conflate the two unthinkingly, and the question of the relationship between them is rarely itself the focus of debate. Thus, for example, Eamonn Callan, Meira Levinson and Alan Ryan have recently written important works on education and liberalism in which, while ostensibly discussing the implications of liberal theory for educational ideas, they are actually concerned to outline the role of education in the liberal state. Alan Ryan, for example, in *Liberal Anxieties and Liberal Education* refers, at the beginning of his discussion, to liberal education as 'the kind of education that sustains a liberal society' (Ryan 1998: 27). However, in the course of the book, he slips into a discussion of 'educating citizens' (ibid.: 123), clearly assuming the framework of the liberal state. A similar process occurs in the writings of several other theorists.

The relationship between liberalism as a system of values and the liberal state as a system of political organization is one which is rarely, if ever, scrutinized, whether by philosophers of education or by liberal theorists in general.

Most theorists, indeed, seem to assume, along with Patricia White, not only that the liberal state is, to all intents and purposes, the only practical framework available, but that theoretically, it has been pretty much established, primarily by Nozick's influential argument (see Nozick 1974) that the state is a necessary evil, and that if it didn't exist, 'we would have to invent [it] – or back into [it] by degrees at least' (White 1983: 8).

'Most political philosophers in the past few generations', Miltrany comments (in Sylvan 1993: 215) 'have what the psychoanalysts might call a "state fixation"'. This is no less true of philosophers of education. But the theoretical implications of conflating 'liberalism' with 'the liberal state' are particularly far-reaching in the case of education, and they hinge above all on the notion of neutrality.

As developed most famously and influentially by Rawls, the liberal notion of neutrality dictates that the state must be neutral regarding conceptions of the good. However, it is important to understand that liberalism, as an ideological position, is not in itself 'neutral' – as indeed it would be logically impossible for any such position to be neutral. So there is nothing neutral about the liberal stance itself. But once 'liberalism' is taken to mean 'the liberal state', the demand for neutrality is logically translated into a demand that individuals and communities be free to pursue their own conceptions of the good within a political framework and institutions which allow them to flourish and interact as fairly and equitably as possible, refraining from any discrimination on the basis of possibly competing conceptions of the good. This, in essence, is the basis of Rawls' defence of 'political liberalism' (see Rawls 1996). If education is then assumed to be one of the central institutions of the liberal state, this position is translated into the demand that education in the liberal state should be, at most, a facilitator for the pursuit of individual autonomy and the development of civic virtues; these are regarded as, ideally, happily coexisting with various different – even conflicting – comprehensive visions of the good.

Of course, the neutrality thesis has been importantly criticized by liberal theorists, and notably by educational philosophers, in recent years. Thus both Eamonn Callan and Meira Levinson argue for a far more substantive vision of the role of education in the liberal state than that traditionally derived from Rawls' political liberalism. Similarly, Robert Reich points out, in his critique of the idea of liberal neutrality, that the very establishment of a state-funded school system is not neutral:

> In the modern age, there exists no social institution, save perhaps taxation, that intervenes more directly and deeply into the lives of citizens than schools ... it is a fantasy that twelve years of education of any sort could possibly leave, as Rawls suggests, all reasonable comprehensive doctrines 'untouched'.
>
> (Reich 2002: 40)

Reich in fact argues that neutrality is theoretically and practically impossible, and that the demands of liberal theory for civic education – primarily as regards fostering autonomy – lead inevitably to the demand for a non-neutral process of education, which in turn has effects on diversity and other aspects of society. Reich makes the point that 'these effects are not unfortunate consequences but the purposeful aim of the liberal state' (ibid.: 42). Yet this argument merely reinforces my earlier claim about the conflation between liberalism and the state: in Reich's analysis, similar to those of Callan and others, it is the state as such that has 'aims' – not liberalism, or even 'liberals' – a point which seems to support the anarchist argument that once a state is established it takes on a life – and aims – of its own, which may, so the argument goes, have little to do with the true needs and aspirations of people and communities.

Reich and other theorists in the liberal tradition seem little aware of the conflation they make between liberalism and the liberal state; one minute they are talking of the demands of liberal theory, and in the next they slip into a discussion of the demands of the state – which, when one pauses to think about it is quite a different thing. There is, as stated, nothing inherently neutral about liberalism; but this issue is often glossed over. Perhaps inevitably, having become the dominant political doctrine in the modern industrialized world, and one which in fact reflects actual social and political organization in much of this world, liberalism seems to have lost its motivating force. Its normative elements more often than not take the form of guidelines for improving or restricting current regulations or practices, or for making choices within the existing framework, not for building radically new practices. Given this dominance of liberalism as a theory and a system, the main narrative associated with this tradition has, as Bauman (1999) notes, become one of 'no alternative'. The idea that the liberal state is, if not the best of all imaginary worlds, at least in effect the best one realistically available, and one which is here to stay, encourages, as Bauman points out, a degree of political apathy.

Richard Flathman has suggested a further reason for the conflation of liberal education with education in the (neutral) liberal state, arguing that the conception of liberal education as non-specific in the sense of being not vocational, not professional or pre-professional – is 'reminiscent of those versions of political and moral liberalism that promote its neutrality toward or among alternative conceptions of the good' (Flathman 1998: 139). Thus, analogously to the liberal state which is agnostic regarding particular conceptions of the good life, the liberal educational curriculum 'seeks to nurture abilities and understandings regarded as valuable to a generous – albeit, again not limitless – array of careers or callings' (ibid.).

But what happens if one pulls apart this conflation? What happens, that is, if, while holding on to what can be broadly described as liberal values, one removes the state from the equation altogether?

Several writers in recent years have theoretically experimented with the idea of removing education from state control. Indeed, we do not need anarchism to prod us into pondering what education would look like without the state. Theorists working broadly within the liberal tradition have questioned the role of the state in controlling and determining educational ends, policies and processes. And, characteristically, those people who, in such debates, come down squarely on the side of state control of schooling, do so out of a carefully argued conviction that social ills such as socio-economic inequality and deprivation can better be minimized by a centrally controlled system than by leaving things to chance or to local initiative, and not out of any political enthusiasm for powerful central government. Thus Patricia White, for example, in *Beyond Domination* (White 1983: 82), claims, on the basis of such convictions, that against the arguments for total devolution of educational control 'there are no moral arguments, but there are practical and political ones'.

The minimal state and social values

Conversely, but starting from the same questioning attitude, James Tooley, in *Reclaiming Education* (Tooley 2000), presents a thought experiment which supposedly leads to the conclusion that educational objectives could be better achieved by private enterprise without the control of the state. The point here is that resolving the question of whether or not state controlled education systems can best achieve what could be construed as liberal goals, including the goal of social equality, is largely an empirical question. Although Tooley argues, rather convincingly, that the state has not so far done a great job in eliminating socio-economic inequalities by means of the education system, it remains to be established (and on the face of it seems quite doubtful) whether a free-market system of education such as that which he advocates could do the job any better. Although Tooley does document evidence suggesting that in areas where private corporations have taken over educational functions, such corporations '*can* deliver equity or equality of opportunity' (ibid.: 64, my emphasis), he offers no argument to convince the reader that the private alternative *will* further socio-economic equality in the absence of state control. Indeed, Tooley's own discussion of the way in which there are often happy coincidences between the profit motives of private educational providers and the improvement of opportunities for disadvantaged members of society (see Tooley 2000: 109–110) simply reinforces the impression that in a free-market system, any such improvements would be largely a matter of chance – a situation unlikely to satisfy anyone genuinely committed to socio-economic equality.

Crucially, in the context of anarchist ideas, even in the work of advocates of removing state control from education, notably that of Tooley, the state is still assumed to be somewhere in the background, albeit in a role perhaps approaching Nozick's notion of the minimal state (see Nozick 1974).

Yet the Nozickian notion of the state that is assumed by so many neo-liberal writers is in itself far closer to the individualist, libertarian picture of individuals in society than to the picture which underlies both the social-anarchist and indeed the egalitarian liberal position. For Nozick, it is important to note, formulates his arguments in the context of the anti-statist critiques not of the social anarchists, but of contemporary libertarians such as Murray Rothbard and Ayn Rand – keen supporters of free-market economy and critics of the collectivist ethos.

The argument of minarchists such as Nozick against such libertarians and individualist anarchists assumes the same picture of human nature which forms the background for the individualist, libertarian position. It is the supposedly inevitable selfish aspects of this human nature which, it is argued, will lead to conflict, thus necessitating some kind of minimal state to prevent disorder and maintain harmony.

The normative value of the social virtues, along with the contextualist view of human nature so central to social-anarchist thought, are entirely absent from both the libertarian and the neo-liberal positions, and thus fail to play a role in Tooley's analysis, which draws heavily on the work of neo-liberal theorists.

Similarly, the view of education which Tooley draws from this perspective, namely that those services usually performed by the state could be supplied far more efficiently and far more morally by private and cooperative enterprise, ignores the charge, shared by social anarchists and Marxists alike, of a systematic bias, in terms of unequal concentration of wealth, inherent in the structure of market relations. The social anarchists, in contrast, viewed market activity as a social relation and thus subject to control by moral obligations.

However radical Tooley's position may seem to be, then, the question he poses is not that of: what kind of society do we want? but the rather less radical one of: given the kind of society we have, what kind of education should we have? The assumption behind such intellectual exercises seems to be very much the basic liberal assumption which constitutes the conclusion of Rawls' work: the ideal of the liberal state as a generally fair framework for negotiating between conflicting conceptions of the good life, managing public affairs with minimum coercion and maximizing individual liberty. As mentioned earlier, the social virtues so central to anarchist – and to much of liberal – thought are not assigned any normative role in Tooley's conceptualization of the education process. The fact that Tooley conflates the term 'education' with that of 'learning' throughout his discussion in *Reclaiming Education*[1] is indicative of his unwillingness to engage with the inherently normative aspects of education, as is the fact that the term 'moral' or 'moral education' does not appear even once in his discussion. If Tooley wants to imply that one can remain 'neutral' regarding the moral and ideological underpinnings of the market-driven society he envisages, this project is arguably undermined both by the point that, as Ruth Jonathan has argued, the 'free markets in education' idea is far from neutral, and indeed 'education is the one social practice where the blind forces of the market are not the expression of liberal freedom, but its nemesis' (Jonathan 1997: 8–9) – as well as by Tooley's self-confessed enthusiasm for Conservative and New-Right political agendas.

In short, although Tooley and similar critics of state control of education may on the face of it seem to be stating a position akin to that of the social anarchists, this is far from the truth. They may indeed be undermining the institutional power of the state, yet they are not doing so out of a commitment to a positive vision of an alternative social arrangement based on justice, equality and mutual aid, but rather out of the rather vague – and potentially dangerous – notion that people should be allowed to run their own affairs as far as possible.

This criticism of Tooley's work touches on a more general problem that I raised in the Introduction, regarding philosophical work on educational issues, namely, that of disassociating discussion of educational concepts and issues from their political and social context. Tooley acknowledges, in his *Disestablishing the School*, that his arguments are largely aimed at 'those who would like to do something to ameliorate educational disadvantage and injustice' (Tooley 1995: 149). Yet while Tooley's arguments suggest that voluntary activity *can* address such disadvantages, this is a very different thing, as mentioned earlier, from trying to design an educational and political programme that *will* address them. However, I would make the further point – and indeed this is one of the central insights of the anarchist perspective on education – that there is no such thing as 'educational disadvantages' *per se*; one cannot address issues of disadvantage, social justice and distribution without considering the broader political context in which they occur.

Of course, the confusion surrounding the possibly anarchist-sounding tone of proposals such as Tooley's also indicates a need for more careful articulation of the positive core of social anarchism – a project to which, I hope, this work has contributed. For in historical periods and places where the state represented a monolithic, oppressive entity, associated with the repression of liberal freedoms – such as, for example, Spain at the beginning of the last century, when Francisco Ferrer set up the Escuela Moderna – social-anarchist aspirations and visions of alternative models were reflected in the very opposition to the state. In many ways, the act of removing social processes, such as education, from the control of the state, seemed in itself to be a radical statement of belief in an alternative. However, when the state in question is a liberal state, the mere act of removing spheres of action from state control is, in itself, not enough to pose an alternative set of values; contemporary social anarchists have, perhaps, to be far more careful and far more explicit than their nineteenth-century counterparts in stating what exactly it is that they object to in current political arrangements, and how their model of the good society and their means for achieving it are different from and superior to those of the dominant (liberal) discourse. Thus, for example, many contemporary anarchist activists take it for granted, due to the traditional anarchist opposition to state monopolies, that community-based or independently run educational initiatives should be supported. However, as the discussion of Summerhill in Chapter 6 suggests, the values and aims implicit in such initiatives may not always be in keeping with those of the social anarchist project.

To use Rawlsian terminology, then, one could say that on the anarchist view, a comprehensive conception of the good is not a given aspect of individual flourishing, different versions of which are to be negotiated amongst by a neutral political system, but rather something constantly being pursued and created, and the quest for which, crucially, is a collective and an open-ended project. Of course, as Will Kymlicka has argued (Kymlicka 1989), a liberal society should be one in which people are not only given the freedom and the capabilities to pursue existing conceptions of the good but also one in which people are free to constantly form and revise such conceptions. In social anarchism, perhaps, the difference is that the conception of the good is, in an important sense, although perhaps not exclusively, one which is arrived at through a communal process of experimentation.

The anarchist educator cannot argue that the school must provide merely basic skills or act to facilitate children's autonomy and abstain from inculcating substantive conceptions of the good. For, on the anarchist view, the school is a part of the very community that is engaged in the radical and ongoing project of social transformation, by means of an active, creative pursuit of the good. This process, which can only be conducted through an experimental and communal engagement, in dialogue and out of a commitment to social values, is at one and the same time a way of establishing the moral basis for a self-governing, decentralized society, and an experiment in creating such a society. From this social-anarchist perspective, there is no 'elsewhere' where children will get whatever substantive values they need in order to flourish. If the values they get from home conflict with those of the school, then this is a part of the process of social creation, not a problem to be negotiated by coming up with a formal, theoretical framework invoking notions such as liberal neutrality. Thus, while Flathman, Callan, Levinson and others are concerned to address the question of whether 'civic, democratic, and other specifically political conceptions of education are vocational rather than liberal and whether such conceptions are appropriate to a liberal regime' (Flathman 1998: 146), they assume that we know and accept just what a liberal regime consists of. From an anarchist perspective, however, it is precisely this 'regime' that we are in the process of exploring, creating and re-creating.

So if one removes the assumption of the framework of the liberal state from the equation entirely, the question 'how should we educate?' is stripped of its demand for neutrality. In other words, one has to first ask who it is who is doing the educating, rather than assuming that it will be the (liberal) state, before one can go on to ask which values will inform the educational process. This accounts for the normative aspect of anarchist educational ideas – an aspect which, as argued, seems to be at odds with the liberal project, but is only so if one accepts the conflation between liberalism and the liberal state.

Of course, a possible objection to this argument would be that anarchists, in effect, simply replace the notion of the state with that of society so that the problems, for the liberal, remain the same. The social anarchists, however, would respond to this criticism with a defence of the qualitative distinction between the state and society. This distinction is perhaps best articulated by Martin Buber, who had considerable sympathy for the anarchist view that 'social transformation begins with the community and is therefore primarily a social rather than a political objective' (Buber, in Murphy 1988: 180). For the anarchists, social relations governed by the state (including a communist state) are essentially different from those constituted by spontaneous forms of social cooperation, and this is so largely due to their hierarchical nature. Thus although most liberals do not hold any essentialist definition of the state, and could perhaps argue that a federated anarchist commune shares the same functions as the liberal state and is therefore subject to the same theoretical considerations, anarchists would disagree. The anarchist position is that hierarchical, centralized functions are inherent features of the modern capitalist state which, once replaced with an organically established, self governing, decentralized system of communities, would lead to qualitatively different types of social relationships, permeating all levels of social interaction.

This is the idea behind Gustav Landauer's famous remark that

> The state is not something which can be destroyed by a revolution, but is a condition, a certain relationship between human beings, a mode of human behaviour; we destroy it by contracting other relationships, by behaving differently.
>
> (quoted in Ward 1991: 85)

Revolutionary tactics: social anarchism and Marxism

The anarchist anti-hierarchical stance also indicates an important difference between the social-anarchist perspective and that of Marxism, with obvious implications for educational theory and practice. As mentioned earlier, anarchists do not regard the revolutionary struggle to change society as a linear progression, in which there is a single point of reference – the means of production – and a single struggle. As Todd May puts it, in Marxism there is 'a single enemy: capitalism' (May 1994: 26), the focus of Marxist revolutionary thought thus being on class as the chief unit of social struggle. Anarchist thinking, in contrast, involves a far more tactical, multi-dimensional understanding of what the social revolution consists in. Connectedly, an anarchist thinker, unlike a traditional Marxist, cannot offer abstract, general answers to political questions outside the reality of social experience and experimentation. In anarchism then, as Colin Ward says, 'there is no final struggle, only a series of partisan struggles on a variety of fronts' (Ward 1996: 26).

The implications of this contrast for education are significant, and are connected to Marx's disparaging view of the anarchists and other 'utopian' socialists. For in the very idea that there may be something constructive and valuable in positing an ideal of a different society whose final form is determined not by predictable historical progress, but by human experimentation, constantly open to revision, the anarchists reject the basic Marxist materialist assumption that consciousness is determined by the material conditions of life – specifically, by the relations of production. The anarchist position implies that, at least to some degree, life may be determined by consciousness – a position which also explains the optimism inherent in the anarchist enthusiasm for education as a crucial aspect of the revolutionary programme.

On the Marxist view, until the relations of production themselves are radically changed, 'the possibility of an alternative reality is not only impossible, but literally unthinkable' (Block 1994: 65), for our thought structures are determined by the reality of the base/superstructure relationship. However, in anarchism, an alternative reality is 'thinkable'; indeed, it is in some sense already here. As the discussion of the anarchist position on human nature makes clear, the human capacity for mutual aid, benevolence and solidarity is reflected in forms of social relations which exist even within the capitalist state, and whose potential for social change is not rendered unfeasible by the capitalist relations of production. It is these capacities which, on the anarchist view, need to be strengthened and built on, a project which can be embarked upon without a systematic programme for revolutionary change or a blue-print for the future, but by forging alternative modes of social organization in arenas such as the school and the workplace.

Much work in radical educational theory in recent years is based on some variant of Marxist reproduction theory, according to which 'all practices in the superstructure may be viewed as products of a determining base, and we have only to examine the products for their component parts, which ought to be easily discerned from the economic base' (Block 1994: 65). Reproduction theorists thus regard schools and education as basically derived from the economic base, which they inevitably reproduce. As Block notes, this idea leads to the generally pessimistic Marxist view of education, according to which even alternative schools are allowed to exist by the system itself, which marginalizes them and thus continues to reproduce the dominant social norms and economic structures.

The anarchist perspective, as mentioned, involves not merely subverting the economic relations of the base, but conceptualizing a social-economic framework that is not structured in a hierarchical way. The pyramid of the Marxist analysis of capitalism is not simply inverted, but abolished. Thus for example, in Marxism, the status of the dominant definitions of knowledge – as reflected, for example, in the school curriculum – is questionable because it is determined by the unjust class system, reflecting the material power of the ruling class. However, in anarchist theory, what renders a national curriculum or a body of knowledge objectionable is the simple fact that it is determined by any central, hierarchical top-down organization. For the anarchist, incorporating 'working-class knowledge' or that of excluded cultural or social groups into the school curriculum of a state education system would be equally suspect – the problem is that there is a curriculum and a national school system at all.

So although anarchists share the Marxist insistence that the structural inequalities of society have to be abolished, they believe that this project can be embarked upon on a micro level; in this they share, perhaps, the faith in the emancipatory power of education common to many liberal theorists.

Goals and visions

These remarks may lead one to believe that the anarchist approach to social change is more of a piecemeal, tactical one, than a strategic one. Todd May in fact argues that the opposite is the case, claiming that the anarchists, faced with the need to adopt either a strategic or a tactical position, have to opt for the former due to their reductionist view of power and their humanist ethics (May 1994: 63–66). Yet I believe that both these readings are too narrow. What the anarchist perspective in fact suggests is that one can be, and in fact has to be, both tactical and strategic; what May refers to as the anarchists' 'ambivalence' between a purely strategic and a purely tactical stance is in fact a kind of pragmatic realism, summed up by Chomsky in his argument that:

> In today's world, I think, the goals of a committed anarchist should be to defend some state institutions from the attack against them, while trying at the same time to pry them open to more meaningful public participation – and ultimately, to dismantle them in a much more free society, if the appropriate circumstances can be achieved. Right or wrong – and that's a matter of uncertain judgement – this stand is not undermined by the apparent conflict between goals and visions. Such conflict is a normal feature of everyday life, which we somehow try to live with but cannot escape.
>
> (Chomsky 1996: 75)

So while certain elements of anarchism – notably its insistence on social improvements 'here and now' – may be reminiscent of Popper's characterization of 'piecemeal social engineering' (Popper 1945: 157–163), the social-anarchist perspective in fact straddles Popper's contrast between utopian social engineering and piecemeal social engineering. It is, as I hope to have shown, utopian in that it holds on to a radical vision of society; however it is not narrowly utopian in Popper's sense as it has no fixed blueprint, and the commitment to constant experimentation is built into its vision of the ideal society. It is 'piecemeal' in the sense that it advocates a form of gradual restructuring, as in the comment by Paul Goodman, quoted in Chapter 4: 'A free society cannot be the substitution of a "new order" for the old order; it is the extension of spheres of free action until they make up most of social life' (in Ward 1996: 18). And, as I think the projects of anarchist educators and the anarchist criticism of Marxist revolutionary theory make clear, it is also piecemeal in Popper's sense that it is concerned with 'searching for, and fighting against, the greatest and most urgent evils of society, rather than searching for, and fighting for, its greatest ultimate good' (Popper 1945: 158).

Chomsky indeed expresses something like this idea in summing up the anarchist stance as follows:

> At every stage of history our concern must be to dismantle those forms of authority and oppression that survive from an era when they might have been justified in terms of the need for security or survival or economic development, but that now contribute to – rather than alleviate – material and cultural deficit. If so, there will be no doctrine of social change fixed for the present and future, nor even, necessarily, a specific and unchanging concept of the goals towards which social change should tend.
>
> (Chomsky, in Guerin 1970: viii)

This perspective, like Popper's piecemeal approach, 'permits repeated experiments and continuous readjustments' (Popper 1945: 163).

Yet at the same time, the anarchist approach is distinct from what Popper characterizes as piecemeal social engineering in that it does not simply concern 'blueprints for single institutions', but sees in the very act of restructuring human relationships within such institutions (the school, the workplace), a creative act of engaging with the restructuring of society as a whole.

The anarchist utopia, then, although it does envisage 'the reconstruction of society as a whole' (Popper 1945: 161), is not utopian in Popper's sense as it is not an 'attempt to realize an ideal state, using a blueprint of society as whole, [...] which demands a strong centralized rule of a few' (ibid.: 159). And while the kind of social restructuring envisaged by the social anarchists is not simply, as Popper characterizes utopian engineering, 'one step towards a distant ideal', (see the discussion on means and ends in Chapter 6), neither is it 'a realization of a piecemeal compromise'. Creating, for example, a school community run on social-anarchist principles is both a step towards the ideal and an embodiment of the ideal itself.

Anarchism, to continue this line of thought, is perhaps best conceived not so much as a theory – in Popper's rationalistic sense – about how society can be organized without a state, but as an aspiration to create such a society and, crucially, a belief that such a society can in fact come about, not through violent revolution or drastic modification of human nature, but as an organic, spontaneous process – the seeds of which are already present in human propensities.

Given these points, one may argue that anarchism, in a sense, needs the theoretical components of liberalism to carry it beyond the stage of aspiration to that of political possibility. For example, the analytical work carried out within the liberal tradition on such key notions as autonomy, individual rights, consent and justice, provides valuable theoretical tools for working out the details of the anarchist project. However, it is not this theorizing which constitutes the core of anarchism but the aspiration itself. In education, this is crucially important. While anarchism perhaps makes little sense without the theoretical framework of the liberal tradition (a tradition which, following Chomsky, it may be a continuation of), it could also be argued that liberalism needs anarchism, or something like the social-anarchist vision, to remind itself of the aspirations behind the theory. Built into these aspirations is, crucially, the belief that things could be different, and radically so, if only we allow ourselves to have faith in people's ability to recreate social relationships and institutions; a sort of perfectibility which, while cherishing traditional liberal values, pushes us beyond the bounds of normal liberal theory. In this context, MacIntyre's comments (MacIntyre 1971) that liberalism is essentially 'negative and incomplete', being a doctrine 'about what cannot be justified and what ought not to be permitted', and that hence 'no institution, no social practice, can be inspired solely or even mainly by liberalism' – seem to make sense.

Utopianism and philosophy of education

I have argued that part of the reason why anarchist education is, on the face of it, objectionable to philosophers within the liberal tradition, is because of the common conflation between liberalism as a body of values, and the liberal state as a framework within which to pursue these values. This conflation, I have argued, could explain why the normative, substantive aspects of anarchist education seem problematic for those wishing to preserve some form of political liberalism. However, there are also those who object to anarchism's political ideal – that of the stateless society – simply on the grounds of its being hopelessly utopian and who would thus argue that it is pointless to try to construct a philosophy of education around this ideal. As mentioned in the Introduction, the charge of utopianism is one of the commonest criticisms of anarchism, and, in my view, raises several interesting philosophical questions. In what follows, I shall attempt to address this charge and to grapple with some of these questions.

Martin Buber was one of the first to note how the concept *utopia* had been

> victimized in the course of the political struggle of Marxism against other forms of socialism and movements of social reform. In his struggle to achieve dominance for his idiosyncratic system of socialism, Marx employed 'utopia' as the ultimate term of perjoration to damn all 'pre-historic' (i.e. pre-Marxian) social systems as unscientific and utilitarian in contrast to the allegedly scientific and inevitable character of his system of historical materialism.
>
> (Fischoff, in Buber 1958: xiii)

In the mid-nineteenth century, indeed, the social-anarchist position could be perceived as an argument over the contested intellectual ground of the developing nation state; its utopianism, for Marx, lay in its rejection of the materialist position. Yet now that the nation state is such an established fact of our political life, and theoretical arguments justifying its existence are so taken for granted that they are rarely even articulated, it is the very distance between the anarchist vision and that of the dominant liberal state tradition that strikes some as utopian. As discussed above, although philosophers of education devote a great deal of energy to the articulation, analysis and critique of liberal values and their educational implications, the framework within which these values are assumed to operate is rarely the subject of debate. It is the anarchist questioning of this framework, then, which constitutes its radical challenge.

Of course, the charge that anarchism is utopian has some truth if one accepts Mannheim's classic account, according to which 'utopian' describes: 'all situationally transcendent ideas which in any way have a transforming effect on the existing historical, social order' (Mannheim 1991: 173).

But there is an important sense in which anarchism is definitely not utopian or, at least, is utopian in a positive, rather than a pejorative, sense. Isaiah Berlin has characterized utopias in a way which, as David Halpin (Halpin 2003) points out, is highly restrictive and problematic and fails to capture the constructive role of utopias as 'facilitating fresh thinking for the future' (ibid.) which Halpin and other theorists are keen to preserve. Nevertheless, Berlin's characterization is useful here as it is indicative of a typical critical perspective on utopian thought and thus serves to highlight the contrast with anarchism. Berlin states:

> The main characteristic of most (perhaps all) utopias is that they are static. Nothing in them alters, for they have reached perfection: there is no need for novelty or change; no one can wish to alter a condition in which all natural human wishes are fulfilled.
>
> (Berlin 1991: 20)

This is clearly in contrast to the anarchist vision of the future society, on two counts. First, due to the anarchist conception of human nature, most anarchist theorists are under no illusion about the possibility of a society without conflict; a society which, as in Berlin's description of utopia, 'lives in a state of pure harmony' (ibid.). Rather, they envisage a particular way of solving conflict. As William Reichert states,

> Anarchists do not suppose for a minute that men would ever live in harmony [...]. They do maintain, however, that the settlement of conflict must arise spontaneously from the individuals involved themselves and not be imposed upon them by an external force such as government.
>
> (Reichert 1969: 143)

Second, it is intrinsic to the anarchist position that human society is constantly in flux; there is no such thing as the one finite, fixed form of social organization; the principle at the heart of anarchist thought is that of constant striving, improvement and experimentation.

In an educational context, this contrast is echoed in Dewey's critique of Plato's *Republic*. As Dewey notes, Plato's utopia serves as a final answer to all questions about the good life, and the state and education are constructed so as to translate it immediately into reality. Although Plato, says Dewey,

> would radically change the existing state of society, his aim was to construct a state in which change would subsequently have no place. The final end of life is fixed; given a state framed with this end in view, not even minor details are to be altered. [...] Correct education could not come into existence until an ideal state existed, and after that education would be devoted simply to its conservation.
>
> (Dewey 1939: 105–106)

This, again, is in clear contrast to the anarchist vision.

Of course, the utopian nature of Plato's account does not detract from its philosophical value. All this suggests that the 'feasibility' of any political vision should not, on its own, constitute a reason for disregarding it as a basis for serious philosophical debate. Many writers on utopias, indeed, have stressed the transformative element of utopian thinking, arguing that the study of utopias can be valuable as it releases creative thought, prodding us to examine our preconceptions and encouraging speculation on alternative ways of conceptualizing and doing things which we often take for granted. Politically speaking, it has been argued that 'utopianism thus offers a specific programme and immediate hope for improvement and thereby discourages quiescence or fatalism' (Goodwin and Taylor 1982: 26).

Thus, as David Halpin says in his discussion of Fourier's nineteenth-century depiction of the Utopian Land of Plenty, where whole roast chickens descended from the sky,

> Fourier was not envisaging concretely a society whose members would be fed magically. Rather, through the use of graphic imagery, he was seeking to mobilize among his readers a commitment to a conception of social life in which being properly fed was regarded as a basic human right.
>
> (Halpin 2001: 302)

There are further aspects of utopianism, specifically in the anarchist context, which are associated with the suspicion or derision of anarchist positions by liberal theorists. For while many liberal and neo-liberal theorists seem amenable to the idea of utopia as an individual project, the social anarchists' faith in the social virtues, and their vision of a society underpinned by these virtues, imply a utopia which is necessarily collective. Nozick's vision of the minimalist state, for example, is clearly utopian in the general sense described earlier. Yet, as Barbara Goodwin points out, the utopian nature of Nozick's minimal state lies

> not in the quality of the individual communities (all of which appeal to some people and not to others) but in each individual having the power to choose and to experiment with the Good Life. Utopia is having a choice between Utopias.
>
> (Goodwin and Taylor 1982: 82)

The anarchist vision, both in its insistence on the centrality of the social virtues, and in its normative commitment to these virtues, seems to be demanding that we extend Nozick's 'utopia of Utopias' to something far more substantive. Indeed, many liberals would agree that it is the lack of just such a substantive vision which is partly to blame for the individualist and often alienating aspects of modern capitalist society. Thus, for example, Zygmunt Bauman has spoken of our era as one characterized by 'the privatization of utopias' (Bauman 1999: 7), in which models of 'the good life' are increasingly cut off from models of the good society. Perhaps the kind of utopianism inherent in social-anarchist thinking can help us to amend this situation.

The anarchist utopian stance, at the same time, arguably avoids the charges of totalitarianism which so worried Popper and Berlin due to two important points: first, the fact that, built into its utopian vision, is the demand for constant experimentation, and the insistence that the final form of human society cannot be determined in advance. Second, the insistence, based on the anarchist view of human nature and the associated conceptualization of social change, that the future society is to be constructed not by radically transforming human relations and attitudes, but from the seeds of existing social tendencies. This is, indeed, in contrast to the Marxist vision, where, as Bauman points out, 'the attempt to build a socialist society is an effort to emancipate human nature, mutilated and humiliated by class society'.

The anarchist rejection of blueprints, while arguably rescuing anarchists from charges of totalitarianism, can at the same time be perceived as philosophically, and perhaps psychologically, somewhat threatening, as Herbert Read points out. The idea that, as Read puts it (Read 1974: 148), 'the future will make its own prints, and they won't necessarily be blue', can give rise to a sense of insecurity. Yet such insecurity, perhaps, is a necessary price to pay if one wants to embark on the genuinely creative and challenging project of reconstructing society, or even reconstructing political and social philosophy.

It has in fact been argued that much mainstream work in political theory, notably in the liberal tradition, is conducted in the shadow of what could be seen as another aspect of the 'sense of insecurity' provoked by the open-endedness of such utopian projects as social anarchism. This view is eloquently argued by Bonnie Honig, in her *Political Theory and the Displacement of Politics:*

> Most political theorists are hostile to the disruptions of politics. Those writing from diverse positions – republican, federal and communitarian – converge in their assumption that success lies in the elimination from a regime of dissonance, resistance, conflict, or struggle. They confine politics (conceptually and territorially) to the juridical, administrative, or regulative tasks of stabilizing moral and political subjects, building consensus, maintaining agreement, or consolidating communities and identities. They assume that the task of political theory is to resolve institutional questions, to get politics right, over and done with, to free modern subjects and their sets of arrangements of political conflict and instability.
>
> (Honig 1993: 2)

In an academic culture dominated by this perspective, it is hardly surprising that a position such as social anarchism, which both challenges the dominant political system with a radically different vision, and holds that this vision, while accessible, cannot be fully instantiated either in theory or by revolutionary programmes, but must be the result of spontaneous, free experimentation is rarely taken seriously. Yet as both Noam Chomsky and Paul Goodman have commented, this type of utopianism is not so far removed from the liberal tradition. Paul Goodman (Goodman 1952: 18–19) argues that American culture has lost the spirit of pragmatism embodied in the thought of James and Dewey. In a climate where, he says, 'experts plan in terms of an unchangeable structure, a pragmatic expediency that still wants to take the social structure as plastic and changeable comes to be thought of as "utopian" '.

Richard Rorty, too, has noted the connections between the type of utopianism embodied in the social anarchist view and the Pragmatism of Dewey and other thinkers. His discussion of this idea captures, for me, the value of this perspective for our educational thought. Rorty argues that what is distinctive about Pragmatism is that it 'substitutes the notion of a better human future for the notions of "reality," "reason" and "nature" ' (Rorty 1999: 27). While nineteenth-century social anarchism, as an Enlightenment tradition, cannot be said by any means to have rejected the notions of reason, reality and nature, I think there is nevertheless an important insight here in terms of the role of utopian hope in social anarchist thought.

The anarchist view that what Fidler refers to as 'awakening the social instinct' is the key role for education, and Kropotkin's insistence that the 'fundamental principle of anarchism' (in Fidler 1989: 37) consists in 'treating others as one wishes to be treated oneself', seems to me in keeping with Rorty's argument that moral progress, for the Pragmatists, 'is a matter of increasing sensitivity' (Rorty 1999: 81). Such sensitivity, Rorty explains, means 'being able to respond to the needs of ever more inclusive groups of people', and thus involves not 'rising above the sentimental to the rational' but rather expanding outwards in 'wider and wider sympathy' (ibid.). This image, which Rorty describes as a 'switch from metaphors of vertical distance to metaphors of horizontal extent' (Rorty 1999: 83) also seems to me in tune with the anarchists' rejection of hierarchical structures, and the image of the ideal anarchist society as one of interconnected networks rather than pyramidal structures. Furthermore, Rorty argues, this element of utopian hope and 'willingness to substitute imagination for certainty' (ibid.: 88) emphasizes the need for active engagement on the part of social agents, articulating a desire and a need 'to create new ways of being human, and a new heaven on earth for these new humans to inhabit, over the desire for stability, security and order' (ibid.).

Rorty's notion of 'replacing certainty with hope' seems to me highly pertinent to the aforementioned discussion of social anarchism and, especially, to the implications of a consideration of the utopian aspects of the social anarchist position for the way we think about education. One aspect of this point is that the utopian – in the sense of radically removed from reality as we know it – aspect of a theory should not in itself be a reason to reject it. Even the evident failure of those utopian projects which have been disastrously attempted should not lead us to reject the utopian hopes which underlie them. As Rorty says,

> The inspirational value of the New Testament and the Communist Manifesto is not diminished by the fact that many millions of people were enslaved, tortured or starved to death by sincere, morally earnest people who recited passages from one or the other text to justify their deeds.
>
> (Rorty 1999: 204)

The anarchist project, arguably, is less liable to such dismal failure for first, if one accepts its account of human nature, this account suggests that the type of society which the social anarchists seek to establish does not go completely against the grain of existing human propensities. Furthermore, as discussed here, the idea of trying to implement this project on a grand scale, by violent means if necessary, is completely incompatible with anarchist principles. For the flip-side of what Ritter refers to as the anarchists' 'daring leap' is the point that, as noted by Buber, the social anarchist

> desires a means commensurate with his ends; he refuses to believe that in our reliance on the future 'leap' we have to do now the direct opposite of what we are striving for; he believes rather that we must create here and now the space *now* possible for the thing for which we are striving, so that it may come to fulfilment then; he does not believe in the post-revolutionary leap, but he does believe in revolutionary continuity.
>
> (Buber 1958: 13)

Whether or not one is convinced by these social anarchist arguments, it seems to me that Rorty's point that such hopes and aspirations as are embodied in this position may constitute 'the only basis for a worthwhile life' (Rorty 1999: 204) is a compelling one. As far as philosophy of education is concerned, it may be true that attempting to construct a position on the role and nature of education around the notion of hope could lead to neglect of the need to work out clear principles of procedure and conceptual distinctions. However, this notion may perhaps insert a more optimistic and motivating element into educational projects characterized by an often overriding concern to formulate procedural principles.

Furthermore, the perspective of starting debates into educationally relevant issues, like the social anarchists, from a position of hope – in other words, taking the utopian position that a radically different society is both desirable and attainable – can have clear policy implications. For example, arguments for equality of opportunity in (state) education, as put forward by liberal theorists, often involve a veiled assumption that socio-economic inequality is an inevitable feature of our life. Thus Harry Brighouse argues (1998) that educational opportunities should be unaffected by matters of socio-economic status or family background. In so doing, he assumes, as he himself readily admits, 'that material rewards in the labour markets will be significantly unequal' (Brighouse 1998: 8). Yet were he to take seriously the aspiration of creating a society in which there were no longer any class or socio-economic divisions, he may be led to placing a very different emphasis on the kind of education we should be providing (e.g. one which emphasized a critical attitude towards the political status quo, and the promotion of certain moral values deemed crucial for sustaining an egalitarian, cooperative society).

Patricia White has discussed the notion of social hope in her 1991 paper, 'Hope, Confidence and Democracy' (White 1991), where she notes the powerful motivational role played by shared hopes 'relating to the future of communities'. Yet while acknowledging a need for such social hope in our own democratic society, White admits that 'liberal democracy is not in the business of offering visions of a future to which all citizens are marching if only they can keep their faith in it' (White 1991: 205). Such a view would, obviously, undermine the liberal commitment to an open future and to value pluralism. However it seems, on the basis of the aforementioned analysis, that the type of utopian hope associated with anarchism may fit White's description of a possible way out of this liberal problem, namely,

> that it is possible to drop the idea that the object of hope must be unitary and inevitable and to defend a notion of hope where, roughly speaking, to hope is strongly to desire that some desirable state of affairs, which need not be inevitable and is not impossible, but in the path of which there are obstacles, will come to pass.
>
> (Ibid.)

In terms of how we conceptualize education, what the earlier discussion suggests is that the interplay between our hopes – or our strategic goals – and our tactical objectives is not a conflict to be decided in advance, but an interesting tension that should itself be made part of educational practice. In certain contexts, tactical decisions may make sense, and thus the type of educational change and action promoted may not appear very radical, but the hope, as a long-term goal, is always there, and even if it is only, as Chomsky states, a 'vision', this vision has tremendous motivating force for those involved in education.

Taking the social-anarchist perspective seriously, then, can help us to think differently about the role of visions, dreams, goals and ideals in educational thought. It suggests that perhaps we should think of education not as a means to an end, nor as an end in itself, but as one of many arenas of human relationships, in which the relation between the vision and the ways it is translated into reality is constantly experimented with. Philosophy of education, perhaps, could be seen as part of this process.

Conclusion

Faith in the power of intelligence to imagine a future which is the projection of the desirable in the present, and to invent the instrumentalities of its realization, is our salvation. And it is a faith which must be nurtured and made articulate: surely a sufficiently large task for our philosophy.

(Dewey 1917: 48)

I hope, in the preceding discussion, to have gone some way towards constructing what an anarchist philosophy of education would look like. There are certain important insights to be drawn from my analysis, both regarding anarchism's significance as a political ideology and regarding educational philosophy and practice.

Situating anarchism: a reevaluation

First, in the course of the preceding chapters, I hope to have dispelled some common misconceptions about anarchism as a political theory, especially with regard to its position on the need for social order and authority and its conception of human nature. Above all, I have argued that the anarchist view of human nature is not naively optimistic but rather embraces a realistic, contextual approach to human virtues and capabilities. The implications of this idea form the core aspects of the anarchist position on education; namely, that systematic educational intervention in children's lives, on the part of social institutions, is necessary in order to sustain the moral fabric of society, and that this education must be, first and foremost, a moral enterprise.

Second, I believe it is clear from my analysis that the values and aspirations underpinning social-anarchist thought are – perhaps surprisingly – fairly close to those which inform the liberal tradition. Anarchism's affinity with liberalism, as well as with certain strands of socialism, suggests that we should perhaps extend our understanding of liberalism beyond the constraints of the liberal state. One does not have to reject liberal values in order to challenge dominant aspects of the political framework which we so often take for granted. The question of what remains of liberalism if one removes the state from the equation is a philosophically puzzling one, but, I suggest, the challenge of trying to answer it may itself be a valuable exercise in re-examining and re-articulating our (liberal) values and prompting us to think through the political implications and scope of these values.

Specifically, examining the implications of the underlying values of social anarchism, in the comparative context of liberal values, may lead us to re-articulate the utopian aspect of the liberal tradition. More broadly speaking, I believe that philosophers, and especially philosophers of education, need to constantly examine and articulate the normative assumptions behind their educational ideas. If, like many liberal theorists, we consciously make compromises in our philosophical treatment of educational notions such as 'equality' – compromises which imply an acquiescence with existing political structures – we should at least articulate our reasons for such compromises, and the way they reflect our substantive ideals. Challenging the political framework within which we commonly formulate such ideas may be one way of prodding us to engage in such a process of articulation.

Anarchism remains a confusing and often frustrating body of ideas, and I do not purport to have resolved the theoretical and practical tensions it involves. Specifically, the charge that social censure will undermine individual freedom in an anarchist society remains a troubling one (eloquently depicted in Ursula Le Guin's science-fictional account of an anarchist colony, *The Dispossessed* (1974)). Similarly, one has to ask oneself whether anarchism, with its Enlightenment understanding of progress and the inevitable triumph of secular, socialist values, is theoretically equipped to deal with the contemporary issues of life in pluralist societies – especially with the question of value pluralism. I have to admit that I find the arguments by Noam Chomsky and others that one cannot resolve such theoretical tensions in advance, but that they have to be worked out through experimentation – an unsatisfactory response to this problem.

These theoretical tensions notwithstanding, I have suggested that both educational practice and philosophy of education may be more challenging and motivating activities if they are guided by a utopian hope; a normative vision, not just of the good life (a phrase commonly employed by philosophers of education), but of the good society – however far removed this may seem from where we are now.

Of course, there is nothing unique to anarchism about the idea of an ideal society. Indeed political liberalism, as formulated by Rawls, is in many ways an ideal theory and a model for the ideal society. It leads to conclusions about the kinds of institutional practices and processes which will enable individuals to live together in what is conceived as the optimal political model, namely, the liberal state. Anarchism's model is similarly ideal but does away with the state. It, like liberalism, begins from intuitions about the moral worth of certain human attributes and values, but its model is strikingly different from that which we have today. Many modern democracies, one could argue, approach something like the Rawlsian model, but need the theoretical framework and arguments of liberal theory to strengthen and underpin their institutions and practices. For anarchism, however, the ideal society is something that has to be created. And education is primarily a part of this creation; it involves a radical challenge to current practices and institutions, yet at the same time a faith in the idea that human beings already possess most of the attributes and virtues necessary to create and sustain such a different society, so do not need to either undergo any radical transformation or to do away with an 'inauthentic' consciousness.

An anarchist philosophy of education?

In my Introduction, I posed the question of whether or not an examination of anarchist ideas could yield a comprehensive, coherent and unique philosophy of education. As indicated by the aforementioned remarks, I believe that while my analysis suggests that anarchism does not perhaps offer a systematic theory of education, it does have significant implications for how we conceptualize education and educational aims, for how we address educational questions in policy and practice, and for how we do philosophy of education.

As far as educational practice is concerned, there are several weaknesses in the anarchist account. Primarily, the sparse attention paid by anarchist writers on education to the issue of pedagogy both exposes this account to theoretical questions about the most appropriate pedagogical approach, and opens the door to questionable pedagogical practices, as witnessed by some graduates of the Stelton school, who suggest (see Avrich 1980) that the actual teaching practices of certain teachers at the anarchist schools were far from anti-coercive. Indeed, the very status of the connection between anarchist ideology and non-coercive pedagogy is one which still demands careful theoretical treatment. Furthermore, the whole question of the teacher–pupil relationship in both its psychological and political dimensions is undertheorized in the literature on anarchist and libertarian education. Although the anarchist account of authority goes some way towards situating and justifying this relationship theoretically, there is clearly a great deal more that could be said on the subject. Similarly, and perhaps most importantly given its central role in creating and sustaining the ideal society, the development of specific approaches to and methods of moral education is sorely lacking from anarchist work on education. Although I have hinted at the form such a programme of moral education may take, and have emphasized its crucial role, I cannot undertake the project of constructing it here.

In spite of these weaknesses in the theoretical framework of anarchist educational practice, I think my analysis establishes that anarchist education is a distinct tradition in the world of what is often loosely referred to as 'radical education'. As such, it differs in important respects from both extreme libertarian positions and various aspects of the free school movement, both in its content and in the conceptualization of education which it embodies.

Above all, an anarchist perspective, I have argued, can help us see questions about the relationship between education and social change in a new light.

Although the anarchist failure to distinguish in any systematic way between social life within as opposed to beyond the state is the cause of much confusion regarding the role of education in promoting and sustaining social transformation, I hope I have gone some way towards drawing this distinction, and clarifying its philosophical significance.

At the same time, I believe that part of anarchism's appeal, and indeed its uniqueness as a perspective on education, lies in its ability to transcend the means/ends model and to perceive every educational encounter as both a moment of striving, through creative experimenting, to create something better, and of celebrating and reinforcing what is valuable in such an encounter.

I can find no better way of illustrating this idea than through an analogy with a very particular instance of education, namely the parent–child relationship. As parents, we are constantly aware of the future-oriented aspect of our relationship with our children. The question of who they will be and how they will turn out is a constant factor in our interaction with them, our concerns, and our motivations and goals for the decisions we make regarding them. Yet to construe this relationship as reducible entirely to this intentional educational aspect would be, surely, to miss the point. For our interaction with our children is also a mutually challenging and stimulating relationship in terms of who they – and we – are now. What makes this relationship so complex is the fact that it involves constant interplay and tensions between the present and the future; between our desires and hopes for our children, our vision of an ideal future in which they will play a part, and our attempt to understand who they are; between our efforts to respect their desires and our inescapable wish to mould these desires; between our own ideals for the future, and the challenges posed for them by the complexities of the present. While the way in which we raise our children is often informed by our commitments, values and aspirations, it is equally true to say that these values and commitments are constantly challenged and questioned by the experience of raising children. In a sense, this inherently confusing, challenging and creative mode of interaction sums up the essence of the anarchist perspective on education. In thus rejecting simplistic distinctions between ends and means, goals and visions, it suggests a certain anti-hierarchical stance not only in its model for the ideal society but also in our very patterns of thinking.

Furthermore, the anarchist stance on the relationship between education and social change has important practical implications. For the anarchist, utopia, as discussed, is not a blueprint for the future society. Therefore the focus of education is not on implementing aspects of this utopia, but on fostering the attitudes and virtues needed to sustain it, alongside a critical attitude to current social principles and practices, out of which the utopian vision grows and which, in turn, are informed by this vision. Education is thus not seen as a means to creating a different political order, but as a space – and perhaps, following Buber, a relationship – in which we experiment with visions of a new political order – a process which itself constitutes an educative and motivating experience both for educators and pupils. I have suggested that this perspective constitutes an alternative to certain dominant views, according to which we tend to regard education as either an end in itself or a means to an end.

Thus even if one remains sceptical as to the feasibility of the social-anarchist model of social organization, the flexibility regarding the exact form and process of this model is the essence of the anarchist position, and it is this, I argue, together with the aspirations and values behind the proposed model, which give meaning to the educational experience.

Critiques of anarchism revisited

Interestingly, one conclusion suggested by my analysis is that the very failure by many commentators to pay adequate attention to the central role of education in anarchist thought has itself contributed to much of the conceptual confusion and apparent tensions surrounding anarchist theory. For the commonly made claim, to the effect that anarchists hold a naïve and optimistic view about the possibility of maintaining a benevolent, decentralized society without institutional control, does not take into account the central and ongoing role of education in promoting, fostering and maintaining the moral foundations deemed necessary to support such a society. In many standard works on anarchism, notably the studies by Miller, Morland and Ritter, education gets barely a passing mention. This is especially striking in Morland's work, which is a detailed study of human nature in social anarchism (Morland 1997). In the light of the complete absence of any discussion of anarchist education in Morland's book, his concluding remark that 'something above and beyond a conception of human nature is required to explain the optimism of the anarchists' (Morland 1997: 198) is quite astonishing. As the present work has suggested, the anarchists' acknowledgement of the need for a substantive educational process, designed along clear moral principles, goes hand-in-hand with their contextualist account of human nature, thus turning what might otherwise be regarded as a sort of naïve optimism, into a complex and inspiring social hope.

A notable exception to this tendency to overlook the centrality of education to the anarchist account is the work of Barbara Goodwin. In her discussion of anarchism in *Using Political Ideas* (Goodwin and Taylor 1982), Goodwin refers to 'the moral basis of anarchist society', arguing that 'the real interest of anarchism lies not in the precise details of communal organization, but in the universal principles on which such communities would be based' (ibid.: 118). In discussing anarchist education in this context, Goodwin acknowledges its important function in promoting and nurturing 'the moral principles which formed the basis of the anarchist order' (ibid.: 128). The present book, I hope, goes some way towards justifying this acknowledgement and exploring just what it consists in. As such, it also shows that articulating the anarchist view on education is an important contribution to the ongoing debate on the viability of anarchism as a political ideology.

In conclusion, I suggest that even if one is ultimately sceptical about the immediate feasibility of an anarchist society, the suggestion that it is theoretically possible, together with the belief that it reflects the true embodiment of some of our most cherished human values, make exploring it an educationally valuable and constructive project.

Notes

2 Anarchism and human nature

1 In an interesting article based on work by Daniel P. Todes, Stephen Jay Gould points out that Kropotkin was not, as is often assumed, an idiosyncratic thinker, but was part of a well-developed Russian critique of Darwin and contemporary interpreters of evolutionary theory. This tradition of critique rejected the Malthusian claim that competition 'must dominate in an ever more crowded world, where population, growing geometrically, inevitably outstrips a food supply that can only increase arithmetically' (Gould 1988: 3). 'Russia', Gould points out,

> is an immense country, under-populated by any nineteenth-century measure of its agricultural potential. Russia is also, over most of its area, a harsh land, where competition is more likely to pit organism against environment (as in Darwin's metaphorical struggle of a plant at the desert's edge) than organism against organism in direct and bloody battle. How could any Russian, with a strong feel for his own countryside, see Malthus's principle of overpopulation as a foundation for evolutionary theory? Todes writes: 'It was foreign to their experience because, quite simply, Russia's huge land mass dwarfed its sparse population. For a Russian to see an inexorably increasing population inevitably straining potential supplies of food and space required quite a leap of imagination'.
>
> (Ibid.)

3 Anarchist values?

1 Illich, given his concern with poverty and social justice and his arguments for the need to decrease the dependency of individuals on corporate and state institutions, is in many ways a part of the anarchist tradition. However, his focus, in addressing chiefly the institutional effects of the modern state, is somewhat narrow and leads to an emphasis on individual autonomy rather than on ideal of forms of communality, suggesting possible theoretical tensions with the social-anarchist position. Illich's critique of schooling focuses on the structure of the modern school and its relationship to control and authority. He has specifically argued that schooling in modern industrial states is geared primarily to the shaping of a type of character which can be manipulated by consumer society and its institutions of authority (see Spring 1975: 26). Schools, thus conceived, encourage dependency which 'creates a form of alienation which destroys people's ability to act' (ibid.). Thus while Illich, with his radical social critique, belongs to the same broad dissenting tradition as many anarchist thinkers, his emphasis on the effects of schooling on the

individual arguably places him somewhat closer to the libertarian tradition than
to the tradition of (social) anarchist education discussed here (see Chapter 6).
2 Bakunin's use of the term 'right' here is particularly interesting given current
debates into the distinction between 'rights' and 'needs', and the general consensus
as to the relative novelty of talk of children's rights.

5 The positive core of anarchism

1 In this thought experiment, designed to illustrate Nozick's central argument that
maintaining a pattern of distributive justice would entail unacceptable restrictions
on people's liberty to do as they wish with their own resources, members of an
imaginary society pay a lot of money to watch a highly talented basketball player
play, resulting in his accumulating a great deal of wealth. On Nozick's account,
although the resulting distribution of resources is unequal, it cannot be regarded
as 'unjust' as it emerged from a series of voluntary exchanges, from an initially just
situation.

7 Education for an anarchist society: vocational training and political visions

1 Although other contemporary philosophers of education have addressed these
issues (e.g. Williams 1994 and White 1997), these two works by Pring and Winch
represent the most substantial philosophical treatment of the field of vocational
education in recent years.
2 A great deal of the literature on the issue of globalization in educational contexts
makes similar assumptions: the economy, we are told, is moving in certain direc-
tions, creating certain changes in the labour market, and education must follow
suit by preparing children for 'an uncertain future', 'flexible job-skills', or 'insecure
employment' (see for example Burbules and Torres 2000: 28).
3 Interestingly, Bakunin seems to have made no acknowledgement of the existence
of any kind of educational process before the age of 5.

8 What's so funny about anarchism?

1 Although the book is ostensibly about education, the private initiatives which
Tooley describes so enthusiastically in fact seem to be more concerned with the
acquisition of skills and training (see Tooley 2000: 102–112) than about education
in a broader sense.

Bibliography

Adan, J. (1992) *Reformist Anarchism 1800–1936; A Study of the Feasibility of Anarchism*, Braunton: Merlin Books.

Avrich, P. (1980) *The Modern School Movement: Anarchism and Education in the United States*, Princeton, NJ: Princeton University Press.

Bantock, G.H. (1984) *Studies in the History of Educational Theory*, London: Allen and Unwin.

Barclay, H. (1990) *People Without Government: An Anthropology of Anarchy*, London: Kahn and Averill.

Bauman, Z. (1999) *In Search of Politics*, Oxford: Polity Press.

Becker, H. and Walter, N. (eds) (1988) *Act for Yourselves: Articles from Freedom, 1886–1907 by Peter Kropotkin*, London: Freedom Press.

Bellamy, R. (1992) *Liberalism and Modern Society: An Historical Argument*, Cambridge: Polity Press.

Beloff, M. (1975) 'The Future of the State; Why it Should Wither', *New Society*, 34, 73–76.

Benhabib, S. (1986) *Critique, Norm and Utopia, A Study of the Foundations of Critical Theory*, New York: Columbia University Press.

Benn, S.I. (1975) 'Freedom, Autonomy and the Concept of a Person', *Proceedings of the Aristotelian Society*, 76.

Bereiter, C. (1974) *Must We Educate?* Englewood Cliffs, NJ: Prentice-Hall.

Berkman, A. (1995) *An ABC of Anarchism*, London: Freedom Press.

Berlin, I. (1991) *The Crooked Timber of Humanity*, London: Fontana.

Block, A. (1994) 'Marxism and Education' in Martusewicz, R. and Reynolds, W. (eds), *Inside/Out: Contemporary Critical Perspectives in Education*, New York: St. Martin's Press.

Bookchin, M. (1990) *Remaking Society: Pathways to a Green Future*, Boston, MA: South End Press.

Bowen, J. and Hobson, P. (1987) *Theories of Education: Studies of Significant Innovation in Western Educational Thought*, Brisbane: Wiley.

Brighouse, H. (1998) *Education and the New Selective Schooling*, London: Philosophy of Education Society of Great Britain.

Buber, M. (1958) *Paths in Utopia*, Boston, MA: Beacon Press.

Bufe, C. and Neutopia, D. (2002) *Design Your Own Utopia*, Tucson, AZ: See Sharp Press.

Burbules, N. and Torres, C.A. (eds) (2000) *Globalization and Education: Critical Perspectives*, New York: Routledge.

Callan, E. (1997) *Creating Citizens: Political Education and Liberal Democracy*, Oxford: Clarendon Press.

Carr, W. and Hartnett, A. (1996) *Education and the Struggle for Democracy; The Politics of Educational Ideas*, Buckingham: Open University Press.

Chomsky, N. (1996) *Powers and Prospects; Reflections on Human Nature and the Social Order*, Boston, MA: South End Press.

Clark, J.P. (1978) 'What is Anarchism?' *Nomos*, 19, 3–28.

Cohen, G.A. (2001) *If You're an Egalitarian, How Come You're So Rich?* Cambridge: Harvard University Press.

Crowder, G. (1991) *Classical Anarchism: The Political Thought of Godwin, Proudhon, Bakunin and Kropotkin*, Oxford: Clarendon Press.

Cullen, S. (1991) *Children in Society: A Libertarian Critique*, London: Freedom Press.

Darling, J. (1982) 'Education as Horticulture: Some Growth Theorists and Their Critics', *Journal of Philosophy of Education*, 16 (2), 173–185.

De George, R. (1978) 'Anarchism and Authority', *Nomos*, 19, 91–110.

DeHaan, R. (1965) 'Kropotkin, Marx and Dewey', *Anarchy*, 5 (9), 271–286.

Dewey, J. (1917) 'The Need for a Recovery of Philosophy', in Boydston, J.A. (ed.) (1980) *The Middle Works*, Vol. 10, Carbondale, IL: Southern Illinois University Press.

——(1939) *Democracy and Education: An Introduction to the Philosophy of Education*, New York: Macmillan.

——(1965) 'The Nature of Aims', in Archambault, R.D. (ed.) *John Dewey on Education*, Chicago, IL: Random House.

Dolgoff, S. (ed.) (1973) *Bakunin on Anarchy*, New York: Knopf.

Dworkin, G. (1988) *The Theory and Practice of Autonomy*, Cambridge: Cambridge University Press.

Dworkin, R. (1978) 'Liberalism', in Hampshire, S. (ed.), *Public and Private Morality*, Cambridge: Cambridge University Press.

Edgley, R. (1980) 'Education, Work and Politics', *Journal of Philosophy of Education*, 14 (1), 3–16.

Edwards, S. (ed.) (1969) *Selected Writings of Pierre Joseph Proudhon*, New York: Anchor Books.

Ehrlich, H.J. (ed.) (1996) *Reinventing Anarchy, Again*, Edinburgh: AK Press.

Ferm, E.B. (1949) *Freedom in Education*, New York: Lear.

Ferrer y Guardia, F. (1909) 'The Rational Education of Children', *The Modern School*, New York: Mother Earth Publishing Association.

——(1913) The *Origins and Ideals of the Modern School*, London: Watts.

Fidler, G. (1989) 'Anarchism and Education: Education Integrale and the Imperative Towards Fraternite', *History of Education*, 18 (1), 23–46.

Flathman, R.E. (1998) *Reflections of a Would-Be Anarchist; Ideals and Institutions of Liberalism*, Minneapolis, MN: University of Minnesota Press.

Fogelman, K. (1991) (ed.) *Citizenship in Schools*, London: Fulton.

Goldman, E. (1906) 'The Child and its Enemies', *Mother Earth*, 2 (9).

Goodman, P. (1952) *Utopian Essays and Proposals*, New York: Random House.

Goodwin, B. (1987) *Using Political Ideas*, Chichester: Wiley.

Goodwin, B. and Taylor, K. (1982) *The Politics of Utopia: A Study in Theory and Practice*, London: Hutchinson.

Gould, A.C. (1999) *Origins of Liberal Dominance*, Ann Arbor, MI: University of Michigan Press.

Gould, S.J. (1988) 'Kropotkin Was No Crackpot', *Natural History*, 97 (6), 12–21.

Guerin, D. (1970) *Anarchism*, New York: Monthly Review Press.

Halpin (2001) 'Utopianism and Education: The Legacy of Thomas More', *British Journal of Educational Studies*, 49 (3), 299–315.

——(2003) *Hope and Education: The Role of the Utopian Imagination*, London: Routledge Falmer.

Hemmings, R. (1972) *Fifty Years of Freedom: A Study of the Development of the Ideas of A.S. Neill*, London: George Allen and Unwin.

Hewetson, J. (1965) 'Mutual Aid and Social Evolution', *Anarchy*, 5 (9), 257–270.

Hirst, P. (1972) 'Liberal Education and the Nature of Knowledge', in Dearden, R.F., Hirst, P.H. and Peters, R.S. (eds) *Education and Reason*, London: Routledge and Kegan Paul.

Hobsbawm, E. (1975) 'Fraternity', *New Society*, 34 (27), 471–473.

Hocking, W.E. (1926) *Man and the State*, New Haven, CT: Yale University Press.

Honig, B. (1993) *Political Theory and the Displacement of Politics*, Ithaca, NY: Cornell University Press.

Ignatieff, M. (1994) *The Needs of Strangers*, London: Vintage.

Illich, I. (1971) *Deschooling Society*, Harmondsworth: Penguin.

Joll, J. (1979) *The Anarchists*, London: Methuen.

Jonathan, R. (1997) *Illusory Freedoms: Liberalism, Education and the Market*, Oxford: Blackwell.

Kekes, J. (1997) *Against Liberalism*, New York: Cornell University Press.

Kelly, H. (1913) 'The Meaning of Libertarian Education', *The Modern School*, 1 (5).

——(1914) Editorial, *The Modern School*, 1 (3).

——(1916) 'What is the Modern School?', *The Modern School*, 33 (3).

Kemp-Welch, T. (1996) 'Bakunin and Kropotkin on Anarchism', in Bellamy, R. and Ross, A. (eds), *A Textual Introduction to Social and Political Theory*, Manchester: Manchester University Press.

Kerr, S. (1913) 'Ferrer and Montessori', *The Modern School*, 1 (5).

Kleinig, J. (1982) *Philosophical Issues in Education*, London: Croom Helm.

Knowles, R. (2000) 'Political Economy From Below: Communitarian Anarchism as a Neglected Discourse in Histories of Economic Thought', *History of Economics Review*, 31.

Kropotkin, P. (1890) 'Brain Work and Manual Work' in *The Nineteenth Century*, March, 456–475.

——(1897) *Anarchism: Its Philosophy and Ideal*, London: J. Turner.

——(1972) *Mutual Aid: A Factor of Evolution*, London: Allen Lane.

——(1974) *Fields, Factories and Workshops Tomorrow*, London: George Allen and Unwin.

Kymlicka, W. (1989) *Liberalism, Community and Culture*, Oxford: Clarendon Press.

Le Guin, U.K. (1974) *The Dispossessed*, New York: Harper Collins.

Levinson, M. (1999) *The Demands of Liberal Education*, Oxford: Oxford University Press.

Lynch, V. and Smalley, K. (1991) 'Citizenship Education' in Fogelman, K. (1991) (ed.) *Citizenship in Schools*, London: Fulton.

McDermot, J. (ed.) *The Philosophy of John Dewey*, Chicago, IL: University of Chicago Press.

MacIntyre, A. (1971) *Against the Self-Images of the Age: Essays on Ideology and Philosophy*, London: Duckworth.

McKenna, E. (2001) *The Task of Utopia; A Pragmatist and Feminist Perspective*, Maryland: Rowman and Littlefield Inc.

Mannheim, K. (1991) *Ideology and Utopia: An Introduction to the Sociology of Knowledge*, London: Routledge.

Marshall, P. (ed.) (1986) *The Anarchist Writings of William Godwin*, London: Freedom Press.

Maximoff, G.P. (ed.) (1953) *The Political Philosophy of Bakunin*, New York: The Free Press.

May, T. (1994) *The Political Philosophy of Poststructuralist Anarchism*, University Park, PA: Pennsylvania State University Press.

Miller, D. (1984) *Anarchism*, London: Dent.

Mill, J.S. (1991) *On Liberty*, Oxford: Oxford University Press.

Morland, D. (1997) *Demanding the Impossible? Human Nature and Politics in Nineteenth Century Social Anarchism*, London: Cassell.

Morris, B. (1993) *Bakunin: The Philosophy of Freedom*, Montreal: Black Rose Books.

Murphy, D. (1988) *Martin Buber's Philosophy of Education*, Dublin: Irish Academic Press.

Neill, A.S. (1926) *The Problem Child*, London: Herbert Jenkins.

Nisbet, R. (1976) *The Social Philosophers*, London: Paladin.

Nozick, R. (1974) *Anarchy, State and Utopia*, Oxford: Blackwell.

O'Hear, A. (1981) *Education, Society and Human Nature: An Introduction to The Philosophy of Education*, London: Routledge and Kegan Paul.

Parekh, B. (1997) 'Is There a Human Nature?' in Rouner, L.S. (ed.) *Is There a Human Nature?*, Indiana: University of Notre Dame Press.

Parker, S.E. (1965) *Individualist Anarchism: An Outline*, London: the author.

Peters, R.S. (1959) *Authority, Responsibility and Education*, Plymouth: George Allen and Unwin.

——(1966) *Ethics and Education*, London: Allen and Unwin.

——(1967) 'Authority' in Quinton, A. (ed.) *Political Philosophy*, London: University Press.

——(1998) 'Freedom and the Development of the Free Man' in Hirst, P. and White, P. (eds) *Philosophy of Education: Major Themes in the Analytic Tradition*, Vol. II, London: Routledge.

Popper, K.R. (1945) *The Open Society and Its Enemies*, London: Routledge and Kegan Paul.

Pring, R. (1994) 'Liberal and Vocational Education: A Conflict of Value', Haldane, J. (ed.) *Education, Values and the State*, The Victor Cook Memorial Lectures, University of St. Andrews: Centre for Philosophy and Pubic Affairs.

——(1995) *Closing the Gap: Liberal Education and Vocational Preparation*, London: Hodder and Stoughton.

QCA (1998) *Education for Citizenship and the Teaching of Democracy in Schools*, Final Report of the Advisory Group on Citizenship, London.

Rawls, J. (1973) *A Theory of Justice*, Oxford: Oxford University Press.

——(1996) *Political Liberalism*, New York: Columbia University Press.

——(2001) *Justice as Fairness: A Restatement*, Cambridge: Harvard University Press.

Raz, J. (1986) *The Morality of Freedom*, Oxford: Clarendon Press.

Read, H. (1974) *Anarchy and Order*, London: Souvenir Press.

Reichert, W. (1969) 'Anarchism, Freedom and Power', *Ethics*, 79 (2), 139–149.

Reich, R. (2002) *Bridging Liberalism and Multiculturalism in American Education*, Chicago, IL: University of Chicago Press.

Ritter, A. (1980) *Anarchism: A Theoretical Analysis*, Cambridge: Cambridge University Press.

Rorty, R. (1999) *Philosophy and Social Hope*, London: Penguin.

Rouner, L.S. (ed.) (1997) *Is There a Human Nature?* Indiana: University of Notre Dame Press.

Ryan, A. (1998) *Liberal Anxieties and Liberal Education*, New York: Hill and Wang.

Sandel, M. (1982) *Liberalism and the Limits of Justice*, Cambridge: Cambridge University Press.

Scruton, R. (1982) *A Dictionary of Political Thought*, London: MacMillan.

Sennett, R. (1980) *Authority*, London: Faber and Faber.

Shotton, J. (1993) *No Master High or Low: Libertarian Education and Schooling in Britain, 1890–1990*, Bristol: Libertarian Education.

Smith, M. (1983) *The Libertarians and Education*, London: George Allen and Unwin.

Spring, J. (1975) *A Primer of Libertarian Education*, New York: Free Life Editions.

Stewart, W.A.C. and McCann, W.P. (1967) *The Educational Innovators*, London: Macmillan.

Swift, A. (2001) *Political Philosophy: A Beginners' Guide for Students and Politicians*, Oxford: Polity Press.

Sylvan, R. (1993) 'Anarchism', in Goodin, R.E. and Pettit, P. (eds) *A Companion to Contemporary Political Philosophy*, Oxford: Blackwell.

Taylor, M. (1982) *Community, Anarchy and Liberty*, Cambridge: Cambridge University Press.

Thomas, M. (2004) 'No-one Telling us What to Do': Anarchist Schools in Britain, 1890–1916, *Historical Research*, 77 (197), 405–436.

Tooley, J. (1995) *Disestablishing the School*, Aldershot: Avebury.

——(2000) *Reclaiming Education*, London: Cassell.

Walden Foundation (1996) *Currents: Walden Center and School*, Berkeley, CA: Walden Foundation.

Wall, G. (1978) 'Philosophical Anarchism Reconsidered', *Nomos*, 19, 273–293.

Walter, N. (1969) 'About Anarchism' in *Anarchy*, 9 (6).

Ward, C. (1990) 'Four Easy Pieces and One Hard One' in *The Raven*, Anarchist Quarterly, 3 (2).

——(1991) *Influences; Voices of Creative Dissent*, Bideford: Green Books.

——(1996) *Anarchy in Action*, London: Freedom Press.

Warnock, M. (1977) *Schools of Thought*, Faber and Faber: London.

Wasserstrom, R. (1978) 'Comments on "Anarchism and Authority"', *Nomos*, 19.

Weiner, L. (1967) *Tolstoy on Education*, Chicago, IL: University of Chicago Press.

White, J. (1982) *The Aims of Education Restated*, London: Routledge and Kegan Paul.

——(1990) *Education and the Good Life: Beyond the National Curriculum*, London: Kogan Page.

——(1997) *Education and the End of Work: A New Philosophy of Work and Learning*, London: Cassell.

White, P. (1983) *Beyond Domination: An Essay in the Political Philosophy of Education*, London: Routledge and Kegan Paul.

——(1991) 'Hope, Confidence and Democracy', *Journal of Philosophy of Education*, 25 (2), 203–208.

Williams, K. (1994) 'Vocationalism and Liberal Education: Exploring the Tensions', *Journal of Philosophy of Education*, 28 (1), 89–100.

Winch, C. (2000) *Education, Work and Social Capital: Towards a New Conception of Vocational Education*, London: Routledge.

Wolff, J. (1996) *An Introduction to Political Philosophy*, Oxford: Oxford University Press.

Wolff, R.P. (1998) *In Defence of Anarchism*, New York: Harper and Row.

Woodcock, G. (1977) (ed.) *The Anarchist Reader*, London: Fontana.

Index

FRIENDS OF PM PRESS

These are indisputably momentous times — the financial system is melting down globally and the Empire is stumbling. Now more than ever there is a vital need for radical ideas.

In the three years since its founding — and on a mere shoestring — PM Press has risen to the formidable challenge of publishing and distributing knowledge and entertainment for the struggles ahead. With over 100 releases to date, we have published an impressive and stimulating array of literature, art, music, politics, and culture. Using every available medium, we've succeeded in connecting those hungry for ideas and information to those putting them into practice.

Friends of PM allows you to directly help impact, amplify, and revitalize the discourse and actions of radical writers, filmmakers, and artists. It provides us with a stable foundation from which we can build upon our early successes and provides a much-needed subsidy for the materials that can't necessarily pay their own way. You can help make that happen – and receive every new title automatically delivered to your door once a month – by joining as a Friend of PM Press. And, we'll throw in a free T-Shirt when you sign up.

Here are your options:

- **$25 a month** Get all books and pamphlets plus 50% discount on all webstore purchases
- **$25 a month** Get all CDs and DVDs plus 50% discount on all webstore purchases
- **$40 a month** Get all PM Press releases plus 50% discount on all webstore purchases
- **$100 a month** Superstar — Everything plus PM merchandise, free downloads, and 50% discount on all webstore purchases

For those who can't afford $25 or more a month, we're introducing **Sustainer Rates** at $15, $10 and $5. Sustainers get a free PM Press t-shirt and a 50% discount on all purchases from our website.

Your Visa or Mastercard will be billed once a month, until you tell us to stop. Or until our efforts succeed in bringing the revolution around. Or the financial meltdown of Capital makes plastic redundant. Whichever comes first.

Demanding The Impossible
Peter Marshall

ISBN: 978-1-60486-064-1
840 pages $28.95

Navigating the broad 'river of anarchy', from Taoism to Situationism, from Ranters to Punk rockers, from individualists to communists, from anarcho-syndicalists to anarcha-feminists, *Demanding the Impossible* is an authoritative and lively study of a widely misunderstood subject. It explores the key anarchist concepts of society and the state, freedom and equality, authority and power and investigates the successes and failure of the anarchist movements throughout the world. While remaining sympathetic to anarchism, it presents a balanced and critical account. It covers not only the classic anarchist thinkers, such as Godwin, Proudhon, Bakunin, Kropotkin, Reclus and Emma Goldman, but also other libertarian figures, such as Nietzsche, Camus, Gandhi, Foucault and Chomsky. No other book on anarchism covers so much so incisively.

In this updated edition, a new epilogue examines the most recent developments, including 'post-anarchism' and 'anarcho-primitivism' as well as the anarchist contribution to the peace, green and 'Global Justice' movements.

Demanding the Impossible is essential reading for anyone wishing to understand what anarchists stand for and what they have achieved. It will also appeal to those who want to discover how anarchism offers an inspiring and original body of ideas and practices which is more relevant than ever in the twenty-first century.

"Demanding the Impossible *is the book I always recommend when asked—as I often am—for something on the history and ideas of anarchism."*
— Noam Chomsky

"Attractively written and fully referenced... bound to be the standard history."
— Colin Ward, *Times Educational Supplement*

"Large, labyrinthine, tentative: for me these are all adjectives of praise when applied to works of history, and Demanding the Impossible *meets all of them."*
— George Woodcock, *Independent*

Revolution and Other Writings: A Political Reader
Gustav Landauer

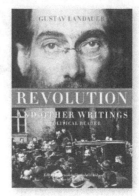

ISBN: 978-1-60486-054-2
360 pages $26.95

"Landauer is the most important agitator of the radical and revolutionary movement in the entire country." This is how Gustav Landauer is described in a German police file from 1893. Twenty-six years later, Landauer would die at the hands of reactionary soldiers who overthrew the Bavarian Council Republic, a three-week attempt to realize libertarian socialism amidst the turmoil of post-World War I Germany. It was the last chapter in the life of an activist, writer, and mystic who Paul Avrich calls "the most influential German anarchist intellectual of the twentieth century."

This is the first comprehensive collection of Landauer writings in English. It includes one of his major works, *Revolution*, thirty additional essays and articles, and a selection of correspondence. The texts cover Landauer's entire political biography, from his early anarchism of the 1890s to his philosophical reflections at the turn of the century, the subsequent establishment of the Socialist Bund, his tireless agitation against the war, and the final days among the revolutionaries in Munich. Additional chapters collect Landauer's articles on radical politics in the US and Mexico, and illustrate the scope of his writing with texts on corporate capital, language, education, and Judaism. The book includes an extensive introduction, commentary, and bibliographical information, compiled by the editor and translator Gabriel Kuhn as well as a preface by Richard Day.

"If there were any justice in this world — at least as far as historical memory goes — then Gustav Landauer would be remembered, right along with Bakunin and Kropotkin, as one of anarchism's most brilliant and original theorists. Instead, history has abetted the crime of his murderers, burying his work in silence. With this anthology, Gabriel Kuhn has single-handedly redressed one of the cruelest gaps in Anglo-American anarchist literature: the absence of almost any English translations of Landauer."
— Jesse Cohn, author of *Anarchism and the Crisis of Representation: Hermeneutics, Aesthetics, Politics*

"At once an individualist and a socialist, a Romantic and a mystic, a militant and an advocate of passive resistance... He was also the most influential German anarchist intellectual of the twentieth century."
— Paul Avrich, author of *Anarchist Voices*

The Paul Goodman Reader
Edited by Taylor Stoehr

ISBN: 978-1-60486-058-0
500 pages $28.95

A one-man think-tank for the New Left, Paul Goodman wrote over thirty books, most of them before his decade of fame as a social critic in the Sixties. A Paul Goodman Reader that does him justice must be a compendious volume, with excerpts not only from best-sellers like *Growing Up Absurd*, but also from his landmark books on education, community planning, anarchism, psychotherapy, language theory, and poetics. Samples as well from *The Empire City*, a comic novel reviewers compared to *Don Quixote*, prize-winning short stories, and scores of poems that led America's most respected poetry reviewer, Hayden Carruth, to exclaim, "Not one dull page. It's almost unbelievable."

Goodman called himself as an old-fashioned man of letters, which meant that all these various disciplines and occasions added up to a single abiding concern for the human plight in perilous times, and for human promise and achieved grandeur, love and hope.

"It was that voice of his that seduced me—that direct, cranky, egotistical, generous American voice... Paul Goodman's voice touched everything he wrote about with intensity, interest, and his own terribly appealing sureness and awkwardness... It was his voice, that is to say, his intelligence and the poetry of his intelligence incarnated, which kept me a loyal and passionate fan."
— Susan Sontag, novelist and public intellectual

"Goodman, like all real novelists, is, at bottom, a moralist. What really interests him are the various ways in which human beings living in a modern metropolis gain, keep or lose their integrity and sense of selfhood."
— W. H. Auden, poet

"Any page by Paul Goodman will give you not only originality and brilliance but wisdom, that is, something to think about. He is our peculiar, urban, twentieth-century Thoreau, the quintessential American mind of our time."
— Hayden Carruth, poet and essayist

"No one writing now in America makes better sense of literary subjects. His ability to combine linguistic criticism, politics, a version of the nature of man, anthropology, the history of philosophy, and autobiographical testament with literary analysis, and to make a closely woven fabric of argument, seems magical."
— Robert Meredith, *The Nation*

From Here To There:
The Staughton Lynd Reader
Edited with an Introduction by
Andrej Grubacic

ISBN: 978-1-60486-215-7
320 pages $22.00

From Here To There collects unpublished talks and hard-to-find essays from legendary activist historian Staughton Lynd.

The first section of the Reader collects reminiscences and analyses of the 1960s. A second section offers a vision of how historians might immerse themselves in popular movements while maintaining their obligation to tell the truth. In the last section Lynd explores what nonviolence, resistance to empire as a way of life, and working class self-activity might mean in the 21st century. Together, they provide a sweeping overview of the life, and work — to date — of Staughton Lynd.

Both a definitive introduction and further exploration, it is bound to educate, enlighten, and inspire those new to his work and those who have been following it for decades. In a wide-ranging Introduction, anarchist scholar Andrej Grubacic considers how Lynd's persistent concerns relate to traditional anarchism.

"I met Staughton and Alice Lynd nearly fifty years ago in Atlanta. Staughton's reflective and restless life has never ceased in its exploring. This book is his great gift to the next generations."
— Tom Hayden

"Staughton Lynd's work is essential reading for anyone dedicated to implementing social justice. The essays collected in this book provide unique wisdom and insights into United States history and possibilities for change, summed up in two tenets: Leading from below and Solidarity."
— Roxanne Dunbar-Ortiz

"This remarkable collection demonstrates the compassion and intelligence of one of America's greatest public intellectuals. To his explorations of everything from Freedom Schools to the Battle of Seattle, Staughton Lynd brings lyricism, rigour, a historian's eye for irony, and an unshakable commitment to social transformation. In this time of economic crisis, when the air is filled with ideas of 'hope' and 'change,' Lynd guides us to understanding what, very concretely, those words might mean and how we might get there. These essays are as vital and relevant now as the day they were written, and a source of inspiration for activists young and old."
— Raj Patel

The Revolution of Everyday Life

Raoul Vaneigem

ISBN: 978-1-60486-213-3
304 pages $20.00

Originally published just months before the May 1968 upheavals in France, Raoul Vaneigem's *The Revolution of Everyday Life* offered a lyrical and aphoristic critique of the "society of the spectacle" from the point of view of individual experience. Whereas Debord's masterful analysis of the new historical conditions that triggered the uprisings of the 1960s armed the revolutionaries of the time with theory, Vaneigem's book described their feelings of desperation directly, and armed them with "formulations capable of firing point-blank on our enemies."

"I realise," writes Vaneigem in his introduction, "that I have given subjective will an easy time in this book, but let no one reproach me for this without first considering the extent to which the objective conditions of the contemporary world advance the cause of subjectivity day after day."

Vaneigem names and defines the alienating features of everyday life in consumer society: survival rather than life, the call to sacrifice, the cultivation of false needs, the dictatorship of the commodity, subjection to social roles, and above all the replacement of God by the Economy. And in the second part of his book, "Reversal of Perspective," he explores the countervailing impulses that, in true dialectical fashion, persist within the deepest alienation: creativity, spontaneity, poetry, and the path from isolation to communication and participation.

For "To desire a different life is already that life in the making." And "fulfillment is expressed in the singular but conjugated in the plural."

The present English translation was first published by Rebel Press of London in 1983. This new edition of *The Revolution of Everyday Life* has been reviewed and corrected by the translator and contains a new preface addressed to English-language readers by Raoul Vaneigem. The book is the first of several translations of works by Raoul Vaneigem that PM Press plans to publish in uniform volumes. Vaneigem's classic work is to be followed by *The Knight, the Lady, the Devil, and Death* (2003) and *The Inhumanity of Religion* (2000).

The Nature of Human Brain Work: An Introduction to Dialectics

Joseph Dietzgen
With an afterword, notes and
bibliography by Larry Gambone

ISBN: 978-1-60486-036-8
144 pages $20.00

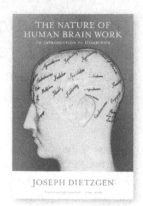

Called by Marx "The Philosopher of Socialism," Joseph Dietzgen was a pioneer of dialectical materialism and a fundamental influence on anarchist and socialist thought who we would do well not to forget.

Dietzgen examines what we do when we think. He discovered that thinking is a process involving two opposing processes: generalization, and specialization. All thought is therefore a dialectical process. Our knowledge is inherently limited however, which makes truth relative and the seeking of truth on-going. The only absolute is existence itself, or the universe, everything else is limited or relative. Although a philosophical materialist, he extended these concepts to include all that was real, existing or had an impact upon the world. Thought and matter were no longer radically separated as in older forms of materialism. The Nature of Human Brain Work is vital for theorists today in that it lays the basis for a non-dogmatic, flexible, non-sectarian, yet principled socialist politics.

"Here is our philosopher!"
— Karl Marx

"...brilliant contributions to the theory of knowledge."
— Anton Pannekoek

"Left... a fine legacy of wisdom in his writings"
— Friedrich A. Sorge

9 781604 861143